# The Book of **LASTS**

# The Book of

# LASTS

Ian Harrison

CASSELL
ILLUSTRATED

**Project Editors** Anna Cheifetz, Victoria Alers-Hankey
**Editor** Barbara Dixon
**Art Editor** Thomas Keenes
**Jacket Design** Abby Franklin
**Picture Research** Vickie Walters, Jennifer Veall with
additional research by Thomas Keenes

The last words quoted in chapter eight and
elsewhere in this book are generally or
traditionally accepted to be the last words
of the people in question, but it should be
remembered that, for a variety of reasons,
people's last words are often disputed.

First published in Great Britain in 2005
by Cassell Illustrated,
a division of Octopus Publishing Group Limited,
2–4 Heron Quays,
London E14 4JP

Text Copyright © Ian Harrison 2005
Design and layout copyright © Cassell Illustrated 2005

The moral right of Ian Harrison to be identified as the author
of this Work has been asserted in accordance with the
Copyright, Designs and Patents Act of 1988

A CIP catalogue record for this book is available from the
British Library.

ISBN 1 84403 259 0
EAN 9781844032594
Printed in China

# Contents

# GENE CERNAN ON BEING PART OF A HISTORIC LAST

On 14 December 1972 I became the last human to stand on the surface of the Moon. I did not expect that more than three decades later I would still be the last, but the fact that mankind has not yet returned there means that my 'last' has become an even more historic landmark than it was at the time. Not only was my departure from the Moon the end of an era but, because it was the last, it also served to emphasise just what a giant leap the Moon landings had been for the human race. And that is why 'lasts' are important: because they invite us to reflect on everything that went before them — the things without which they would not be 'lasts'.

In addition to honouring the past, 'lasts' can also invite us to look forward. As well as meaning 'the last ever', the word last can also mean 'the last to date' — and the implication that something may be repeated sets a goal for those who come after. For example, John Young was the last man to walk on the Moon until I did; and I will only be the last man to walk on the Moon until someone else does. A 'last' that is a last ever, such as the last dodo or the last Ford Model T, is a memorial to its kind — but a 'last' that is a last to date, like my Moonwalk, sets a challenge for the future.

In the case of my 'last', I look forward to that challenge being met. Being the last person to have left his footprints on the Moon holds a special place in history but I would very much like to be around when mankind takes the next step. It's not as if I hold a record that I don't want to see broken; being the last just means that I closed out an era in history — and when we do return to the Moon, the last Apollo mission will still be a significant landmark because it was truly the end of a pioneering era.

When I stood on the Moon looking back at the Earth, I felt as if I was standing on a plateau where science had met its match; the world and that small part of the universe I was privileged to be witness to was 'just too beautiful to have happened by accident'. I was both honoured and saddened by the fact that I represented the end of Apollo, one of mankind's greatest adventures, and

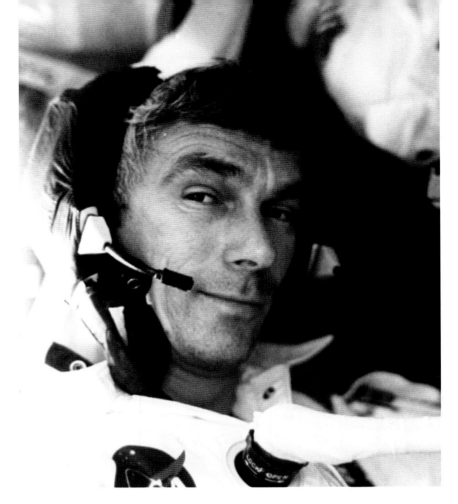

**Astronaut Gene Cernan in the
Apollo 17 command module**

when the time came to leave the Moon I wished I had the opportunity to stay longer. Now, when I look up at the Moon at night over 30 years later, I often wonder whether it was reality or simply a dream. Yet, it was indeed my home for over three days of my life. When we did leave I knew that I personally would never pass this way again, although I did expect that mankind would have done so by now; in fact, I predicted we would be on our way to Mars by the turn of the century. I still believe my basic prediction is correct even if my timetable is somewhat off the mark.

Obviously 'lasts' have a greater significance for me than for many other people, but I believe it's important for everyone to recognize the last of an occurrence or an event that was significant in the history of mankind — whether it be the last day of a war, the last of a famous aircraft to fly, the last man out of Saigon, or the last of a classic automobile. The last of any event that has had a major impact on history or is nostalgic in peoples' lives is important because it does indeed mark the end of an era — and in almost every instance the beginning of a new era of progress.

**Captain Gene Cernan**

# Chapter One

# Last of All

The dodo, a large, flightless bird about the size of a turkey, has become an archetypal symbol of extinction, a fact encapsulated in the phrase 'as dead as a dodo'. This is not because the species was any more significant than others, but because of the speed and nature of its demise.

# DODO & OTHER BIRDS

Raphus cucullatus was a stubby, comical-looking bird with a hooked black bill, short yellow legs, grey-blue plumage and a tuft of pale-coloured feathers for a tail. Its strange appearance and the ease with which it was caught gave rise to its more popular name, dodo, which derives from the Portuguese *doudo*, meaning 'silly'.

The first reports of the dodo came from Portuguese sailors c.1507, and it later became known to the Dutch as the 'nauseous bird', supposedly because no matter how it was cooked it still tasted terrible. Nonetheless, being defenceless and fatally tame because it had no natural predators, the dodo was an easy source of fresh meat for the many sailors who passed its habitat, the island of Mauritius in the Indian Ocean. The island was settled in 1598 by the Dutch (who named it after Prince Morris of Nassau) and less than 100 years later, in 1681, the last Mauritius dodo had been killed.

Two variations of the dodo had evolved separately on nearby islands: the white dodo (*Raphus solitarius*) on the island of Réunion, and the Rodrigues solitaire (*Pezophops solitaria*) on Rodrigues island. Although these varieties lasted longer than the Mauritius dodo, the last white dodo died on a ship to France in 1746, and the last Rodrigues solitaire met its demise in 1790, marking the final extinction of the species.

**Above** A replica of a dodo, made at the British Museum in London, is packaged in preparation for export to the island of Mauritius (October 1952)

## DID YOU KNOW?

● The tree *Calvaria major*, indigenous to Mauritius, is known as the dodo tree. Botanists noticed that no new dodo trees had grown since the extinction of the bird, and surmised that the tree's seeds would only germinate after the outer casing had been crushed in the gizzard of the dodo. In 1973 one botanist fed the fruit to turkeys, which digested the seeds in the same way, so providing a means of saving the dodo tree from meeting the same fate as its avian namesake

**Opposite** A dodo among various other birds in a detail from *Landscape with Birds* by Flemish painter Roelant Savery (1628)

The Tasmanian tiger was a wild marsupial said to look like a dog with the head of a wolf, the stripes of a tiger and the tail of a kangaroo. The species was hunted almost to extinction as a menace to livestock and the last known example died in Hobart Zoo, Tasmania, in 1936.

**The Last** # TASMANIAN TIGER & OTHER ANIMALS

## DID YOU KNOW?

- In his book *Ghost of Chance*, William S. Burroughs (USA) writes of the Garden of Lost Biological Chances, where 'the last Tasmanian wolf limps through a blue twilight, one leg shattered by a hunter's bullet. As do the almosts, the might-have-beens, who had one chance in a million and lost'

- There have been several hundred unconfirmed sightings of Tasmanian tigers since 1936, but nine systematic searches by highly respected naturalists, parks officers and wildlife photographers between 1937 and 1993 have failed to uncover any hard evidence that the Tasmanian tiger still exists. There has even been talk of trying to revive the species by cloning a specimen that has been preserved in alcohol

Variously nicknamed the 'Tasmanian wolf', the 'kangaroo wolf' and the 'zebra wolf', the Tasmanian tiger is officially known as the thylacine (*Thylacinus cynocephalus*). The Latin name translates as 'pouched dog with a wolf's head', referring to the fact that this strange-looking creature carried its young in a pouch facing its tail. The thylacine was once common across the whole of mainland Australia and New Guinea, where it is thought it was hunted to extinction by dingoes. However, the thylacine population on Van Diemen's Land (now Tasmania) thrived – until white Europeans settled on the island in 1803.

The problems began when the Europeans introduced sheep to the island in 1824; the thylacine hunted the sheep and the farmers hunted the thylacine. In 1830 the island's governing body, the Van Diemen's Land Co., introduced a bounty to combat the threat to livestock, and the thylacine population began to diminish. In 1863 naturalist John Gould (England) predicted: 'When the comparatively small island of Tasmania becomes more densely populated ... the numbers of this singular animal will speedily diminish, extermination will have its full sway, and it will then, like the Wolf in England and Scotland, be recorded as an animal of the past.'

And so it was. In 1909 the government ended its bounty scheme, but the species was already moribund; in 1930 the last known killing of a Tasmanian tiger in the wild took place, and in 1933 the last to be captured was hunted down in the Florentine Valley and sold to Hobart Zoo – the world's last known Tasmanian tiger died in captivity at the zoo on 7 September 1936. The thylacine was then (somewhat belatedly) added to the endangered species list and, although there have been many unconfirmed sightings since, was declared officially extinct 50 years later, in 1986.

**c.8000BC** The last woolly mammoth expires

**c.1700BC** The last mammoth (smaller than the woolly mammoth) expires, on Wrangel Island off Siberia

**1627AD** The last aurochs, *Bos primigenius*, dies in Poland. (The aurochs, a species of wild ox, had been hunted since prehistoric times for its meat and skin. The last herd lived in the Jaktorow Forest, Poland, and had diminished to 25 in number by 1599)

**1768** The last Steller's sea cow, *Hydrodamalis gigas*, dies in the Commander Islands of the Bering Sea as the species is finally hunted to extinction for its meat and fat

**▌TIMELINE: SOME ANIMAL EXTINCTIONS**

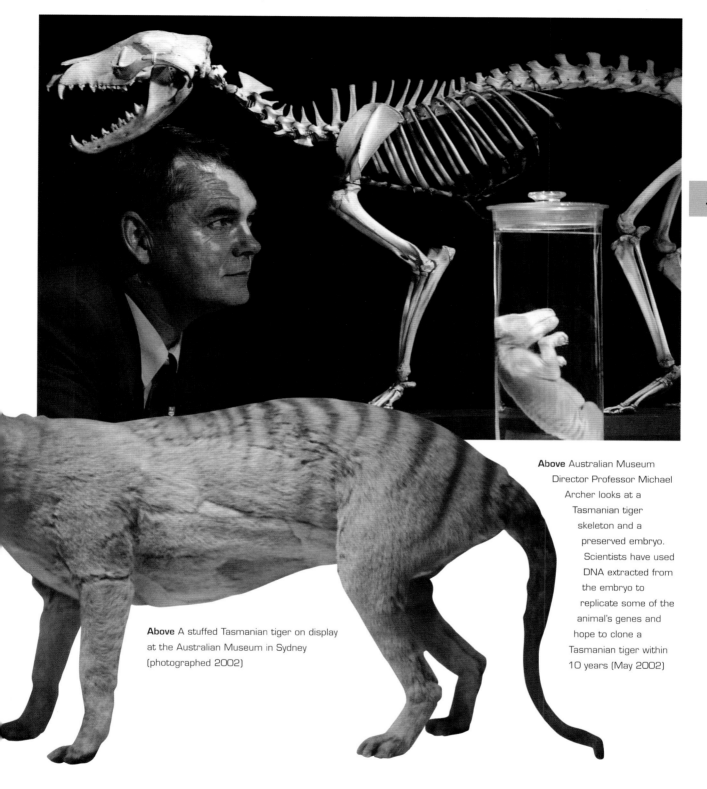

**Above** Australian Museum Director Professor Michael Archer looks at a Tasmanian tiger skeleton and a preserved embryo. Scientists have used DNA extracted from the embryo to replicate some of the animal's genes and hope to clone a Tasmanian tiger within 10 years (May 2002)

**Above** A stuffed Tasmanian tiger on display at the Australian Museum in Sydney (photographed 2002)

**1883** The last known quagga, *Equus quagga*, dies in Amsterdam Zoo, Netherlands. (The quagga was a form of brown-and-white striped zebra native to southern Africa – the last known killing of a quagga in the wild took place in 1878 in South Africa)

**1894** Last confirmed sighting of a Jamaican iguana, in Jamaica

**1933** The last Tasmanian tiger to be captured is hunted down in Tasmania and sold to Hobart Zoo

**1936** The last captive Tasmanian tiger, and the last known example of the species, dies in Hobart Zoo on 7 SEPTEMBER. The Tasmanian tiger is added to the endangered species list

**1986** The Tasmanian tiger is declared officially extinct

**Lasts of** # THE OLYMPICS

Sport was an important part of the religious festivals of ancient Greece, the greatest of which was held at Olympia in honour of the god Zeus. 'Olympiads' were held every four years from c.776BC until they were banned as pagan festivals by the Roman Emperor Theodosius I in 393AD.

**728BC** Olympia, Greece. For the last time the Olympics comprises a single event

**692BC** Olympia, Greece. For the last time the Games lasts for just one day

**385AD** Olympia, Greece. Varazdates (Armenia) is the last ancient Olympic champion to have his name recorded for posterity; there is no record of the victors at the last two Olympiads

**393** Olympia, Greece. Last ancient Olympiad

**1896** Athens, Greece. The first Olympiad of the modern era is the last Olympiad to bar women from competing

**1900** Paris, France. Cricket, croquet, live pigeon shooting, underwater swimming, swimming obstacle race, equestrian high jump and equestrian long jump are contested as Olympic sports for the first and last time

**1904** St Louis, USA. Thomas Hicks (USA) is the last athlete to win the Olympic marathon in a time of more than three hours. Golf and standing triple jump are contested as Olympic sports for the last time

**1908** London, England. Lacrosse is played as an Olympic sport for the last time; Canada is the last winner

**1912** Stockholm, Sweden. Standing high jump and standing long jump are contested as Olympic sports for the last time; Platt Evans (USA) and Constantin Tsiklitiras (Greece) respectively are the last winners

## The Last Ancient Olympics

The first record of sport as part of the Olympic festival of Zeus dates from 776BC, when a baker called Koroibos (a.k.a. Coroebus) won the only event, a 192-metre running race known as the *stadion*. From this single race, the ancient Olympics gradually developed into a spectacular sporting event that took place in a stadium that archaeologists estimate held some 20,000 spectators. The last time the 'Games' comprised only a single event was in

**DID YOU KNOW?**

● Women were banned from taking part in or even watching the ancient Olympics, but nonetheless it was possible for a woman to win one of the coveted wreaths of olive leaves, because the prize for the chariot race was awarded to the owner of the horses, not the driver of the chariot. Some women disguised themselves as men in order to attend the games, but the penalty if they were discovered was to be thrown off a cliff to certain death

● The first and last time that croquet was contested at the Olympics was at the Paris Games in 1900 (*see: Timeline*). The gold medals for all three categories were won by France – perhaps not surprisingly, as all the competitors in the event were French

728BC (four years later a race of two *stadions*, known as a *diaulus*, was added to the programme), while the last time the Games lasted just a single day was in 692BC, after which they were extended to two days.

By 632BC the Games had been extended to five days, and over the next six centuries the Olympics continued to increase in profile. The ancient Olympics had passed their zenith by the time of the Roman occupation, but for more than 400 years the Romans gave this Greek tradition their blessing. Effigies of Roman gods replaced those of Greeks at Olympia, and the Emperors Nero and Tiberius are known to have taken part in the Games. (Noone dared compete against Nero and in 67AD he was crowned winner of the chariot race, despite not completing the course.) However, once the Roman Empire adopted Christianity in 391, the Games were doomed. After the Games of 393, Roman Emperor Theodosius I declared that the event was anti-Christian and issued a decree from Milan banning the Olympics from being held again.

His decree was to last until the 17th century, when the 'Cotswold Olympic Games' were inaugurated in England, but the Games were not truly resurrected until 1896, when the first modern Olympics was held in Athens.

*See also: Nero's Olympic Chariot Race, page 216*

**1920** Antwerp, Belgium. The tug-of-war is contested as an Olympic sport for the last time; Britain is the last winner

**1924** Paris, France. Rugby union and men's cross-country running are contested as Olympic sports for the last time; the USA (rugby union), Paavo Nurmi (Finland, individual cross-country) and Finland (team cross-country) are the last winners

**1936** Berlin, Germany. Polo is contested as an Olympic sport for the last time; Argentina is the last winner

**1980** Moscow, USSR. Allan Wells (Scotland) is the last person to win the men's 100 metres in a time of more than 10 seconds

*See also: Many That Are First Shall Be Last, page 202*

**Left** At the foot of Mount Olympus, Greece, the First Priestess of the Temple hands the Olympic torch to the first of the runners who will carry it to Melbourne, Australia, where it will be used to open the 1956 Olympic Games (4 November 1956)
**Below** A Greek pottery amphora dating from the 5th century BC, depicting a foot race

The Romans initiated many civilized ideas that have survived until, or reappeared in, modern times, such as roads and central heating. They also initiated several less civilized ideas that haven't, such as gladiatorial combat. The last such fight in Rome took place in 404AD.

**The Last**

# ROMAN GLADIATORIAL GAMES

● Women, as well as men, fought in Roman gladiatorial games, but few contemporary writers gave detailed accounts of gladiatrices because their contribution was considered trivial. The Roman satirist Juvenal ridiculed the very concept of the gladiatrix:

*How can a woman be decent
Sticking her head in a helmet,
denying her sex she was born with?
...Hear her grunt and groan as she
works at it, parrying, thrusting;
See her neck bent down under the
weight of her helmet.
Look at the rolls of bandage and
tape, so her legs look like tree
trunks,
Then have a laugh for yourself after
the practice is over.*

The last women to fight in the Colosseum did so in 200AD, the year that gladiatrices were banned by Emperor Septimius Severus

Gladiatorial combat was one of ancient Rome's most popular spectator sports, and in these fights to the death several hundred gladiators were killed every year to satisfy the public thirst for bloodshed. Such was the fame and adulation to be won by a successful gladiator that some free men chose to fight, but most gladiators were slaves, prisoners of war or condemned criminals who were trained in special gladiatorial schools. The most famous gladiator of all, Spartacus (Thrace, now Greece/Bulgaria), was sold to the owner of a troupe of gladiators after being convicted of robbery.

Initially, gladiatorial games were justified on the basis that they hardened Romans to pain and death, making them better warriors, but gradually the games came to be seen as a corrupting influence. The Christian writer Tertullian (Carthage, now part of Tunisia) questioned whether it was right that Romans should 'gaze down with most tolerant eyes on the bodies of men mangled, torn in pieces, defiled with their own blood', and highlighted the hypocrisy of combat as punishment: 'He who comes to the spectacle to signify his approval of murder punished, will have a reluctant gladiator hounded on with lash and rod to do murder.'

In 399 Emperor Honorius abolished the gladiatorial schools, presumably hoping to create a slow decline, but at a series of games at the Colosseum, Rome, in 404 he was prompted into more immediate action. A monk named

**Right** An aerial view of the Colosseum in Rome, Italy, as it appears today

Telemachus jumped into the arena to separate two gladiators and was stoned to death by the crowd for spoiling the entertainment. Honorius banned future gladiatorial games forthwith, although some gladiatorial fights continued illegally outside Rome, and criminals continued to be condemned to fight against wild animals at the Colosseum until the last recorded animal games there in 523.

**Above** American actors Woody Strode (left) and Kirk Douglas (right) face off in a scene from *Spartacus* (1960)

**264BC** The first recorded gladiatorial games take place, in a Roman cattle market as part of the funeral of an aristocrat

**73–71BC** The gladiator Spartacus (Thrace) leads a slaves' revolt against the Roman Empire. He is defeated by Marcus Licinius Crassus in 71 and executed by crucifixion

**200AD** Emperor Septimus Severus bans female gladiators

**399** Emperor Honorius abolishes the gladiatorial schools

**404** The last gladiatorial games in Rome take place at the Colosseum, before such games are banned by Emperor Honorius. Gladiatorial games continue illegally outside Rome for some years

**523** The last recorded animal games to be held at the Colosseum take place, although outside Rome such games continue into the following decade

▮ TIMELINE: ROMAN GLADIATORIAL GAMES

To name the last Roman emperor is no simple matter, because of the way the Roman Empire declined. In fact, the story is of three 'last' emperors: the last ruler of a united Roman Empire, the last ruler of the Western Roman Empire and the last ruler of the Eastern Byzantine Empire.

## The Last ROMAN EMPEROR

TIMELINE: THE LAST ROMAN EMPERORS

**363AD** Julian (the Apostate), the last pagan Roman emperor and the last of the Constantine dynasty, is killed in battle

**392** The last pagan pretender, Eugenius, is proclaimed emperor by the rebel general Arbogastes, but never officially assumes the title. Eugenius is executed by Emperor Theodosius I, the Great, in 394 and Arbogastes commits suicide soon afterwards

**395** The last ruler of a united Roman Empire, Theodosius the Great, dies. His sons Arcadius and Honorius become emperors of the East and West respectively, and the Empire reverts permanently to two parts

**475** The last effective ruler of the Western Roman Empire, Emperor Julius Nepos, is killed in a coup by Odoacer, leader of the Imperial Guard. Romulus Augustulus is elected as successor

**476** The last titular Roman emperor of the West, Romulus Augustulus, is forced by Odoacer to abdicate

**1453** The last emperor of the East (Byzantine Empire), Constantine XI, is killed on 29 MAY, the last day of the Roman Empire

**1806** The last Holy Roman emperor, Francis II (Francis I of Austria), is deposed by Napoleon, who also announces the abolition of the Holy Roman Empire

**Above** The last Roman emperor of the West, Romulus Augustulus

As the Roman Empire grew it became too large to be ruled by a single emperor, so Emperor Diocletian divided control of the Empire, naming Maximian as emperor of the West, while retaining for himself seniority and control of the East. Each named an heir, giving rise to the tetrarchy, or 'rule of four'. Diocletian intended this to be a permanent arrangement, but some of his successors did not wish to share power and the Empire was reunited by various emperors over the next 100 years.

The last ruler of a united Empire was Theodosius I, the Great, who became emperor of the East in 379. His brother-in-law Valentinian II became emperor of the West in 383, but in 392 a rebel general named Arbogastes killed Valentinian and proclaimed a new emperor, Eugenius, the last pagan pretender to the Imperial throne. Eugenius was executed in 394, never having officially assumed the title, thus Theodosius ruled as the last sole Roman emperor from the death of Valentinian in 392 until his own death in 395, after which the Empire reverted permanently to two parts.

The last emperor of the West was Romulus Augustulus (meaning 'little emperor'), who in 476 was forced to abdicate by Odoacer, the treacherous leader of the Imperial Guard, causing the fall of the Empire. The Empire in the East lasted another 1,000 years, but shrank until it was not much greater than its capital city, Constantinople (previously Byzantium, now Istanbul). Constantine XI, the last emperor of what was by then known as the Byzantine Empire, was killed defending the city on 29 May 1453, the last day of the Roman Empire.

A coda to the story of the Western Roman Empire is that in 800 Charles the Great, King of the Franks, revived the idea by establishing the Holy Roman Empire. The last Holy Roman emperor was Francis II (Francis I of Austria), who was deposed in 1806 by Napoleon.

## DID YOU KNOW?

● The modern custom of wearing wedding rings on the third finger of the left hand (or the third finger of the right in some countries) derives from the Roman belief that a nerve led directly from that finger to the heart

● The erstwhile titles kaiser (Germany) and tsar or czar (Russia) both derive from the name Caesar, after the Roman dictator, Julius Caesar. The Romans used the name to refer to the heir to the incumbent emperor

**Below** Detail of the base of the Obelisk of Theodosius in Istanbul, Turkey. The obelisk was taken from Egypt to Constantinople (now Istanbul) by Emperor Theodosius, the last ruler of a united Roman Empire, who installed it on a marble base carved with figures of himself and his family as they watched events in the Hippodrome

As Byzantium and then Constantinople, this great city was besieged no less than 22 times in some 1,700 years, latterly as the capital of the Byzantine Empire. The last siege was broken on 29 May 1453, when the Ottoman Turks captured the city and rebuilt it as Istamboul.

**The Last** # SIEGE OF CONSTANTINOPLE

### DID YOU KNOW?

● In a deliberate echo of Rome, its predecessor as capital of the Roman Empire, the city of Constantinople was built on seven hills. The city was originally to have been named New Rome before the decision was made to name it instead after Emperor Constantine I

Constantinople was founded in 330AD, when the 1,000-year-old city of Byzantium was chosen as the new capital of the Roman Empire. Byzantium was rebuilt and named Constantinople, after Emperor Constantine I, but the name of Byzas the Megarian, after whom the original city was named, survived in the title of the Eastern Roman Empire, which was ruled from Constantinople and became known as the Byzantine Empire.

Despite the gradual dissolution of the Empire by various attackers over the next 900 years, Constantinople itself thrived, being situated on a seemingly impregnable triangular peninsula with water on two sides and strong landward defences on the third. Eventually, in 1204, the Crusaders

| **c.660BC** Founded by Byzas the Megarian (Greece) and named Byzantium after its founder | **330AD** Byzantium is so-called for the last time before being chosen as the new capital of the Roman Empire, rebuilt, and renamed Constantinople after Emperor Constantine I | **1204** Constantinople is sacked and captured by the Crusaders | **1261** Constantinople is regained by the Byzantines | **1453** Constantinople is so-called for the last time after being captured by the Ottoman Turks on 29 MAY, following the last siege of the city, and rebuilt as Istamboul (Istanbul). This date also marks the last of the Byzantine (and, by extension, the Roman) Empire |

■ **TIMELINE: CONSTANTINOPLE**

managed to breach the sea walls and sack the city, but the Byzantines regained their capital in 1261 and held it for a further two centuries, during which time the Empire diminished to little more than the city itself.

The end came with the rise of the Ottoman Empire, which by the 15th century virtually surrounded Constantinople. In 1452 Sultan Mehmet II built a fortress on the Bosphorus, which enabled the Ottomans to control supplies to Constantinople, and the following year Mehmet began what would be the last siege of the great city. Despite Mehmet's devastating firepower, the siege lasted more than seven weeks before the walls were breached on 29 May 1453. The last Byzantine emperor, Constantine XI, was killed in the fighting, marking the last day of the Byzantine Empire – and the last day of Constantinople, which was subsequently renamed Istamboul (Istanbul).

**DID YOU KNOW?**

● Byzas the Megarian, founder of Byzantium (later Constantinople), had been told by the Delphic oracle to found a city 'opposite the city of the blind'. Byzas took the oracle to mean Chalcedon (now Kadiköy, Turkey), whose founders had built their city on one side of the Bosphorous, apparently blind to the strategic advantages of the peninsula on the other, where Byzas founded the city named after him

**Left** Sultan Mehmet II, the last besieger of Constantinople (painting attributed to Gentile Bellini)

**Below** The Haghia Sophia, which reflects the religious changes in Constantinople: it was originally built as a Christian basilica, but Islamic minarets were added after the Ottoman conquest. The building is now a museum

More than a dozen sophisticated civilizations flourished in Central and South America before the arrival of Christopher Columbus in the 15th century. The last two were the Aztecs in Central America and the Incas in South America; for both, contact with Europeans was disastrous.

## Lasts of THE AZTECS & INCAS

| c.1200 Beginnings of the Aztec Empire in central Mexico. Manco Capac becomes first emperor of the Incas | 1325 According to legend, the Aztec city of Tenochtitlán is established in this year | 15th century The Aztec Empire expands under the rule of Emperor Montezuma I | c.1438 Expansion of Inca Empire begins | 1519 Hernán Cortés (Spain) arrives in Mexico and imprisons Montezuma II, the last Aztec emperor to wield any power | 1520 Montezuma II is killed | 1521 The last Aztec emperor, Cuauhtémoc, surrenders and Cortés completes his conquest of the Aztecs |

**TIMELINE: AZTEC & INCA EMPIRES**

## The Last of the Aztecs

The Aztec Empire reached its zenith in the early 16th century under Montezuma II, the ninth Aztec emperor and the last to wield any power. When Spanish conquistador Hernán Cortés (Hernando Cortez) arrived in search of riches in 1519, his timing was perfect – Montezuma and his people thought that the Spaniards were the fulfilment of an ancient Aztec prediction that the wind god Quetzalcoatl (white and bearded, like Cortés) would return at about that time, and so welcomed them without a fight.

Cortés imprisoned Montezuma, but the harshness of the Spanish rule he imposed provoked a revolt in 1520, during which Montezuma was killed and the Spanish were driven from the capital, Tenochtitlán. But Cortés regrouped and returned in April 1521, razing Tenochtitlán to the ground by August and later establishing Mexico City in its place. Cuauhtémoc, Montezuma's successor and the last Aztec emperor, surrendered on 13 August, marking the end of the Aztec Empire, and in 1535 Mexico officially became the viceroyalty of New Spain.

## The Last of the Incas

The South American counterpart of the Aztec Empire was that of the Incas, created by the last and largest of the pre-Columbian civilizations. Like the Aztec, the Inca Empire began in the early 13th century, expanded greatly during the 15th and fell to the Spanish in the 16th. In 1532, 11 years after the conquest of the Aztecs by Cortés, Spanish conquistador Francisco Pizarro marched into Peru, captured Atahualpa, the last Inca emperor to wield power, and in 1533 had him put to death for treason. Leaderless, the Incas quickly succumbed, and in 1535 their former empire officially became part of the Spanish viceroyalty of Peru. The last significant uprising was led by Manco, nominally the last Inca emperor although he was merely a puppet-emperor installed by the Spanish. The uprising was quelled in 1537–38, marking the complete conquest of Peru and the end of the Inca Empire.

**Opposite** Native drawing of Spaniards fighting against Aztecs (1519–21)
**Below** Inca Emperor Atahualpa about to be strangled by Francisco Pizarro's soldiers (engraving 1595)

| 1532 Francisco Pizarro (Spain) arrives in Peru | 1533 Atahualpa, the last Inca emperor to wield power, is executed by strangulation, having been found guilty of treason | 1535 Mexico becomes the viceroyalty of New Spain. The former Inca Empire becomes part of the viceroyalty of Peru | 1537–38 Pizarro's brothers complete the conquest of the Incas by putting down the last Inca uprising, initiated by Manco, who had become disenchanted after being installed by the Spanish as a puppet successor to Atahualpa | 1544 Manco, nominally the last Inca emperor, is stabbed to death | 1824 Peru becomes the last Spanish colony in Central or South America to achieve independence | 1836 The last descendant of Montezuma II dies in New Orleans, USA |
| --- | --- | --- | --- | --- | --- | --- |

As monarchies evolved over thousands of years, there have been many royal lasts. Two of the most dramatic and far-reaching were the last days of the French and Russian monarchies, brought about by the French Revolutions of 1789 and 1848 and the Russian Revolution of 1917.

## TIMELINE: ROYAL LASTS

**1043** Edward the Confessor, who ascended the English throne in 1042, is crowned at Winchester, the last crowned monarch of England (or, later, Britain) to date not to be crowned at Westminster Abbey. (Edward V and Edward VIII were not crowned.) Westminster Abbey is established by Edward from 1044 to 1065

**1066** The last Anglo-Saxon king, Harold II, is killed at the Battle of Hastings and succeeded by William the Conqueror (France). Harold is often referred to as 'the last English king'

**1186** The last High King of Ireland, Ruadri Ua Conchobar (Rory O'Connor) is deposed. The last native Irish provincial king, Cathal O'Connor, King of Connacht, continues resistance against the English until 1224

**1282** The last Welsh Prince of Wales, Llewellyn ap Gruffydd, a.k.a. Llewellyn the Last, is killed by the English in battle near Builth, Wales. In 1301 Edward I of England appropriates the title Prince of Wales (which has previously been used to denote the ruler of Wales) for his newborn son, since when the title has been bestowed on most male heirs to the English (and, later, British) throne

**c.1400** Owain Glyndŵr proclaims himself Prince of Wales prior to his unsuccessful revolution against Henry IV, but his title is not officially recognized (*see: 1282*)

**1485** At the Battle of Bosworth on 22 AUGUST Richard III becomes the last English king to die in battle

BASTILE

## The last French monarch

The first French Revolution saw the temporary end to more than 1,000 years of French monarchy. On 17 June 1789 the Third Estate, representing a bourgeoisie discontented with the absolute power of the monarchy and a feudal system that was being abused by the first two Estates (the clergy and the nobility), declared itself to be the National Assembly. On 9 July King Louis XVI used his troops to intimidate the Third Estate, triggering the anger of the ordinary people of Paris, known as the sans-culottes ('without trousers'). On 14 July the sans-culottes stormed that hated symbol of oppression, the Bastille prison, an event that is celebrated to this day to commemorate the liberation of the people.

The revolutionaries had taken political control, but while Louis XVI lived the Revolution was in danger of stalling. In July 1791 he and his queen, Marie-Antoinette, were arrested as they tried to escape from Paris. A Republic was proclaimed in 1792 and the King was brought to trial in December on charges of treason against this new Republic. The inevitable

**Above** Soldiers shoot at the Bastille during the French Revolution

**Opposite** Cartoon entitled *French Democrats Surprising the Royal Runaways* (1794)

- Marie-Antoinette's extravagance came to be identified with the miseries of the French people prior to the Revolution, and she was executed by the revolutionaries nine months after her husband, Louis XVI. As she approached the guillotine she tripped over her executioner's foot and her last words are recorded as: 'Monsieur, I beg your pardon. I did not do it on purpose'

- For some 50 years the family of 19th-century British Royal Physician Sir Henry Halford used part of Charles I's backbone as a salt cellar. Charles I was buried in St George's Chapel at Windsor Castle following his execution in 1649. After the restoration of the monarchy, Charles II wanted to rebury his father in Westminster Abbey, but the body could not be found. When, in 1813, workmen accidentally broke the tomb of Henry VIII, where Charles' coffin was discovered next to Henry's, Halford was asked to identify the body. He removed the vertebra that had been severed when Charles was beheaded, set it in gold and used it as a salt cellar until Queen Victoria heard the story and ordered that the bone be returned to the tomb

verdict was reached and on 21 January 1793 Louis XVI woke to his last dawn before being guillotined in the Place de la Révolution.

The First Republic lasted a mere 12 years, before Napoleon Bonaparte had himself crowned Emperor I of France in 1804. The following decade he was twice forced to abdicate and the monarchy was restored, with Louis XVIII as king. It survived until 1848, when Louis Philippe, the last French king, was deposed in the February revolution. The Second Republic was declared that year and Napoleon's nephew Louis was elected president, but this Republic lasted just four years before Louis proclaimed himself Emperor and established the Second Empire in 1852. Louis, who as Napoleon III was the last self-proclaimed ruler of France, was ousted in 1870 after defeat in the Franco–Prussian War, leading to the establishment of the Third Republic.

**1509** Henry VII dies, ending his reign as the last monarch of England only; his successor, Henry VIII, later declares himself King of England and Ireland

**1513** At the Battle of Flodden on 9 SEPTEMBER, James IV becomes the last Scottish king to die in battle

**1543** Catherine Parr marries Henry VIII, to become his sixth and last wife

**1567** The last monarch of Scotland only, King James VI, ascends the Scottish throne. In 1603 he is crowned James I of England and Ireland, making his predecessor to the English throne, Elizabeth I, the last monarch of England not to be also monarch of Scotland

**1649** Charles I, the last British monarch to date to be executed, is beheaded at Whitehall on 30 JANUARY. Charles was known to his opponents, the Parliamentarians, as 'the last man', meaning the last king of Britain; in fact, the monarchy was restored in 1660, with Charles II, 'the Son of the Last Man', as king

**1727** George I (son of the elector of Hanover, Germany) dies, bringing to an end his reign as the last non-English-speaking British monarch

**1789** The French Revolution begins. The Bastille is stormed on 14 JULY, marking the symbolic last day of feudalism in Europe (feudalism is officially abolished on 4 AUGUST)

**1792** Louis XVI of France is deposed and the First Republic is proclaimed

**1793** Louis XVI is executed on 21 JANUARY, marking a temporary end to more than 1,000 years of French monarchy; it is restored in 1814. The last attempt to rescue Louis' queen, Marie-Antoinette, from the guillotine is made on 28 AUGUST by Chevalier de Rougeville (France). Her last day is 16 OCTOBER, when she is guillotined

**1848** The last king of France, Louis Philippe, is deposed in the February Revolution, heralding the establishment of the Second Republic (*see: 1870*)

*continued...*

*...continued*

**1870** The last emperor of France, Napoleon III, is deposed after defeat in the Franco–Prussian War, heralding the establishment of the Third Republic

**1871** King Wilhelm I ends his reign as the last monarch of Prussia when he assumes the title Kaiser (Emperor of Germany)

**1893** The last monarch of Hawaii, Queen Liliuokalani, is deposed and the Republic of Hawaii is proclaimed the following year. In 1993 the USA officially apologizes for the overthrow of the monarchy

**1912** The last emperor of China, the infant Pu-i, abdicates on 12 FEBRUARY after the previous year's Chinese Revolution, ending 3,000 years of Chinese monarchy

**1917** Following the Revolution, the last crowned tsar of Russia, Nicholas II (Nikolai II), abdicates on 15 MARCH for himself and on behalf of his son and successor, Alexis. Technically, Michael, his younger brother, rules for one day as the last (uncrowned) tsar before refusing the throne

**1918** The last German kaiser, Wilhelm II, is forced to abdicate. The last king of Austria, Karl, is deposed and a republic proclaimed

**1936** Edward VIII, the last British monarch to date to abdicate and the last to date not to be crowned, abdicates on 11 DECEMBER to end his 325-day reign. On 3 JUNE 1937 he marries American divorcée Wallis Simpson, his relationship with whom has been the cause of the constitutional crisis. Additionally, Edward VIII is the last British monarch also to be monarch of all Ireland; in 1937 a new Irish constitution establishes Eire as a sovereign state, and in 1949 Eire is proclaimed a republic

**1946** The last monarch of Italy, King Umberto II, is exiled to Portugal after the Italian people vote for a republican government

**1947** Michael, the last monarch of Romania and the last reigning Eastern European monarch, is forced to

## The last tsar

The Russian Revolution was no less bloody than the French had been. By 1917 Nicholas II, the last crowned tsar, was ruling over a discontented nation and, as with the French Revolution, the armed dispersal of protesters was the trigger for fully fledged revolution. Demonstrators had taken to the streets in Petrograd (a.k.a. St Petersburg) in February and March 1917 and when troops were sent to disperse them more than 300,000 of the soldiers simply joined the protesters. Then, on 13 March, sailors on board the battle cruiser *Aurora* mutinied. Without the support of the military the Tsar knew he had lost power – on 15 March he was forced to abdicate in favour of a provisional government that called itself a *soviet*, meaning 'council', and the world witnessed the beginning of communism.

Nicholas abdicated not only on his own behalf, but also on behalf of his son and successor Alexis, leaving his brother Michael (Mikhail Alexandrovich) as next in line. Technically, Michael ruled as the last (uncrowned) tsar for a single day before he too refused the throne, ending the 300-year-old Romanov dynasty. Unfortunately for the Romanovs, as with Louis XVI, the very existence of the ousted royals jeopardized the revolution by implying the possibility of a restoration. In order to prevent this, on 16 July 1918 the entire family was taken to the basement of the house where they had been imprisoned, and they were told: 'Your relations have tried to save you. They have failed, and we must now shoot you.'

abdicate and Romania is declared a people's republic. He and his family live in exile in Switzerland

**1952** The last reigning monarch of Egypt, King Farouk, is deposed in a bloodless military coup. His 17-month-old son succeeds to the monarchy, but never reigns as king

**1967** The last monarch of Greece, Constantine II, is exiled. He is formally deposed and a republic proclaimed in 1973; the monarchy is officially abolished by referendum in 1974

**1969** The last king of Libya, Idris, is deposed by Colonel Muammar Gaddafi (Moamer al-Khaddhafi)

**1979** The last shah of Iran, Muhammad Reza Shah Pahlavi, is deposed and the country declared an Islamic republic

*See also: The Last State to Join the Union, page 142*

## DID YOU KNOW?

● The last monarch to be killed by a monkey was **King Alexander of Greece**, who died in **1920** after being bitten by his pet

**Above** The Shah of Iran and Empress Farah wave from their carriage as they ride through the streets of Tehran after their coronation ceremony. The Shah's egret-plumed crown is covered with 3,755 jewels. The Empress's crown has 1,469 diamonds and 177 rubies, emeralds and pearls (1 November 1967)

**Left** Russians hold portraits of Tsar Nicholas II and his family during a religious procession in St Petersburg on 24 August 2000. Four days earlier the Russian Orthodox Church had canonized the Tsar and his family for their murders at the hands of the Bolsheviks in 1918

**Lasts of**

# TV SOAPS, SITCOMS & SERIALS

Since the 'soap opera' format transferred from radio to television during the 1940s, soaps, sitcoms and serial dramas have become a staple of television entertainment. Since the 1940s many classics have come and gone, their last episodes often attracting record viewing figures.

Soap operas have been characterized as 'never-ending stories of extraordinary events befalling quite ordinary folk with extraordinary frequency'. With their roots in melodrama, soap operas came to be so-called during the 1930s, when American washing powder manufacturers began sponsoring hugely popular long-running radio dramas. The format proved equally successful on television, where it was soon followed by another seemingly ever-renewable entertainment format, the situation comedy, or sitcom.

The most successful TV soap to date in terms of exposure is *Dallas* (USA), which, during the 1980s, was watched by a then record 76% of the American viewing public and has since been broadcast in more than 90

countries worldwide. *Dallas* was first broadcast by ABC (USA) on 2 April 1978, and focussed on the lust, power and wealth of oil-rich Texans. When it was broadcast in Britain, 27 million viewers tuned in on 22 November 1980 to discover 'who shot JR' (J.R. Ewing, played by Larry Hagman). The last new episode of *Dallas* was first screened in the USA on 3 May 1991.

One of the most popular TV sitcoms to date is *Friends* (USA), whose last, hour-long episode (barring any come-backs) was first broadcast by NBC (USA) on 6 May 2004, prompting Steve Beverly (USA), a professor of communication arts, to declare: '*Friends* has left its signature on American TV history.' Jennifer Aniston (USA), who played the character of Rachel, was somewhat more emotional. Prior to filming the last episode she said: 'This is gutting us. We're like delicate china and we're speeding towards an inevitable brick wall. It's painful in the weirdest way because it was the most fun and joyous place to be. It was the time of my life.' Lisa Kudrow (USA), who played Phoebe, agreed: 'It's a deeper loss than I was expecting. A really deep-down loss.'

**Opposite** Americans gather at an open air 'television theatre' for a communal viewing of the last episode of *Friends*

**Right** Actor Larry Hagman as J.R. Ewing in *Dallas*

**TIMELINE: LAST EPISODES OF TV SHOWS**

**1968** The last new episode of *The Man from UNCLE* is first broadcast in the USA on 15 JANUARY

**1969** The last new episode of the original *Star Trek* (USA) is first broadcast in the USA on 2 SEPTEMBER (the Klingon word for last is 'oav')

**1974** The last new episode of *Monty Python's Flying Circus*, entitled 'Party Political Broadcast', is first broadcast in Britain on 5 DECEMBER

**1977** The last new episode of *Porridge* is first broadcast in Britain on 25 MARCH

**1979** The last new episode of *Fawlty Towers*, entitled 'Basil the Rat', is first broadcast in Britain on 25 OCTOBER. The last line of this last episode goes to Basil Fawlty's wife, Sybil, as Manuel, the waiter, drags the unconscious Basil out of the room: 'I'm afraid it's started to rain again'

**1981** The last new episode of *The Waltons* (not including TV movies) is first broadcast in the USA on 4 JUNE

**1983** The last new episode of *M*A*S*H*, entitled 'Goodbye, Farewell and Amen', is first broadcast in the USA on 28 FEBRUARY

**1991** The last new episode of *Dallas* is first broadcast in the USA on 3 MAY

**1993** The last new episode of *Cheers* is first broadcast in the USA on 20 MAY

**1998** The last new episode of *Seinfeld*, first broadcast on 14 MAY in the USA, attracts a record 108 million viewers

**2000** The last new episode of *One Foot in the Grave*, in which Victor Meldrew is killed, is first broadcast in Britain on 20 NOVEMBER. A short special is broadcast on 16 MARCH 2001, in which Meldrew appears, *Sixth Sense*-style, as a ghost

**2004** The last new episode of *Sex and the City* is first broadcast in the USA on 22 FEBRUARY. The last new episode of *Friends* is first broadcast in the USA on 6 MAY. The last new episode of *Frasier* is first broadcast in the USA on 13 MAY

In the course of motoring history, many makes and models have come and gone, but the most significant, being the first car to be mass-produced on a moving assembly line, was the Ford Model T. The last example of this famous model rolled off the production line in May 1927.

**The Last** 

# FORD MODEL T & OTHER CARS

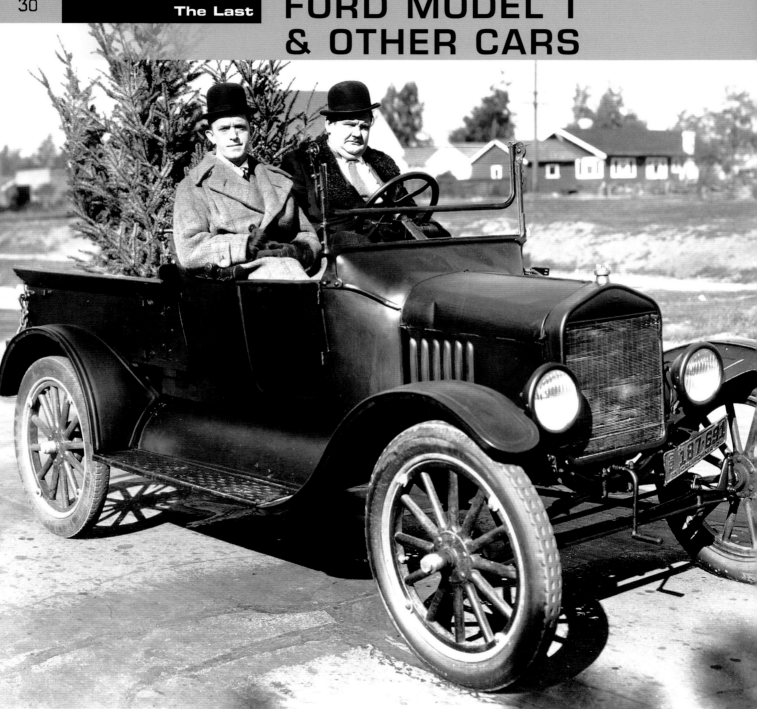

Opposite Stan Laurel and Oliver Hardy in a Ford Model T, in a scene from *Big Business* (1929)

**Left** *Volkswagen,* by Andy Warhol (1977)

TIMELINE: LAST CARS

**1927** The last Ford Model T rolls off the production line on 31 MAY, the 15,007,033rd Model T to be built

**1972** Volkswagen celebrates the production of the 15,007,034th Beetle, surpassing the record set by the Ford Model T

**1973** The last Fiat 500, once Italy's favourite car, is built in MARCH

**1974** The last of the classic Citroën D-series is built, replaced by the CX

**1975** The last E-Type Jaguar rolls off the production line after 72,500 have been built, to be replaced by the XJ-S

**1979** The last German-built Volkswagen Beetle, a cabriolet, is made in APRIL (production continues overseas). An all-new Beetle is launched in the 1990s

**1980** The last MGB is produced in the autumn, after more than 460,000 have been built. The memory of the MGB is revived in 1992 with the launch of the MG RV8, based on a modified MGB body

**1988** The last French-built Citroën 2CV rolls off the production line (production continues overseas)

**2002** In FEBRUARY the last car (a Fiesta) rolls off the production line at Ford's plant in Dagenham, Essex, England. It is the 10,980,368th vehicle to be made at Dagenham before the plant is converted to engine manufacture

The year 1908 has been described as one of the most significant dates in motoring history, for it was on 1 October that year that Henry Ford (USA) launched the legendary Model T. The previous year, Ford had pledged to launch 'a motor car for the great multitude': a car cheap enough for anyone on a reasonable salary to buy, made from the best materials and 'the simplest designs that modern engineering can devise'. Simplicity of design enabled Ford to set up the first moving assembly line in 1913, revolutionizing the car industry, although the relative inflexibility of mass production over manual construction led to Ford's famous comment that the Model T was available in 'any colour you like as long as it's black'.

Mass production led to reduced prices and increased sales, which peaked at 1.8 million in 1923. However, times moved on and the 'Tin Lizzy', as the Model T was affectionately known, began to appear dated. By 1926 sales were flagging, and in May 1927 came another significant date in motoring history when the 15,007,033rd and last Ford Model T rolled off the production line. Ford, of course, went from strength to strength, but the famous Model T was no more.

The Model T remained the most popular model ever built until February 1972, when Volkswagen (Germany) celebrated production of the 15,007,034th example of the perennially popular Beetle, or 'Bug'. The last German-made Beetle (before its 1990s reincarnation) was built in April 1979, but production continued overseas, and on 15 May 1981 the 20 millionth Beetle rolled off the production line in Mexico.

**DID YOU KNOW?**

● In the vision of the future presented by Aldous Huxley (England) in his novel *Brave New World*, the assembly-line principles of mass production pioneered by Henry Ford have acquired religious status. The inhabitants of this world pray to Our Ford, dates are defined as AF (Anno Ford), people of rank are addressed as 'your fordship' and the sign of the cross is replaced by the sign of the T

● In 1991 a panel of motoring industry experts from 37 countries named the Volkswagen Beetle Car of the Century

**The Last**

# LE MANS SPRINT START

The Le Mans 24-hour race is one of the world's most famous motor races. For many years the race began with the drivers sprinting across the track to their cars, but growing safety awareness put a stop to this dramatic tradition and the last sprint start took place in 1969.

The first Le Mans Grand Prix d'Endurance, as the 24-hour race is officially known, took place in 1923 on the new Circuit de la Sarthe in Le Mans, France, and for more than 40 years a key ingredient in the excitement of the 24-hour race was the famous sprint start. The cars would be parked in echelon (i.e. at 45° to the track) and the drivers would line up on the opposite side of the track. When the flag dropped for the start of the race, the drivers would sprint across the tarmac to their cars, fire up their engines and take off for the most gruelling test in motor racing. However, safety became a more important consideration than spectacle, and 1969 proved to be the last year of the sprint start – that year the race also began two hours earlier than usual in order for racing fans to be home in time for the presidential elections the following day.

At 14:00 on 14 June 1969 all but one of the 45 drivers sprinted across the Le Mans track in the last start of its kind. To highlight the safety issue, Jacky Ickx (Belgium) pointedly walked across the track and fastened his safety harness before starting his engine. Two Porsche 917s (since voted the best racing car of all time) led the race for the first 21 hours, but for the last three hours it was a battle between the legendary Ford GT 40 and a Porsche 908. On the last lap, Ickx (co-driver Jacky Oliver, England) took the lead in the Ford to win the last Le Mans 24-hour race to have begun with a sprint to the car, despite the fact that he had walked to his.

**DID YOU KNOW?**

● Multiple Le Mans-winner Derek Bell (England) has good reason to remember his first test session in a Porsche 917 at Hockenheim, prior to the 1970 Le Mans 24-hour race: 'I was running at about 170mph in the dusk, when the headlight beam picked out a sight so unbelievable that for a split second I thought I must be hallucinating. There was a bloke cycling across the road, as cool as you like! At that speed I just dared not swerve a fraction, so I missed him by what seemed like the width of a fag paper. The look of sheer panic on his face is something that has stayed in my mind ever since'

**Above** For the last
time, drivers in the Le
Mans 24-hour race sprint
across the track to their cars
to start the race (June 1969)
**Left** Jackie Ickx (Belgium), the winner
of the last Le Mans 24-hour race to
have begun with a sprint start
(photographed 1967)

# Lasts of STEAM RAILWAYS

The age of steam is fondly remembered as the golden age of the railways. Steam has survived on private preserved lines, and in parts of the less-developed world, but the end of steam railways as a commercially operated means of transport in the developed world began in the 1950s.

**1938** *Mallard*, operated by LNER (Britain), becomes the last steam locomotive to hold the world rail speed record, setting a record of 126mph in JULY

**1945** In MARCH the last steam locomotive to pull America's famous 'Twentieth Century Limited' service between New York and Chicago makes its final run

**1949** CP5935 is completed for the Canadian Pacific Railway as the last standard gauge steam locomotive to be built for a Canadian railway

**1956** The Class P36 No.0251 is completed as the last mainline steam locomotive to be built for Soviet Railways

**1958** The Norfolk & Western Railroad, America's last remaining Class One railway to operate steam traction only, finally breaks with tradition and orders its first diesel-electric locomotives

The fact that steam was replaced as early as March 1945 on America's famous 'Twentieth Century Limited' service between Chicago and New York was a sign of things to come. The advantages of the new diesel-electric locomotives were aggressively marketed by their manufacturers and by the end of the 1950s steam on commercial railways was moribund in the USA, although the Norfolk & Western Railroad, America's last remaining Class One railway to operate steam traction only, held out as late as 1958 before ordering its first diesel-electric locomotives.

The following decade Britain waved goodbye to steam; the country's last steam locomotive was completed in 1960 and the last commercial use of steam on overground railways came just eight years later, when steam was retired from engineering duties on 8 August 1968.

The protracted end of the age of steam provoked a great deal of emotion, even among those initiating the change. British Railways broke with tradition by giving a name, rather than simply a number, to the last steam locomotive to be built in Britain – a Class 9F freight locomotive that was painted in green, rather than the standard black freight livery, and was given the name of *Evening Star* to commemorate the sun going down on the age of steam. *Evening Star* was named on 8 March 1960, just four years before the withdrawal of steam locomotives from service began. Britain's last regular steam passenger service ended on 30 May 1967, and on 11 August 1968, three days after the retirement of steam from engineering duties, British Railways ran a commemorative 'Farewell to Steam' service, marking the official end of steam rail travel in Britain.

**Above** The Twentieth Century Limited Streamlined Locomotive of the New York Central System (undated photograph)
**Right** Detail from *Guildford Shed*, one of a series of paintings by English artist David Shepherd commemorating the end of steam in Britain

## DID YOU KNOW?

● For several years, *Evening Star* was the only 9F to have a name, until artist David Shepherd (England) rescued No.92203 from being scrapped and named it *Black Prince*. No.92203 was built in 1959, the 17th from last steam locomotive to be built in Britain, and was just eight years old when Shepherd asked British Rail whether he could buy a 9F. BR took 92203 straight out of service and sold it to him for just 5% of what it had cost to build. Shepherd, who upset a lot of railway purists by giving 9F a name, says: 'She's now known as *Black Prince* because she's carried the name for four times her working life. Of course she's Black Prince. She *knows* she's *Black Prince*'

**1960** The Class 9F *Evening Star* is completed as the last steam locomotive to be built in Britain

**1961** The last scheduled steam passenger train on the London Underground system runs on 11 SEPTEMBER, albeit not underground but on the overground section of the Metropolitan Line. Europe's last mainline steam locomotives are built: 10 Garratt freight locomotives built for Spanish National Railways (RENFE) and two locomotives built by Turkish Railways (TCDD)

**1967** Britain's last regular scheduled commercial steam passenger service, on the Brockenhurst to Lymington branch line in Hampshire, ends on 30 MAY

**1968** On 8 AUGUST steam is used for engineering duties on British overground railways for the last time. On 11 AUGUST British Railways runs a commemorative 'Farewell to Steam' service, a return trip from Liverpool to Carlisle

**1969** Chinese Railways introduces the Class AY, the last standard Chinese steam locomotive to enter production

**1971** The last steam train on the London Underground makes a commemorative run on 6 JUNE, from Barbican to Neasden, to commemorate the retirement of steam from engineering duties on the underground (passenger duties ended 10 years earlier)

**1973** The Class AD60 No.6042 is withdrawn on 18 MARCH as Australia's last steam locomotive in regular service on government railways

**1975** The last of commercial steam traction in Spain

**1986** The last of commercial steam traction in Hungary

**1992** The last of commercial steam traction on South Africa's main lines

**2000** The last scheduled steam service in India runs on 3 FEBRUARY

**The Last** 

# FACE ON MOUNT RUSHMORE

America's Mount Rushmore National Memorial is world-famous for the faces of four American presidents hewn out of the side of the granite mountain. But for all its fame, few people can state the order in which the presidents were carved, or whose was the last face to appear.

**1867** Born John Gutzon de la Mothe Borglum on 25 MARCH near Bear Lake, Idaho, USA, of Danish parents. Later studies art in San Francisco, USA, and at the Académie Julian in Paris, France

**1904** Wins a gold medal at the St Louis World's Fair (a.k.a. Louisiana Purchase Exhibition) for his sculpture *Mares of Diomedes*

**1908** Completes a giant head of Abraham Lincoln in the US Capitol Rotunda

**1909** Completes a memorial statue of General Philip Sheridan of the Union Army

**1916** Commissioned to carve a memorial to the Confederate army into the side of Stone Mountain in Georgia, USA, but is dismissed before the sculpture is completed. (Stone Mountain is eventually completed in 1970 and features three 27-metre figures of Confederate heroes Jefferson Davis, General Robert E. Lee and General Thomas 'Stonewall' Jackson)

**1923** Discusses with South Dakota State Historian Doane Robinson (USA) the idea of creating a patriotic sculpture from an outcrop of granite 'fingers' known as the Needles. They moot the possibility of depicting American heroes such as frontiersmen Jim Bridger and Kit Carson, US army scout Buffalo Bill Cody and explorers Lewis and Clark

**1927** Commissioned to carve the Mount Rushmore National Memorial,

Sculptor Gutzon Borglum (USA) once declared that: 'American art should be monumental, in keeping with American life.' He certainly lived up to his own ideal with the gigantic sculpture on Mount Rushmore in the Black Hills of South Dakota, which he began in 1927. Borglum died in 1941 shortly before the completion of the monument, making it in one sense his last work, although it was not the last commission on which he was working.

On 10 August 1927 US President Calvin Coolidge dedicated the steep granite cliff of Mount Rushmore that was to be the site of the sculpture. Work began that same year and continued, intermittently, for the next 14 years. Borglum led a team of workers who blasted the basic shapes out of the mountain with dynamite and then, working from one-twelfth scale models, drilled and chiselled them into the heads of the four presidents chosen to represent the first 150 years of American history. George Washington was the first to emerge, in 1930, followed by Thomas Jefferson in 1936 and Abraham Lincoln in 1937. Borglum's friend Theodore Roosevelt was the last face to appear, in 1939.

Each head is about 18 metres tall, which means that if the presidents had been sculpted full figure to the same scale, each would stand 142 metres tall. Borglum's favourite was Lincoln, whose nose is 6 metres long and whose eyes are nearly 4 metres wide. Although Borglum saw the last face emerge he did not live to see the completion of his epic sculpture: he died in March 1941 and it was left to his son, Lincoln Borglum, to oversee the completion of the memorial in October that year.

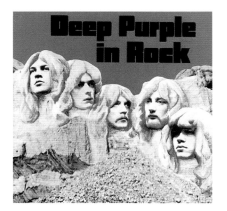

**DID YOU KNOW?**

● Rock band Deep Purple used a parody of Mount Rushmore for the cover of their 1970 album *In Rock*, depicting the faces of the band members carved out of the mountain. An extra face was added to the four of the real Mount Rushmore in order to accommodate the five band members: (left to right) Ian Gillan, Ritchie Blackmore, Jon Lord, Roger Glover and Ian Paice

**Left** Gutzon Borglum in his studio (c.1930s)
**Below** Aerial view of Mount Rushmore, showing: (left to right) Presidents Washington, Jefferson, Roosevelt and Lincoln (photogaphed August 1967)

originally known as The Shrine of Democracy, a development of the idea discussed with Robinson. Completes the sculpture *Wars in America* in Newark, New Jersey

**1930** The face of George Washington emerges from Mount Rushmore

**1936** The face of Thomas Jefferson emerges from Mount Rushmore

**1937** The face of Abraham Lincoln emerges from Mount Rushmore

**1939** The last face emerges from Mount Rushmore, that of Theodore Roosevelt

**1940** Completes the Trail Drivers Memorial in San Antonio, Texas

**1941** Dies on 6 MARCH, aged 73, before completing work on Mount Rushmore. His son, Lincoln, completes the work seven months later

Transportation was a particularly harsh punishment by which criminals, often convicted of relatively minor offences, would be exiled to the New World to provide hard labour – usually for life. This form of punishment, which bordered on slavery, was abolished in the 1860s.

**Lasts of**

# TRANSPORTATION & PENAL COLONIES

TIMELINE: PENAL COLONIES

**1776** The last British transportation of convicts to America takes place, before ceasing due to the American War of Independence (1775–83)

**1810** The last hanging takes place of a convict guilty of escaping a penal colony after transportation and returning to Britain. Illegally returning to Britain remains a capital offence until 1834

**c.1856** Convict labour is used for the last time by free Australians in the east (Van Diemen's Land)

**1857** The last of Britain's wooden prison hulks is decommissioned. (Steel ships are later used, during the 1970s, as floating prisons in Belfast Lough, Northern Ireland)

**1868** On 10 JANUARY the last convict ships, carrying some 162,000 British convicts (c.137,000 men and c.25,000 women) transported to Australia, arrive in Fremantle

**1953** The last day of the notorious French penal colony Devil's Island, off the coast of French Guiana, comes when it is decommissioned on 22 AUGUST

**1963** The last use of Alcatraz Island, San Francisco Bay, USA, as a prison comes when Alcatraz Federal Prison is decommissioned in MARCH

## The last convict ships

Britain's transportation of convicts to penal colonies abroad began in 1597, when the inhabitants of the American colonies would pay for the right to use convicts as labourers. The last transportation of convicts to America took place in 1776, after the outbreak of the American War of Independence, and convicts awaiting transportation were instead imprisoned on board decommissioned naval vessels moored in Britain's estuaries. These ships, which became known as prison hulks, were intended as a temporary measure, but their use was to last another 81 years; the last one was decommissioned in 1857.

By the time American independence was recognized in 1783, the hulks were as overcrowded as the prisons, and the British government realized that an alternative to American transportation was required. Africa was considered, but eventually it was decided to send convicts to Australia, which

**DID YOU KNOW?**

● One of the few convicts to escape from Devil's Island was Henri Charrière (France), who had been condemned at the age of 25 for a murder he had not committed and was imprisoned there during the 1930s. He later published an account of his escape, using his nickname as the title: *Papillon* ('Butterfly'). After its publication a French government minister claimed that 'the present hopeless moral decline in France is due to the wearing of miniskirts and the reading of *Papillon*'

had been claimed for Britain by Captain James Cook (England) 13 years earlier, in 1770. The first fleet of convict ships set sail for Australia in 1787 and landed in New South Wales in January 1788, marking the birth of a nation.

Transportation was seen as such a harsh and unfair punishment that free Australians in the east stopped using convict labour (New South Wales c.1840 and Van Diemen's Land c.1856), and in Britain public opinion during the 1860s forced its official abolition. In 1865 Prime Minister Lord Palmerston agreed to phase out transportation, by which time Western Australia was the last remaining penal colony. The last convict ships left Britain two years later, in 1867, and landed in Fremantle on 10 January 1868, a far more worthy judicial milestone than the arrival of the first transportees 80 years earlier.

**Opposite** Illustration from French magazine *Le Petit Journal*, showing convicts embarking for transportation to Guyana (January 1904)
**Above** Black-eyed Sue and Sweet Poll take leave of their lovers, who have been sentenced to transportation to Botany Bay, Australia (engraving 1792)

America is the last remaining industrialized Western nation to condone capital punishment, except in a dozen states where it has been abolished. Unless any of the other Western nations revert to the barbarism of previous centuries, the lasts recorded here will remain lasts.

## Lasts of CAPITAL PUNISHMENT

**DID YOU KNOW?**

• As he stepped onto the gallows in 1856, the last words of serial killer William Palmer (Britain) were: 'Are you sure it's safe?' Gallows humour also extended to the electric chair. In 1928 the last words of George Appel (USA) as he was strapped into the chair were: 'You're about to see a baked Appel.' And just prior to his execution in 1966, James French (USA) told a reporter: 'I have a terrific headline for you in the morning – "French Fries" '

• Albert Pierrepoint (Britain), who dispatched Ruth Ellis and was one of Britain's last executioners, said after his retirement: 'I do not now believe that any of the hundreds of executions I carried out has in any way acted as a deterrent against future murder. Capital punishment, in my view, achieved nothing except revenge'

*See also: Last Suppers, page 126*

Punishment by death is the ultimate penalty for any crime, but even within this category of punishment there are degrees, some forms of death being more barbaric than others. The last person in Britain to be judicially executed by beheading on the block was 80-year-old Simon Fraser, 11th Lord Lovat (Scotland), for his part in the Jacobite Rebellion of 1745. Noticing that his executioner appeared nervous, Lovat reportedly told him: 'Cheer up thy heart, man. I am not afraid. Why should you be?' Just over 40 years later Britain's last judicial burning at the stake took place, of a woman named Murphy who had been convicted of minting false coins.

Hanging, the firing squad and, in France, the guillotine remained standard forms of judicial execution in Europe until well into the 20th century, and the first two are still on the statute books for use in America. In 1955 Ruth Ellis (Wales) became infamous as the last woman to be judicially executed in Britain (by hanging), but Britain's last executions (of two men) took place in 1964, although capital punishment, except for treason, was not officially abolished until 1965. In France, the last use of the guillotine came as late as 1977 with the execution of convicted murderer Hamida Djandoubi (Tunisia) at Baumetes Prison, Marseilles; capital punishment was abolished in 1981.

The firing squad was the preferred method for military executions following courts martial. The last British soldier to be shot for desertion was Private L. Harris of the 10th Battalion, West Yorkshire Regiment, on 7 November 1918 at the end of the First World War, just four days before Armistice Day. The last American soldier to be shot for desertion was Private Eddie Slovik, on 31 January 1945 in France towards the end of the Second World War. It was the first US military execution for desertion since the American Civil War the previous century and the only one in the Second World War, although there were some 70 Second World War executions for rape and murder. In 1987 Slovik was given a posthumous pardon and reburied in his home state of California.

**Left** 28-year-old model, nightclub hostess and murderess Ruth Ellis, the last woman to be hanged in Britain, pictured before her arrest

**Opposite** The execution of King Louis XVI of France (c.1793, unattributed)

**Overleaf** Goya's painting *The Third of May, 1808*, commemorating the execution of citizens of Madrid, Spain, by French soldiers (1814)

**1682** Britain's last judicial executions for witchcraft take place on 18 AUGUST, when Temperance Lloyd, Mary Lloyd and Susannah Edwards (all Britain) are hanged in Exeter, although the British law punishing witchcraft with death is not repealed until 1736, and supposed witches are lynched by mobs as late as 1863

**1747** The last person in Britain to be judicially executed by beheading on the block is Simon Fraser, 11th Lord Lovat (Scotland), at the Tower of London on 9 APRIL, for treason (the beheading of bodies *after* execution by hanging continues until 1820)

**1775** Europe's last judicial execution for witchcraft takes place on 11 APRIL, when Anna Maria Schwägel (Germany) is beheaded

**1789** The last person in Britain to be judicially burned at the stake is a woman called Murphy, for forgery (minting false coins)

**1842** Midshipman Philip Spencer (USA) is the last member of the US Navy to be hanged for mutiny

**1868** Britain's last judicial public execution by hanging is that of Michael Barrett (Ireland), outside Newgate Prison, London on 26 MAY; legislation to prevent public executions receives royal assent three days later

**1918** The last British soldier to be shot for desertion is Private L. Harris, at 06:30 on 7 NOVEMBER, just four days before the end of the First World War

**1939** The last public execution by guillotine is that of convicted murderer Eugene Weidmann in Versailles, France, at 16:50 on 16 JUNE

**1945** The last American soldier to be shot for desertion is Private Eddie Slovik, at Ste-Marie-aux-Mines, France, on 31 JANUARY

**1955** The last woman to be judicially executed in Britain is Ruth Ellis (Wales), hanged at Holloway Prison, London, at 09:00 on 13 JULY for the murder of her former lover, David Blakely

**1962** Canada's last judicial execution takes place with the hanging of two

men in Toronto on 11 DECEMBER. Capital punishment is officially abolished for most offences on 14 JULY 1976, but retained for military offences including treason and mutiny. It is abolished altogether with the acceptance of an international treaty on 10 DECEMBER 1998

**1964** Convicted murderers Gwynne Owen Evans and Peter Anthony Allen (both Britain) are the last people in Britain to be judicially executed, hanged at 08:00 on 13 AUGUST for their joint crime, Evans at Strangeways Prison, Manchester, and Allen at Walton Prison, Liverpool

**1965** Capital punishment is officially abolished in Britain, except for treason, and abolished altogether with the acceptance of an international treaty on 10 DECEMBER 1998

**1967** Ronald Joseph Ryan (Australia) is the last person to be judicially executed in Australia, at 08:00 on 3 FEBRUARY in Pentridge Prison, Victoria. Western Australia is the last state to officially abolish capital punishment, in 1984, although the last execution in WA had taken place in 1964. Capital punishment is officially abolished nationwide in 1985

**1972** Capital punishment is officially abolished in Sweden and Finland

**1977** The last (non-public) execution by guillotine is that of convicted murderer Hamida Djandoubi (Tunisia) at Baumetes Prison, Marseilles, France, on 10 SEPTEMBER

**1978** Capital punishment is officially abolished in Denmark

**1979** Capital punishment is officially abolished in Norway

**1981** Capital punishment is officially abolished in France

**1982** Capital punishment is officially abolished in the Netherlands

**1994** Capital punishment is officially abolished in Italy

**1996** Capital punishment is officially abolished in Belgium

The Bible is divided into two parts, the Old and New Testaments, but some versions include the Apocrypha in a separate section, so there are actually three 'last books of the Bible': Malachi in the Old Testament, Revelation in the New and The Prayer of Manasses in the Apocrypha.

**44**   **The Last**   # BOOK OF THE BIBLE

● In 1632 printers Robert Barker and Martin Lucas (England) were fined £300 for omitting a single word from their edition of the Bible, which became known as the Adulterer's Bible. The word 'not' was missing from the seventh commandment, which therefore read: 'Thou shalt commit adultery'

● In 1971 a US firm published what became known as the Bathroom Bible after their alteration of a Hebrew euphemism in I Samuel 24:3, which in the authorized version read: 'Saul went in [to a cave] to cover his feet.' This was translated for the modern version as: 'Saul went into a cave to go to the bathroom'

● Apocrypha comes from the Greek, meaning 'things that are hidden', but its Biblical use has led to the modern meaning of 'without authority', from which we get the phrase 'apocryphal story' for tales of doubtful provenance, including so-called 'urban myths'

'Bible' means book (from the Greek *biblos*), but the Bible is no ordinary book, it is a self-contained library comprising an entire collection of books. The Old Testament, which is recognized as a holy book by both Jews and Christians, comprises 39 separate books in four groups. These groups are the Pentateuch (or Books of Moses), the Historical Books, the Books of Wisdom and, lastly, the Prophets. The last book of this last group is Malachi, which encourages faithfulness to God's Covenant and teachings, and prophesies the arrival of the Messiah.

The 14 books known collectively as the Apocrypha do not appear in the original Hebrew Bible, and, whereas the 39 'canonical' (i.e. officially recognized) books were written in Hebrew, the Apocrypha were written in Greek. For these reasons, the Apocrypha are often included in a separate section between the Old and New Testaments, although some versions of the Bible include them as part of the Old Testament. The last book of the Apocrypha (though it does not usually appear in Roman Catholic bibles) is The Prayer of Manasses (sometimes Manassas), a prayer of repentance for the wicked acts of King Manasseh of Judah.

The 27 books of the New Testament describe the life and teachings of Jesus Christ, the Messiah, and are split into two sections: the Gospels, which means 'good news', and the Epistles. The last of the four Gospels is that of St John, and the last book of the New Testament is the Book of Revelation, or The Revelation of St John the Divine, a.k.a. The Apocalypse. This book prophesies the Last Judgement and the rule of the Messiah, and is full of rich symbolism including the Four Horsemen of the Apocalypse: War, who rides a white horse; Slaughter, on a red horse; Famine, on a black horse; and the last, Death, riding on a pale horse.

| 11th–5th centuries BC | 5th century BC | c.58AD | c.64 | c.96 | c.100 |
|---|---|---|---|---|---|
| The first five books of the Old Testament, known as the Pentateuch, are written. They are Genesis, Exodus, Leviticus, Numbers and, the last, Deuteronomy | The Book of Malachi is completed and later appears as the last book of the Old Testament, though other books, such as Esther, are completed later | St Paul writes his Letter to the Romans, the earliest document in the New Testament. Though the Epistles, written mainly by Paul, appear after the Gospels in the New Testament, most of them are in fact written earlier than the Gospels | The first of the Gospels, that of Mark, is completed | St John the Divine (probably a pseudonym) completes the Book of Revelation, or Apocalypse, which later appears as the last book of the New Testament | John completes the fourth and last of the Gospels |

**TIMELINE: BOOKS OF THE BIBLE**

**Above** *St John Devouring the Book,* by Albrecht Dürer, one of his illustrations of *The Revelation of St John the Divine* (woodcut, 1498)

Modern secular society is moving towards the acceptance of Sunday as the last day of the week, reinforced by the printers of many calendars and diaries and by the fact that Sunday is considered part of the 'weekend'. But technically Saturday, not Sunday, is the last day of the week.

**The Last DAY OF THE WEEK**

| Sunday From the Anglo-Saxon *Sunnandaeg*, meaning sun's day | Monday From the Anglo-Saxon *Monandaeg*, meaning moon's day | Tuesday From the Anglo-Saxon *Tiwesdaeg*, from Tiw, the god of war | Wednesday From the Anglo-Saxon *Wodnesdaeg*, from Woden, the Anglo-Saxon form of the Norse Odin, the god of storms | Thursday From the Anglo-Saxon *Thuresdaeg*, from Thor, the god of thunder | Friday From the Anglo-Saxon *Frigedaeg*, from Frigg or Freya, the goddess of marriage | Saturday From the Anglo-Saxon *Saterdaeg*, from Saturn, the god of time |
|---|---|---|---|---|---|---|

■TIMELINE: THE WEEK

Although we owe the division of the year into months to the Romans, it is not so with the days of the week. The early Romans had no concept of weeks, and days were simply designated working days or non-working days. It was not until after the Roman Empire adopted Christianity that a seven-day week was introduced, by Emperor Constantine I in the 4th century AD, to enable the prescribed observance of a day of rest on the Lord's Day. The Romans called this day *Dies Dominica* from which comes the French name *Dimanche* for Sunday.

Although Constantine introduced a seven-day week to the Roman Empire, he did not invent the idea. It originated much earlier with the Jews, who followed the teachings of Genesis that God created the world in six days and rested on the seventh. Thus Saturday, the Jewish Sabbath (from *shabath*, meaning 'to rest'), was the last day of the week and Sunday, the Christian Lord's Day, was the first. Although the Lord's Day was declared a day of rest, the reasoning was not the same as that for the Jewish Sabbath; Sunday was celebrated as the day of the resurrection of Christ, not as God's day of rest after the Creation.

In modern times there is some confusion as to which is technically the last day of the week. Many diaries and calendars are printed with Sunday at the start of the week and many with it at the end, while dictionaries that define Sunday as 'the first day of the week' also define it as part of 'the weekend'. It seems that we now have a choice as to whether we consider Saturday or Sunday to be the last day of the week, but in practice it makes little difference because weeks are cyclical and therefore have no real beginning or end.

**DID YOU KNOW?**

● Although secular calendars consider each day to begin and end at midnight, the Jewish and Christian ecclesiastical calendars consider each to begin and end at sunset, which is why we say 'fortnight' rather than 'fortday'. 'Se'n night' was once a common phrase for a week, but has fallen into disuse, while fortnight, a contraction of fourteen-night, is still used in English-speaking countries to describe a two-week period

**Opposite** *Personifications of the days of the week*, an illustration by George R. Halkett for *Rumpelstiltskin*
**Right** God creating day and night, from the Book of Genesis, as illustrated in the Souvigny Bible (12th century)

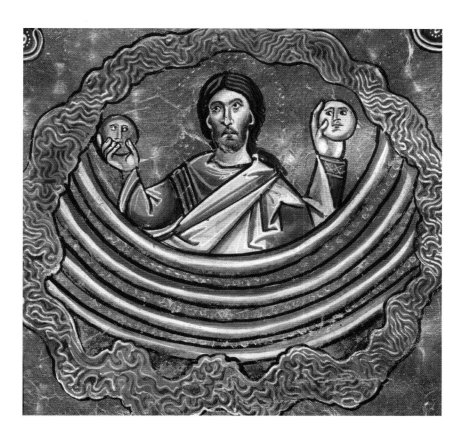

Most Western European alphabets and, therefore, the American alphabet, can be traced back to the Phoenician and North Semitic alphabets via the ancient Greek, whose first two letters give us the word 'alphabet'. But it was not until c.100AD that the Romans made Z the last letter.

**The Last** 

# LETTER OF THE ALPHABET

The Bible's Book of Revelation, chapter 1 verse 8, states: 'I am the Alpha and the Omega, the first and the last' (sometimes translated as 'the beginning and the ending'). The verse refers to the first and last letters of the Greek alphabet, but had Revelations been written at a different time the phrase might have been: 'I am the Alpha and the Tau', as it was often quoted in medieval literature. Tau was the last letter of the ancient Phoenician and Greek alphabets (it is still the last letter of the Hebrew alphabet) and remained so until the Greeks later adopted Omega as the last letter of their alphabet.

One of the symbols the ancient Greeks took from the North Semitic alphabet via the Phoenician was an arrow-like hieroglyphic that was the seventh letter of the Phoenician alphabet and which they called *zayin*. The Greeks adopted it as the sixth letter of their alphabet c.800BC, called it *zeta* and gave it the form 'Z'. The Greek alphabet was subsequently developed by the Romans, who at first dropped the letter, but later reinstated it at the end of their alphabet for use when writing words borrowed from Greek. And so, c.100AD, Z became the last letter of the Roman alphabet and remains so

**Right** Neon sign for a pizza bar in Tuscany, Italy
**Opposite** The letters Alpha and Omega, illuminated by Pedro for the King of Castile's *Book of Hours* (manuscript 1055)

today in most modern alphabets of Western Europe and the Americas.

The letter Z has different names on each side of the Atlantic – *zed* in England and *zee* in the USA – and was previously known by various names in England, including *izzard* and *ezod*. The letter is variously represented: in semaphore by one horizontal and one lowered flag to the right, in Morse Code by two dashes and two dots, in Braille by ⠵ and by the word Zulu (previously Zebra) in the phonetic alphabet.

**c.1700BC** The North Semitic alphabet develops

**c.1000BC** The Phoenicians develop a 22-letter alphabet influenced by the North Semitic alphabet

**c.1000–800BC** The ancient Greeks adapt the Phoenician alphabet and introduce it to Europe. The last letter of the Greek alphabet is Tau and, later, Omega

**c.800BC –114AD** The Romans learn the Greek alphabet from the Etruscans and develop an alphabet of 20 letters, which later gains 3 more letters

**c.250BC** The Roman alphabet is decreased to 21 letters, of which the last is X

**c.100AD** The Greek letters upsilon and zeta (Y and Z) are reinstated in the Roman alphabet as its last two letters

**9th century** St Cyril and St Methodius (Greece) devise the Glagolithic alphabet, which, c.900, is modified and renamed Cyrillic, after St Cyril. It is now used in Russia and most of Eastern Europe. Its last letter is Я, which transliterates as 'ya'

**c.16th century** The last letter to be added to the western European and American alphabet is the letter J/j, which now emerges in continental European languages as a soft consonant, having developed from the medieval practice of adding a tail to the first 'I/i' where two were written together. It is common in English by the mid-17th century, though most dictionaries treat it as a variant of 'I/i'

**18th century** The letters V (which emerged during the 15th century) and J are finally accepted by many dictionaries as letters in their own right, although they do not gain universal acceptance as such until the mid-19th century

# LAST BUT NOT LEAST...

## The Last Western Country to Grant Women the Vote

In 1971 Switzerland became the last Western country to grant women the right to vote in federal elections.

**Above** Swiss suffragettes, who had invaded the Federal Palace in Berne, demonstrate at the entrance to the Parliament Hall (undated photograph)

## The Last Electric and Steam-powered Land Speed Records

The land speed record was officially inaugurated in 1898, when it was set at 39.24mph by Count Gaston de Chasseloup-Laubat (France) in an electric car. The last electric car to hold the record was *Jenatzy*, named after its driver, Camille Jenatzy (Belgium), who set the record on 29 April 1899 and held it until 13 April 1902, when it was taken by Léon Serpollet (France) in his steam-powered car *Oeuf de Pâques* ('Easter Egg'). The last steam-powered land-speed record was set on 23 January 1906 at Daytona Beach, USA, when Fred Marriott (USA) reached an amazing 121.57mph in his steam-powered car *Rocket*. Marriott's record stood for 3$^{1}/_{2}$ years before it was beaten by the internal combustion engine on 8 November 1909, when Victor Hemery (France) took his Blitzen-Benz (Germany) to 125.95mph at Brooklands, England.

## The Last Steam-powered Flight

Strange though it may seem, steam did have its part to play in the pioneering of flight. The first heavier-than-air craft to take off under its own power was a steam-powered monoplane built by Clément Ader (France). Ader made his successful take-off in 1890, and the last steam-powered 'flight' came just four years later, in 1894. Inventor Hiram Stevens Maxim (USA–Britain) once said: 'If a domestic goose can fly, so can a man', and from 1889–94 he developed a steam-powered aircraft that succeeded in lifting off the ground, but it never achieved free flight. By then the internal combustion engine was already making its mark, and it was this form of propulsion that took the Wright brothers into the air nine years later, on 17 December 1903.

## The Last Gentlemen v. Players Cricket Match

The last annual Gentlemen v. Players cricket match between amateurs and professionals at Lord's Cricket Ground, London, took place in 1962. The fixture had first been played in 1806 and became an annual event in 1819, but the abolition of amateur status in first-class cricket rendered the fixture obsolete.

## The Last Television Cigarette Advertisement

It has long been known that smoking cigarettes damages people's health, and one early means of attempting to reduce consumption was to ban television advertisements for cigarettes. Britain's last television commercials for cigarettes were screened on the night of 31 July 1965, and the USA followed suit five years later, when President Nixon signed a bill passed by Congress banning such advertising from 1 January 1971. America's last televised cigarette advertisement was for Virginia Slims, and was screened during the *Tonight Show* on 31 December 1970.

**Right** Advertisement for Viriginia Slims cigarettes (c.1972)

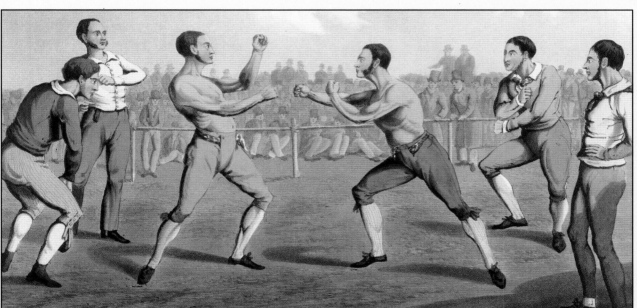

## The Last Bare-knuckle Fight and the Last 15-round Professional Boxing Match

Boxing developed out of bare-knuckle prizefights that were contested with no rounds and few, if any, rules. The first rules of boxing, including the concept of rounds, were introduced by Jack Broughton (England) in 1743, but the idea of restricting the number of rounds did not come until 1867, with the introduction of the Queensberry Rules and the advent of padded gloves. However, it was another 22 years before the wearing of gloves finally superseded bare-knuckle fighting in 1889,

when Jem Smith (England) won the last internationally recognized bare-knuckle prizefight, in Bruges, Belgium. For bouts fought under the Queensberry Rules the number of rounds was restricted, at first to 21, then to 15 and finally to 12. The last professional world championship match to last 15 rounds was the IBF strawweight title, in Bangkok, Thailand, on 29 August 1988, when Mahasamuth Sithnaruepol (Thailand) beat Inkyu Hwang (South Korea) on points.

**Above** *Bare-knuckle Boxers in Boxing Match*, by Henry Alken (undated 19th-century print)

# Chapter Two

# Historic Last Days

## The Last Day of **POMPEII**

Pompeii was not the only city to be buried by the eruption of Mount Vesuvius, but it is the best known. The last days of three cities came between 24 and 26 August 79AD with a volcanic eruption that covered Pompeii and Stabiae in smothering ash and buried Herculaneum in boiling mud.

Pompeii was a prosperous Roman city on the Bay of Naples, sited less than one mile from the foot of Mount Vesuvius and some six miles from the neighbouring cities of Herculaneum and Stabiae. The last days of these three cities were recorded in all their horrific detail by the Roman writer Pliny the Younger (Italy) as part of the world's earliest recorded scientific account of a volcanic eruption.

The first explosion heralding the eruption came on 24 August 79AD. According to Pliny, the explosion shook the buildings 'as if they had been torn from their foundations' and created a thick cloud of dark ash. He wrote of a 'black and dreadful cloud [which] burst open in twisted and quivering gusts to reveal long flames resembling large flashes of lightning' and went on to decribe how the cloud descended and covered the earth 'like a flood'. Over the next two days this flood of hot ash, cinders and poisonous fumes buried Pompeii and Stabiae and killed thousands in their homes. Pliny described the landscape as being 'covered by a thick layer of ash that resembled snow'. This deadly coat of cinders sealed off the cities and preserved many of the bodies until they were discovered, some 1,700 years later, by an engineer called Alcubierre (Italy), eerily mummified by the ash that had even preserved the agonized expressions of the dying.

Meanwhile, Herculaneum was buried not by ash but by an unstoppable stream of lava and boiling mud, up to 30 metres deep in places, which filled the town and the harbour, preserving it even more completely than its more famous neighbour, Pompeii.

**DID YOU KNOW?**

● Pliny the Younger witnessed the eruption of Etna from a distance of some 20 miles, but his uncle and adoptive father, Pliny the Elder, was in command of a Roman fleet that rescued some of the populace. He went ashore at the town of Stabiae in order to witness the eruption more closely and was killed by the poisonous fumes released by the eruption

● Before the havoc wrought by Vesuvius, Pompeii was notorious for another reason: sports hooliganism. The Roman historian Tacitus records that during the 1st century a battle broke out in the amphitheatre at Pompeii between home sports fans and visiting fans from neighbouring Nuceria

port of Vestmannaeyjar under a rain of ash. All but one of the 4,500 inhabitants are evacuated safely, but having been buried in ash Vestmannaeyjar is dubbed 'the Pompeii of the north'

**1980** Mount St Helens, Washington State, USA, erupts on 19 MAY, killing eight people and devastating an area of 230 square miles

**1985** Mount Nevado del Ruiz, Colombia, erupts on 13 NOVEMBER, killing almost 23,000 people

**2004** The Grímsvötn volcano, buried nearly 200 metres beneath Iceland's biggest glacier, erupts on 1 NOVEMBER, creating a seven-mile column of ash that disrupts transatlantic air traffic

**Above** The last major eruption of Mount Vesuvius, Italy, to date (March 1944)

**Below** *The Last Day of Pompeii,* by Karl Bryullov (1830–33)

The Inquisition, an organ of the Roman Catholic church established for the prosecution of heretics, was first established in 13th-century France and Germany, but this medieval Inquisition was tame compared to the terrors of the Spanish Inquisition, whose last day was 15 July 1834.

# THE INQUISITION

**Above** *Pope Gregory IX Consecrating the Chapel of Subiaco*, by Consolo
**Opposite** *St Dominic Presiding Over an* Auto Da Fé, by Pedro Berruguete (1475)

During the 12th and 13th centuries a number of Roman Catholics began to rebel against their church. Some secular authorities refused to punish these heretics and so, between 1229 and 1231, Pope Gregory IX (Italy) set up a church commission known as the Inquisition to investigate suspects and force them to recant their heresy. This Inquisition comprised temporary tribunals set up in France, Germany, Italy and parts of Spain. It was superseded in the 15th century by the notorious Spanish Inquisition, championed by King Ferdinand of Aragon (Spain), sanctioned by decree of Pope Sixtus IV (Italy) in 1478 and established in 1480.

The Spanish Inquisition is now universally condemned for the abuse of power by its inquisitors, the injustice of its tribunals and the barbarity of its methods of inquisition, punishment and execution. The Inquisition regularly held public ceremonies, called *autos da fé* ('acts of faith'), that involved a procession and a mass at which the accused repented of their sins, followed by the burning of those who refused to recant, including not only lapsed Catholics but also Jews and Muslims who refused to practise Catholicism.

The 16th and last permanent tribunal of the Spanish Inquisition was established in Madrid in 1640, but the Inquisition began to lose its power towards the end of the following century. The Inquisition of Portugal held its last *auto da fé* in 1765, and the last of the Inquisition in France came with its suppression in 1772. Progress towards enlightenment continued with the last day of the Inquisition of Portugal in 1821 and the last day of the hated Spanish Inquisition on 15 July 1834, with the issue of a decree by Queen Isabel II (Spain) suppressing the Inquisition, paying off all its officials and seconding all its property to the public purse.

## DID YOU KNOW?

● The astronomer, mathematician and philosopher Galileo Galilei (Italy) was twice taken before the Inquisition for supporting the views of Nicolaus Copernicus (Poland) that the earth moved around the sun rather than vice versa. The first time, in 1616, Galileo was acquitted of heresy, but ordered not to 'hold or defend' the Copernican theory. The second time, in 1633, he was found guilty and forced under threat of torture to recant. Legend has it that after his recantation Galileo muttered under his breath the words that have also been attributed as his last, when he died in 1642: *'Eppur si muove'*, meaning 'yet it does move'. On 31 October 1992 Pope John Paul II (Poland) formally retracted the sentence against Galileo

**TIMELINE: THE INQUISITION**

**1229–31** Pope Gregory IX (Italy) establishes local and temporary Inquisitions in France and Germany

**1237** The Inquisition spreads to the realm of Aragon, Spain

**1252** Pope Innocent IV (Italy) authorizes the Inquisition to use torture to extract evidence or confessions and later establishes a permanent Inquisition in Italy

**1478** Pope Sixtus IV (Italy) issues a decree founding the new Castilian or Spanish Inquisition, which is established in 1480 and eventually comprises 16 permanent tribunals

**1539** The Inquisition of Portugal is established on a temporary basis

**1547** The Inquisition of Portugal is made permanent by decree of Pope Paul III

**1560** The Inquisition of Portugal is established in Goa and, later this century, in Brazil

**1570** The Spanish Inquisition is established in Peru

**1571** The Spanish Inquisition is established in Mexico

**1640** The 16th and last permanent tribunal of the Spanish Inquisition is established, in Madrid

**1765** The Inquisition of Portugal holds its last *auto da fé*

**1772** The last day of the Inquisition in France

**1808** The Spanish Inquisition is temporarily suppressed by Napoleon (France) when he enters Madrid

**1814** King Ferdinand VII (Spain) restores the Spanish Inquisition after his own restoration to the throne the previous year

**1821** The last day of the Inquisition of Portugal, which is abolished by decree

**1834** The last day of the Spanish Inquisition is 15 JULY. The last Secretary of the Inquisition is Juan Antonio Llorente (Spain)

As with many lasts relating to social practices, it is only possible to date the last official example in certain places. Slavery continues to this day, legally and illegally, in parts of the world, but slavery was officially outlawed worldwide by the League of Nations in 1926.

## The Last Days of SLAVERY

**TIMELINE: ABOLITION OF SLAVERY**

**1772** The last year of legal slavery within the British Isles. Lawyer and abolitionist Granville Sharp (England) wins a legal ruling that secures the freedom of any slave who sets foot in the British Isles, effectively making slavery illegal in Britain

**1780** Maine, Massachusetts and Pennsylvania become the first American states to abolish slavery

**1787** With others, Sharp establishes the Society for Effecting the Abolition of the Slave Trade

**1789** William Wilberforce (England) tables a parliamentary motion to abolish the slave trade, but vested interests mean that it is not passed; the same happens in 1791

**1804** Denmark is the first European country to end its involvement in the slave trade

**1806** Wilberforce finally succeeds in passing a bill banning Britons from trading in slaves; it becomes law the following year

**1807** Wilberforce's 1806 bill becomes law on 25 MARCH, marking the last year of legal British slave trading; the last British slave ship, the *Kitty Amelia*, leaves Liverpool. The US government passes legislation outlawing the importation of slaves. Both laws come into force on 1 JANUARY 1808

**1814–15** In Austria, at the Congress of Vienna, Britain persuades most other European nations to abolish slave trading

The campaign to end the evils of slavery was led by luminaries such as Granville Sharp (England), who succeeded in outlawing slavery within the British Isles (but not the Empire) as early as 1772. However, British involvement in slave trading continued until it was abolished by parliament in March 1807 – the last day of legal British slave trading was 31 December 1807, before the bill came into force on 1 January 1808. Earlier, however, Denmark had had the honour of being the first European country to abolish slave trading, in 1804. The following decade abolitionists took their campaign into Europe where, at the 1814–15 Congress of Vienna,

Austria, they managed to persuade most other European nations to condemn the slave trade, France and Spain ending their involvement in 1818 and 1820 respectively.

On 28 August 1833 the British Parliament passed the Slavery Abolition Act, which replaced slavery in the British Empire with a seven-year bonded apprenticeship, leading to the last day of legal slavery on 31 July 1834. The last vestiges of slavery in the Empire were removed on 1 August 1838 when the apprenticeship, too, was abolished.

Meanwhile, across the Atlantic, in 1780 Maine, Massachusetts and Pennsylvania had become the first American states to abolish slavery and the federal government had banned the import of slaves (but not slavery itself) throughout the USA from 1808. Half a century later, slavery was one of the main issues leading to American Civil War between the pro-slavery southern states and the anti-slavery north – victory for the northern states led to the last day of legal slavery across the USA on 31 January 1865, before Abraham Lincoln (USA) signed the 13th Amendment on 1 February, which is still celebrated in the USA as National Freedom Day.

It was 1926 before slavery was officially outlawed worldwide under the terms of the International Slavery Convention promulgated that year by the League of Nations.

**Left** Former slaves Jennie Jacobs (left), 96, and Phyllis Pollitt, 99, prepare to celebrate the birthday of Abraham Lincoln, in an old people's home in Philadelphia, USA (February 1940)
**Above** Africans bound and being forced to walk to the coast to be sold into slavery

**1816** The American Colonization Society is founded to campaign against slavery

**1818** France abolishes slave trading

**1820** Spain abolishes slave trading

**1833** Wilberforce breathes his last just three months before British Parliament passes the Slavery Abolition Act, on 28 AUGUST **1833**. The American Anti-Slavery Society is founded

**1834** The last day of legal slavery in the British Empire comes on 31 JULY, before the previous year's Slavery Abolition Act comes into force on 1 AUGUST, replacing slavery with a seven-year 'apprenticeship'

**1838** The last vestiges of official slavery in the British Empire come when the apprenticeship is abolished from 1 AUGUST

**1845** France abolishes slavery (as opposed to merely slave trading, see: *1818*)

**1848** France frees all the slaves in its remaining colonies

**1865** Slavery is abolished across the USA when Abraham Lincoln (USA) signs the 13th Amendment on 1 FEBRUARY

**1873** The last slaves are traded at the last known African slave market, in Zanzibar. Spain ends slavery in Puerto Rico

**1886** Spain ends slavery in Cuba

**1888** Brazil abolishes slavery

**1926** Slavery is outlawed worldwide by the International Slavery Convention of the League of Nations

**1956** A Supplementary Convention to the 1926 League of Nations agreement aims to eradicate all forms of servitude that approximate to slavery

The Raj was the name given to British rule in India, which began with the British East India Company and was taken over by the Crown in 1858. Mahatma Gandhi's nationalist movement made independence inevitable, leading to the last day of the Raj on 14 August 1947.

**The Last Day of**

# THE RAJ

**Above** Mahatma Gandhi with his two granddaughters, Ava and Manu (c.1947) **Opposite** Soldiers of the 1st Battalion Somerset Light Infantry (the last British troops to leave India) display their colours during the last parade in Bombay (February 1948)

**DID YOU KNOW?**

● When Mahatma Gandhi visited London, England, he stayed at the Hyde Park Hotel on Knightsbridge. He did not demand many luxuries, but the hotel did go to the length of milking a goat for him each day

The name raj comes from *rajya*, the Sanskrit word for government or rule. The British Raj in India lasted in its various forms for some 200 years, and the alternative championed by Mahatma Gandhi (India, properly Mohandâs Gandhi) was Home Rule, or *Swaraj*. Under British rule, a strong Indian nationalist movement developed whose cause was intensified during the 1920s by Gandhi's famous campaign of non-violent civil disobedience. In 1947 Gandhi succeeded in forcing his goal of independence.

The last day of the Raj came very suddenly, after less than a year of frantic planning hastened by the fear that civil war might break out before the original deadline of June 1948. A new deadline was set for midnight on 14 August 1947 and on that night a conch shell was blown to mark the opening of the new Indian Constituent Assembly, with Jawaharlal Nehru as prime minister. Each member swore 'to dedicate myself to the service of India and her people' and Nehru announced: 'At the stroke of the midnight hour, when the world sleeps, India will awake to life and freedom.'

The handover of power was overseen by Lord Mountbatten (Britain), who in February had been appointed the last viceroy of India. One of his last duties, before relinquishing his title of viceroy to become the first governor general of the new independent dominion of India, was to deliver a message of congratulation from King George VI to the people of Pakistan, a newly formed independent dominion resulting from the partition of India between Muslims (Pakistan) and Hindus (India). The celebrations were marred by violence as Muslims and Hindus tried to move to the 'right' side of the new border, but nonetheless independence had been achieved, something that Gandhi described as '...the noblest act of the British nation'.

**1600** British East India Company is established, initially as a trading company

**1701** British East India Company begins exerting political control after being granted rights over several districts near Calcutta

**1757** Robert Clive (England, known as Clive of India) wins the Battle of Plassey to give the East India Company control of Bengal

**1784** The British government passes the India Act, making the East India Company responsible to parliament

**1857** Indian Mutiny takes place: mutiny in the Bengal army against British officers spreads throughout the country into a revolt against the rule of the East India Company

**1858** British authority is restored, the administrative powers of the East India Company are abolished and India is brought under British sovereignty

**TIMELINE: THE RAJ**

**1885** The Indian National Congress (INC) is formed to promote Indian nationalism

**1919** The British government passes the 1919 Government of India Act, giving Indians some measure of provincial self-government

**1919–22** Mahatma Gandhi (India) becomes leader of the INC and conducts a campaign of civil disobedience in demand for independence

**1935** The British government passes the 1935 Government of India Act, giving Indians greater internal self-government, but retaining British control of external affairs and national defence

**1947** On 20 FEBRUARY Lord Mountbatten is appointed the last viceroy of India. The Raj ends at midnight on 14 AUGUST, as India is partitioned into two independent dominions within the British Commonwealth: India and Pakistan. King George VI relinquishes the title Emperor of India, making him the last British monarch to hold the title

The word apartheid is now used for any segregationalist policy, but it has its roots in South Africa's erstwhile policy of racial segregation, deriving from the Afrikaans *apart* and *heid*, meaning, literally, 'aparthood'. The last day of official aparthood in South Africa came in 1993.

# APARTHEID

**Below** African National Congress leader Nelson Mandela leaves Victor Verster Prison, accompanied by his wife, Winnie, and a crowd of supporters (February 1990)

Apartheid was an inhuman policy of racial segregation that was instigated in 1948 by South Africa's National Party under Prime Minister Daniel Malan (South Africa) and continued by his successors until 1989, when Prime Minister F.W. de Klerk (South Africa) came to power and began dismantling the hated machinery of this iniquitous system.

De Klerk almost immediately desegregated many public facilities as well as lifting a 30-year-old ban on the African National Congress (ANC), which had been formed in 1912 to campaign for the rights of South Africa's black majority. The action that reverberated around the globe was the freeing of

| **1940s** The Afrikaans word *apartheid* is coined, meaning 'aparthood' or 'separateness' | **1948** The National Party, under Prime Minister Daniel Malan (South Africa), officially adopts apartheid as government policy | **1950** The entire South African population is classified by race and segregated under the Group Areas Act | **1960** The ANC is banned following the Sharpeville massacre, when police shoot and kill 69 anti-apartheid demonstrators | **1964** ANC activist Nelson Mandela (South Africa) is sentenced to life imprisonment for political crimes including sabotage and treason | **1984** A new South African constitution gives segregated representation to Asians and 'coloureds', but continues to exclude blacks |
| --- | --- | --- | --- | --- | --- |

**TIMELINE: APARTHEID IN SOUTH AFRICA**

● A measure of just how much South Africa had changed after apartheid came with the 1995 Rugby Union World Cup when Nelson Mandela, wearing the green and gold of the national team, welcomed the world to his 'Rainbow Nation'. When South Africa played New Zealand in the final on 24 June at Ellis Park, Johannesburg, the atmosphere was felt across the globe. South Africa won the World Cup with a drop-goal in extra time, and afterwards captain François Pienaar said: 'There's a lot of work still to do in South Africa, but I'm proud of what happened ... It was a massive step forward, and it has become a symbol of a united South Africa'

**Above** F.W. de Klerk and Nelson Mandela (May 1994)

ANC leader Nelson Mandela (South Africa), who, after 27 years in prison, served his last full day on 10 February 1990 and walked free on the afternoon of 11 February, saying: 'I greet you in the name of peace, democracy and freedom for all' and calling for a peaceful and definitive end to 'the dark hell of apartheid'.

Reform came more quickly than even Mandela could have hoped when on 1 February 1991, to cries of 'traitor' from many white MPs, de Klerk announced that he would repeal the last of the remaining apartheid laws. With apartheid legislation repealed, the last barrier to a free democracy was the constitution. The last day of constitutional apartheid was 22 December 1993, when the South African Parliament voted by 237 votes to 45 to dissolve the existing constitution and to re-form under an interim 'majority rule constitution' pending free multi-racial elections the following year. As expected, the ANC easily won those elections. De Klerk was appointed vice president and Nelson Mandela was elected South Africa's first black president, a fitting symbol of the very last of official apartheid in South Africa.

| | | | | |
|---|---|---|---|---|
| **1989** Under Prime Minister F.W. de Klerk (South Africa), public facilities are desegregated and many **ANC** activists released | **1990** Mandela serves his last day in prison and is freed on 11 FEBRUARY. De Klerk lifts the 30-year-old ban on the **ANC** | **1991** The last of apartheid legislation: on 1 FEBRUARY de Klerk announces that he will repeal the remaining apartheid laws | **1993** The last day of the apartheid constitution: on 22 DECEMBER the South African Parliament votes to dissolve itself and re-form under a new constitution, paving the way for free elections the following year. De Klerk and Mandela share the Nobel Peace Prize for negotiating the transition | **1994** The ANC wins South Africa's first multi-racial free elections in MAY and Mandela is voted South Africa's first black president, marking the symbolic end of apartheid just five months after its constitutional end |

The Soviet Union came into being in 1922 when the former Russian Empire was renamed the Union of Soviet Socialist Republics (USSR). It exercised an iron grip over eastern Europe and northern Asia from the end of the Second World War until its last month of power, December 1991.

## The Last Day of THE SOVIET UNION

### DID YOU KNOW?

● Many of Mikhail Gorbachev's political problems stemmed from the fact that he was unable to ensure the nation had an adequate supply of food, which created unrest across the USSR. In 1991 he asked whether people would start a revolution simply for sausages – the answer was yes. Contemplating resignation after the formation of the CIS, Gorbachev used another culinary analogy when he issued a warning to journalists about the danger of unscrupulous business and political leaders 'carving up the country like a pie'

● Boris Yeltsin and his fellow rebel leaders were relatively gracious in victory, calling for Gorbachev's resignation in reasonably polite terms: 'We want a president of a country who has done a lot of good as well as made mistakes to leave with dignity.' However, underlying this polite request was the suggestion that if he didn't leave with dignity he would be forced to leave without it

From 1928 until his death in 1953, Joseph Stalin (Georgia), general secretary of the Communist Party, exerted total political control over the Soviet Union by executing or imprisoning his critics and political opponents. Repression lessened under his successors, but nonetheless the Communist Party maintained its totalitarian regime and it was not until Mikhail Gorbachev (USSR) came to power in 1985 that those wanting democracy had any hope of gaining influence.

Gorbachev introduced wide-ranging reforms with his policies of *perestroika* (restructuring) and *glasnost* (openness), aimed at revitalizing the stagnant economy and ending the Cold War between the Soviet bloc and the West. His goal was to achieve 'a revolution within the revolution', in the hope that reform could be brought about under the control of the Communist Party. However, radical constitutional changes introduced in 1988–89 reawakened long-suppressed nationalism among the member republics, with pressure for greater independence coming, in particular, from Boris Yeltsin (USSR), who in 1990 was voted President of the Russian Republic.

But if Gorbachev was moving too slowly for the reformists, he was moving too quickly for hardline communists who, backed by the military and the KGB, attempted a coup on 19 August 1991 in an attempt to restore Communist

**Right** Mikhail Gorbachev (left) and Boris Yeltsin in the Russian Parliament (August 1991)
**Opposite** Soviet actress Tatyana Dogileva posing at Mosfilm Studios among busts of Soviet icons: (left to right) Lenin, Marx, Gogol, Mayakovski and Stalin

**1985** Communist Party leader and State President Konstantin Chernenko (Russia) dies. Mikhail Gorbachev (USSR) is appointed Communist Party leader and introduces policies of *perestroika* (restructuring) and *glasnost* (openness), paving the way for change

**1988** An All-Union Party Congress approves radical constitutional changes. Gorbachev is elected head of state. Open opposition to the communist regime begins in several Caucasus and Baltic republics

**1989** Open multi-party elections are held in a move towards 'socialist democracy', bringing to power coalition governments committed to reform. Hungary legalizes opposition parties. The Berlin Wall is breached. Communist regimes collapse in Poland, Czechoslovakia, Bulgaria, Romania and East Germany
*See also: The Last Day of the Berlin Wall, page 66*

**1990** Nationalist and anti-communist candidates are successful in multi-party local elections across the USSR. Boris Yeltsin (USSR) is elected president of the Russian Republic – he immediately leaves the Communist Party and urges Gorbachev to grant Soviet republics more independence. Gorbachev is awarded the Nobel Peace Prize for improving relations between the USSR and the West, leading to the end of the Cold War

**1991** Many Soviet republics declare independence. On 19 AUGUST hardline communists, supported by the armed forces and the KGB, attempt a coup. Yeltsin puts down the coup, takes power from Gorbachev and forces the dissolution of the USSR. Three dates are often cited as the last day of the USSR: 8 DECEMBER, when three states announce the formation of the CIS; 21 DECEMBER, when 11 states sign a document officially founding the CIS; and 25 DECEMBER, when Gorbachev resigns

Party control after several republics declared independence. The coup was defeated by reformists led by Yeltsin, who reinstated Gorbachev, but undermined his power, forming the Commonwealth of Independent States (CIS) on 8 December and declaring the end of the USSR, claiming somewhat prematurely: 'The USSR, as a subject of international law and a geopolitical reality, has ceased to exist.' On 21 December the leaders of 11 former Soviet republics signed a declaration officially founding the CIS, marking the last day of the USSR in all but name. CIS leaders also demanded that Gorbachev resign by the end of the year. He did so on 25 December, when the red flag was lowered over the Kremlin for the last time, marking the official last day of the Soviet Union.

# THE BERLIN WALL

The Berlin Wall was far more than a physical barrier dividing a German city; it was also the embodiment of the political barrier dividing East from West during the Cold War. After 28 years as a hated symbol and agent of oppression, the wall was finally breached on 9/10 November 1989.

**TIMELINE: BERLIN 1989**

**11 SEPTEMBER Hungary** opens its borders, allowing a mass exodus of East Germans to the West

**7 OCTOBER Soviet President Mikhail Gorbachev** visits East Berlin and urges the government to introduce reforms, sparking off pro-reform rallies across East Germany

**18 OCTOBER Erich Honecker, German** Communist Party leader since 1971, is replaced by Egon Krenz

**4 NOVEMBER One million people** protest in East Berlin against communist oppression

**7 NOVEMBER The East German** government resigns en masse

**9 NOVEMBER At midnight, all border** points are opened, including crossing points through the Berlin Wall, most famously Checkpoint Charlie

**10 NOVEMBER Bulldozers move in to** create additional crossing points and begin demolishing the wall

**11 NOVEMBER Largest movement of** Europeans ever recorded in a single day as people move freely from East to West and back

Since the partition of Germany in 1949 a growing tide of refugees had fled communist East Germany via West Berlin. On the night of 13 August 1961 the East German authorities sealed this border with the West by erecting temporary barriers across Berlin. Later, these temporary barriers were replaced by twin four-metre high reinforced concrete walls with a no-man's land between them, stretching some 29 miles across the city – a physical representation of the metaphorical Iron Curtain dividing East from West, communism from capitalism.

In the 28 years of its existence, more than 70 people died trying to escape over the Berlin Wall, but from midnight on 9 November 1989 East Germans were able to walk through the checkpoints unopposed – as he crossed to the West, one young East German spoke for thousands when he yelled: 'I'm no longer in prison.'

The last day of the wall – the culmination of two months of sweeping political upheaval sparked by the opening of Hungary's borders – began with a press conference at which Gunter Schabowski (Germany) announced that from midnight that night there would be freedom of movement across the country's borders without special dispensation – even across the wall. Crowds soon gathered on both sides of the divide and, as the clocks struck 12, the checkpoints were opened. Thousands of people swarmed over and through the wall, while others began demolishing it with whatever tools were to hand, a process continued officially the following day using bulldozers. On the night of 9/10 November 1989 the Iron Curtain was at last lifted and the hated barrier that had been the Berlin Wall became a gateway to freedom.

## DID YOU KNOW?

● In a survey conducted in 2004 of just over 2,000 former East and West Germans, nearly 20% of those interviewed said they would like to see the Berlin Wall reinstated. The poll found that 25% of West Germans and 12% of East Germans did not want to be part of a united country and that many West Germans resented paying for reunification while a similar number of East Germans said that their finances were no better than under communism. (Former West Germans are sometimes referred to in the east as 'arrogant Wessies', while easterners are known in the west as 'Jammer Ossies' – whining Easterners)

**Opposite top** The Berlin Wall is reinforced with a second concrete wall built parallel to the first (March 1967)
**Opposite bottom** Germans celebrate by standing on the hated wall (November 1989)

When they work, bridges are among the marvels of engineering. When they don't, the results can be spectacular and deadly. Infamous last days of bridges include the collapse of the Tay Bridge, on 28 December 1879, and of the Tacoma Narrows Bridge, on 7 November 1940.

## Last Days of BRIDGES

### DID YOU KNOW?

● Not only was the collapse of the Tay Bridge one of its century's worst bridge collapses, it also spawned one of its century's worst poems. William McGonagall (Scotland) commemorated the disaster in verse, beginning:

*Beautiful railway bridge of the Silvery Tay,*
*Alas I am so sorry to say,*
*That 90 lives have been taken away,*
*On the last Sabbath day of 1879*

### The last day of the Tay Bridge

In June 1879 engineer Thomas Bouch (England) was knighted for his achievement in designing the Tay Bridge, Scotland, which had opened two years earlier as the world's longest bridge. Six months after Bouch was knighted, the bridge collapsed.

The last day of what Scottish poet William McGonagall called the 'Beautiful railway bridge of the Silvery Tay' was 28 December 1879. As dusk fell, a storm was gathering strength over Dundee, with winds rising to Force 11 and gusting to over 100mph across the Tay Estuary. At 19:00, signalman Thomas Barclay (Scotland) gave the mail train the signal to cross the bridge and he and his colleague John Watt (Scotland) watched the lights of the train as it pulled away onto the bridge. Then they saw sparks and four large flashes, after which the lights of the train disappeared.

The Tay Bridge had 13 high girder spans at the centre to allow clearance

**1014** King Ethelred II (England) and his ally King Olaf Tryggvesson (Norway) pull down London Bridge to divide the forces of the attacking Danish Vikings

**1660** Last day of repairs to the Pont St-Bénézet, France, better known as the Pont d'Avignon, some 350 years after construction. Only four of the 22 medieval arches will survive to the 21st century

**1854** The last day of the Wheeling Suspension Bridge, Ohio, USA, then the world's longest single span, which collapses at 15:00 on 17 MAY, six years after completion. Noone is killed or injured and a new bridge opens in 1860

**1876** The last day of the Ashtabula Bridge, Ohio, USA, which collapses on the night of 29 DECEMBER, 11 years after completion, killing 90 people on the 11-carriage Pacific Express train, which falls into the Ashtabula Creek 23 metres below

**1879** The last day of the Tay Bridge, Scotland, which collapses on the night of 28 DECEMBER, two years after completion, killing 75 people

**1907** The last day of the Quebec Bridge, Canada, which collapses on 29 AUGUST while under construction, killing 86 people

**1940** The last day of the Tacoma Narrows Bridge in Washington State, USA, which collapses on 7 NOVEMBER, just four months after opening

**1945** The last day of the bridge over the River Kwai, Burma, built by Allied prisoners-of-war and destroyed by Allied forces on 13 OCTOBER

**1970** The last day of the Milford Haven Bridge, Wales, which collapses during construction on 2 JUNE, killing four people. The last day of the West Gate Bridge, Melbourne, Australia, which collapses during construction on 15 OCTOBER, killing 35 people

**1989** The last day of several bridges in San Francisco, USA, which collapse on 17 OCTOBER as a result of the Loma Prieta earthquake

for shipping and it was this part of the bridge that had collapsed, sending the mail train and its passengers plunging into the icy water below: 75 people died, but only 46 bodies were recovered. The inquiry into the disaster concluded that the bridge had been 'badly designed, badly constructed and badly maintained' and as a result Bouch was dismissed as engineer of his new project, the Forth Rail Bridge, and died a year later a broken man.

## The last day of the Tacoma Narrows Bridge

The Tacoma Narrows Bridge across Puget Sound, Washington State, USA, opened to traffic on 1 July 1940 and was nicknamed 'Galloping Gertie' because the bridge deck was so flexible that the road would undulate in even relatively minor winds. It became something of an attraction and motorists would drive there especially to experience the galloping bridge, but on 7 November 1940 Galloping Gertie tore herself to pieces.

The wind rose to a moderately high 44mph (the bridge was supposedly designed to withstand 120mph) and the familiar gallop developed into an uncontrolled bucking and writhing. Motorist Leonard Coatsmith (USA) abandoned his car and managed to crawl on his hands and knees to safety before the bridge was closed to traffic. The movement escalated until the bridge deck was rising and falling up to 9 metres and the deck was twisting up to 90 degrees before some of the suspension hangers tore loose, sending a 180-metre section of concrete decking plunging into the Puget Sound.

This was one of the world's most famous bridge collapses, partly because it has been shown around the globe on newsreel footage and on television, having been filmed by Professor Farquharson (USA) of the University of Washington.

**Opposite** Steam launches and a diver's barge search for bodies and survivors of the Tay Bridge Disaster. Drawing from *The Illustrated London News* (1880)

**Above** The Tacoma Narrows Bridge writhes, twists and tears itself to pieces, taking Leonard Coatsmith's car with it (November 1940)

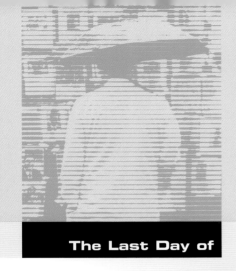

The last day of New York's World Trade Center is burned into the collective memory of the developed world, for this was not simply the last day of a symbolic landmark, it was also the last day of nearly 3,000 innocent people slaughtered in the name of religion.

**The Last Day of**

# THE WORLD TRADE CENTER

• A competition to design a new World Trade Center was won by architect Daniel Libeskind (Poland–USA) with a project entitled 'Memory Foundations', comprising two open spaces and seven buildings that include the 540-metre-high Freedom Tower, whose height commemorates the date of the American Declaration of Independence. Two of the buildings will be sited to create a wedge of light that will shine precisely across Ground Zero on 11 September each year between 08:46, when the first plane hit, and 10:28, when the second tower collapsed, in what Libeskind calls a 'perpetual tribute to altruism and courage'

**Opposite top** Port Authority police embrace at the funeral of a fellow officer killed in the World Trade Center (19 September 2001)
**Opposite bottom** Notices at Bellevue Hospital, New York, showing some of those missing in the attack on the World Trade Center

The facts have been documented, the reasons analyzed, the human cost counted and the debris cleared. But the enormity of what happened on 11 September 2001 does not diminish, and its after-effects continue. The day began like any other, but, at 08:46, that Tuesday morning turned from one that few people would have remembered into one that noone could forget.

This was the last day of American Airlines Flight 11, which took off at 07:59 from Boston bound for Los Angeles. But, like three other flights that day, Flight 11 did not reach its destination. Hijackers took control of the plane at approximately 08:15 and told the passengers: 'Call home. You will be dying.' At 08:46 they flew the plane into the North Tower of the World Trade Center, which collapsed at 10:28.

It was the last day of United Airlines Flight 175, which took off from Boston 15 minutes after Flight 11, also bound for Los Angeles. At approximately 09:00, one passenger called his parents to tell them the plane had been hijacked. At 09:03 it hit the South Tower of the World Trade Center, which collapsed at 09:59.

It was the last day of American Airlines Flight 77, which took off from Dulles at 08:20, disappeared from radar screens en route to Los Angeles, and then reappeared heading in the opposite direction, towards Washington, DC. At 09:43 it hit the Pentagon, ploughing through three of the five concentric rings of offices.

And it was the last day of United Airlines Flight 93 from Newark to San Francisco, one of whose passengers called his wife and told her: 'I know we're all going to die... There's three of us who are going to do something about it.'

| **05:53** The hijackers begin to assemble. The first of them pass through security at Portland Jetport, Maine, and fly to Logan International Airport, Boston | **07:59** American Airlines Flight 11 from Boston–Los Angeles takes off 14 minutes behind schedule, with 81 passengers and 11 crew | **08:14** United Airlines Flight 175 from Boston–Los Angeles takes off 16 minutes behind schedule, with 56 passengers and 9 crew | **c.08:15** Hijackers take over AA Flight 11 | **08:20** American Airlines Flight 77 from Dulles–Los Angeles takes off 10 minutes behind schedule, with 58 passengers and 6 crew | **08:41** United Airlines Flight 93 from Newark–San Francisco takes off 42 minutes behind schedule, with 38 passengers and 7 crew | **c.08:42** Hijackers take over UA Flight 175 |

**TIMELINE: 9/11 (EASTERN DAYLIGHT TIME)** (NOTE: TIMES VARY BETWEEN PUBLISHED ACCOUNTS OF 9/11)

At 10:06 the plane crashed near an abandoned mine without reaching its intended target.

No words are sufficient to describe the events of that day, but two numbers have come to represent the anguish, the suffering and the heroism, and to serve as an epitaph for those who died: 9/11.

| **08:46** AA Flight 11, a Boeing 767, hits the North Tower of the World Trade Center | **c.09:00** Hijackers take over AA Flight 77 | **09:03** UA Flight 175, a Boeing 767, hits the South Tower of the World Trade Center | **09:43** AA Flight 77, a Boeing 777, hits the west wing of the Pentagon, Washington, DC | **09:59** The South Tower collapses | **10:06** UA Flight 93, a Boeing 757, crashes into the ground near Shanksville, Pennsylvania, while flying towards Washington, DC | **10:28** The North Tower collapses | **17:20** The 47-storey Building 7 of the World Trade Center collapses |
|---|---|---|---|---|---|---|---|

**The Last Day of**

# THE FIRST WORLD WAR

The First World War began with the assassination of one man, the heir to the Austro-Hungarian throne, and rapidly spiralled into a conflict that killed an estimated 10 million troops from all around the globe. The 'war to end all wars' ended with German surrender on 11 November 1918.

**TIMELINE: 1918**

22 JUNE **France halts the German advance on Paris**

31 JULY **Germany retreats across the River Marne**

8 AUGUST **Allies push back Germany near Amiens, France**

27–30 SEPTEMBER **Allies break through the Hindenburg Line**

30 SEPTEMBER **Bulgaria surrenders to the Allies**

4 OCTOBER **Kaiser Wilhelm II (Germany) appeals to President Woodrow Wilson (USA) to settle terms for an armistice**

17 OCTOBER **Hungary declares independence from the Austro-Hungarian Empire**

30 OCTOBER **Austria pulls out of Italy**

31 OCTOBER **Turkey surrenders; the Dardanelles are reopened to Allied shipping**

3 NOVEMBER **Austria signs an armistice with the Allies**

6 NOVEMBER **Germany pulls back its troops on all fronts**

9 NOVEMBER **Kaiser Wilhelm II abdicates; Germany is declared a republic**

11 NOVEMBER **Germany surrenders to Marshal Foch (France)**

When the end came, it came more quickly than many had dared to hope. As late as August 1918 the Allies were planning to fight on into 1919 or even 1920, but the Central Powers had suffered more heavily than the Allies had realized, and in October Kaiser Wilhelm II (Germany) appealed to President Woodrow Wilson (USA) to agree terms for an armistice. The following year Wilson was awarded the Nobel Peace Prize for his part in the peace process.

At 05.00 on 11 November 1918, the last day of the war, a party of Germans led by Mathias Erzberger made their way towards a heavily guarded railway carriage in the forest of Compiègne, France. There they met the Allied Commander in Chief, Field Marshal Ferdinand Foch (France), admitted defeat and formally surrendered by signing the armistice. After more than four years of bloody war, and the loss of an entire generation of young men, the guns finally fell silent across the battlefields of Europe at the 11th hour of the 11th day of the 11th month. Nearly a century later, the millions who died are still remembered across the world at that very hour with poppies and a two-minute silence.

**Below** Foch's train, in which the armistice was signed, arrives at Compiègne station (11 November 1918)

**Opposite top** Allied Commander in Chief Field Marshal Ferdinand Foch at the signing of the armistice, marking the last day of the First World War

On that last day of war, author Virginia Woolf (England) encapsulated the conflicting emotions that peace brought when she wrote in her diary: 'Twenty-five minutes ago the guns went off, announcing peace … The rooks wheeled round, and wore for a moment the symbolic look of creatures performing some ceremony, partly of thanksgiving, partly of valediction over the grave.'

**DID YOU KNOW?**

● On 22 June 1940, during the Second World War, France was forced to surrender to Germany. Adolf Hitler (Germany) humiliated the French by presenting the terms of his armistice in the same railway carriage, in the forest of Compiègne, in which the 1918 armistice had been signed, marking the last day of the First World War. Hitler sat in the chair used 22 years earlier by Field Marshal Foch and imposed terms described by the French delegation as 'merciless'

*See also: The Last Day of the Second World War, page 76*

**Last Days of**

# WARSHIPS

Probably the most famous last day of any warship is that of the German battleship *Bismarck*, irrevocably linked to the last day of the British battle cruiser HMS *Hood*. *Bismarck* sank *Hood* on 24 May 1941 and, as a result, *Bismarck* was sunk by *Hood*'s companions-in-arms three days later.

Named after the first of a dynasty of British naval officers, HMS *Hood* was the largest warship in the world at 42,800 tonnes when completed in 1923. By the Second World War *Hood* was still the pride of the British fleet, but no longer the world's largest warship: that accolade now went to the *Bismarck*, completed early in 1941 at 45,700 tonnes as one of Germany's last two battleships (the other being *Tirpitz*) and named after the first chancellor of the German Empire.

In May 1941 *Hood* sailed with the newly built battleship HMS *Prince of Wales* on routine duties protecting Allied merchant convoys in the North Atlantic. On 18 May *Bismarck*, accompanied by the heavy cruiser *Prinz Eugen*, sailed from Gdynia, Poland, to attack those same convoys. As *Bismarck* and *Prinz Eugen* emerged from the Denmark Strait on 24 May, they encountered and engaged the British ships. *Prince of Wales* was damaged, but *Hood* fared much worse: a salvo of shells hit the munitions magazine and the ship exploded, sinking within minutes with the loss of more than 1,300 lives.

**Below** Adolf Hitler attends the launch of the *Bismarck* at the Blohm & Voss shipyard, Hamburg, Germany (February 1939)

**Opposite** The last picture of HMS *Hood*, seen from HMS *Prince of Wales* going into action against the *Bismarck* (May 1941)

**1943** The last day of the German battle cruiser *Scharnhorst* is 26 DECEMBER, when it is sunk off North Cape, Norway, by the British battleship HMS *Duke of York*

**1944** The last day of Germany's last major warship, the *Tirpitz*, is 12 NOVEMBER, when it is sunk in Tromsø fjord, Norway, by the RAF acting on information from the Norwegian Resistance

**1945** The last day of USS *Indianapolis*, the last major battleship to be sunk during the Second World War, comes just after midnight on the night of 29/30 JULY, when it is torpedoed and sunk by Japanese submarine I-58

**1982** The last day of Argentinian cruiser *General Belgrano* is 2 MAY, when it is controversially sunk by British submarine HMS *Conqueror* during the Falklands War. Two days later an Exocet missile sinks British destroyer HMS *Sheffield*, the first major British warship to be sunk since the Second World War

The Royal Navy immediately vowed to 'pursue and destroy' the *Bismarck*. On 25 May *Prinz Eugen* escaped into mid-ocean while *Bismarck*, which had been damaged in the earlier engagement, desperately tried to reach the safety of Brest, France. British ships continued the pursuit and, after 1,750 miles, engaged *Bismarck* 550 miles west of Land's End, England, on 26 May. Aerial attacks from the aircraft carrier HMS *Ark Royal* damaged *Bismarck*'s rudder, reducing its speed and allowing the British to close in. At 08:00 on 27 May, HMS *King George V* and HMS *Rodney* sighted the *Bismarck* and opened fire, destroying all resistance within an hour. The *coup de grâce* was a torpedo from HMS *Dorsetshire*, as a result of which *Bismarck* sank with a similar loss of life to the *Hood* – HMS *Dorsetshire* picked up a mere 110 survivors.

**DID YOU KNOW?**

● One witness to the sinking of HMS *Ark Royal* (*see: Timeline 1941*) said: 'It was as though an athlete in the prime of his powers with a score of laurels to his credit had been knifed in the back in a dark alley'

● The Argentine government described the sinking of the *General Belgrano* (*see: Timeline 1982*) as 'a treacherous act of armed aggression', while British Prime Minister Margaret Thatcher hailed the successful removal of 'a very obvious threat to British forces'

The Second World War began at dawn on 1 September 1939 with the German invasion of Poland, as a result of which Britain and France declared war on Germany. Fighting in Europe ended six long years later, on 8 May 1945, and the war in Japan on 14 August 1945.

**The Last Day of**

# THE SECOND WORLD WAR

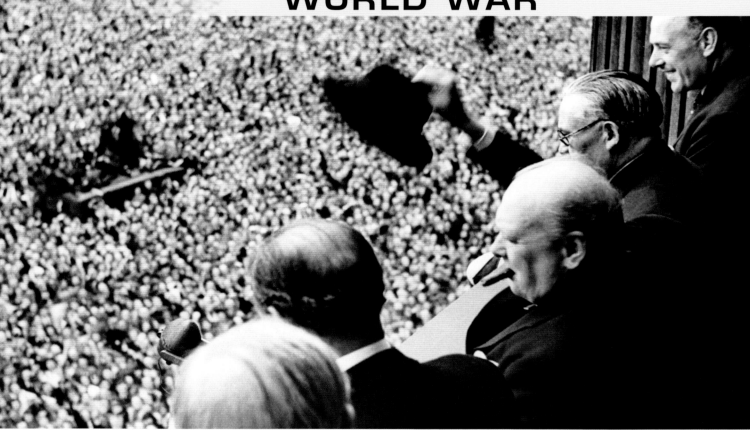

**Above** From a balcony in the Ministry of Health Building, British Prime Minister Winston Churchill and members of his war cabinet acknowledge a huge crowd gathered in Whitehall, London, to celebrate peace (May 1945)

**Opposite** In Times Square, New York, a jubilant American sailor and a nurse celebrate VJ Day in style (2 September 1945)

Because the Second World War was fought in two theatres – Europe and the Pacific – there were two official and four actual 'last days', the first of which was when Germany surrendered, in Europe in the small hours of 7 May 1945. Although German forces in many parts of Europe had already surrendered, it wasn't until that night that German emissary General Alfred Jodl signed an unconditional surrender in Rheims, France, saying: 'With this signature, the German people and the German armed forces are, for better or worse, delivered into the victors' hands.' The German surrender was ratified in Berlin the following day, making 8 May officially the last day of the war in Europe (although some fighting did continue after that date).

In the Pacific, Japan held out longer than Germany had done and fighting continued for a further three months, even after atom bombs had been

**28 APRIL** Mussolini's last day: the Italian dictator Benito Mussolini is shot and his body taken to Milan, Italy, where it is strung up by the ankles in the Piazza Loretto

**29 APRIL** German forces in Italy surrender

**30 APRIL** Adolf Hitler's last day: the German dictator becomes his own last victim when he commits suicide in his bunker in Berlin. His last statement includes a form of suicide note: 'My wife and I choose to die in order to escape the shame of overthrow or capitulation'

**4 MAY** German forces in Holland, Denmark and north-west Germany surrender

**6 MAY** German forces in Norway surrender

**7 MAY** Germany surrenders unconditionally in Rheims, France

**8 MAY** German surrender is ratified in Berlin, marking the official end of the war in Europe. This last day of war is celebrated in Europe as Victory in Europe (VE) Day; in the USA President Truman announces that **9 MAY**, the first day of peace, will be celebrated as VE Day; Soviet countries also celebrate **9 MAY** as VE Day

**6 AUGUST** An atomic bomb is dropped on Hiroshima, Japan

**9 AUGUST** An atomic bomb is dropped on Nagasaki, Japan

**14 AUGUST** Japan agrees to unconditional surrender, celebrated in Europe as Victory in Japan (VJ) Day

**19 AUGUST** The Soviet Sixth Guards complete the rout of the Japanese Kwantung Army in central Manchuria, the last major battle of the Second World War

**2 SEPTEMBER** In Tokyo Bay, on board **USS** *Missouri*, the Japanese surrender is formally signed, marking the official last day of the Second World War, celebrated in the USA as VJ Day

## DID YOU KNOW?

● The last entry in the diary of Anne Frank (Germany) was made on Tuesday, 1 August 1944, and ended: 'I keep on trying to find a way of becoming what I would so like to be, and what I could be, if ... there weren't any other people living in the world. Your Anne.' On 4 August the Nazis raided the house in Amsterdam, Holland, where she and her family were hiding. In March 1945, two months before her 16th birthday, Anne died of typhus in the Bergen-Belsen concentration camp

● The last Second World War soldier to surrender was Lee Kuang-Huei (Taiwan), who fought for the Japanese and surrendered in 1975, 30 years after the end of the war. He had been living on a remote Indonesian island, unaware that the war had ended. When discovered, he asked to be executed because he felt his capture was a dishonour to the Emperor

dropped on Hiroshima and Nagasaki. The last battle of the war began on 13 August in central Manchuria between Soviet and Japanese forces and finally reached a conclusion on 19 August, five days after Emperor Hirohito's announcement of unconditional Japanese surrender on 14 August. Although the surrender document was not formally signed by Japanese representatives until 2 September, marking the official last day of the war, it was on 14 August that US President Truman declared: 'This is the day we have been waiting for since Pearl Harbor', and Britain's new prime minister, Clement Attlee, who had defeated Churchill in a surprise election result just two weeks earlier, announced: 'Japan has today surrendered. The last of our enemies is laid low.'

# THE VIETNAM WAR

Like all wars, the Vietnam War was notorious for its barbarity and the appalling loss of life. Peace talks began in Paris, France, in 1968, but the war was to continue for seven more years before the last US troops to be evacuated were airlifted from Saigon on 30 April 1975.

**TIMELINE:: THE VIETNAM WAR**

**1954** Vietnam is divided along the 17th parallel between communist North Vietnam and US-backed South Vietnam. Over the next decade, tension mounts as the North Vietnamese, together with South Vietnamese communist guerillas (the Viet Cong), begin the struggle to overthrow the government of South Vietnam and reunite the country

**1964** The USA officially enters the Vietnam War after the destroyer USS *Maddox* is attacked on 2 AUGUST by North Vietnamese forces in the Gulf of Tonkin

**1968** Peace talks begin in Paris, France, between representatives of the USA and North Vietnam

**1969** The USA begins to reduce its military presence in Vietnam after protest at home over the horrendous number of casualties

**1973** A cease-fire agreement is reached at peace talks in Paris, France, allowing for the full withdrawal of US troops and the release of prisoners of war

**1975** The North Vietnamese capture Saigon on 30 APRIL. The last 11 troops to be evacuated are airlifted from the roof of the US Embassy by helicopter. Marine Sergeant John J. Valdez (USA) is last to board the last helicopter. South Vietnam surrenders

**1976** The Socialist Republic of Vietnam is proclaimed, with thousands of South Vietnamese becoming political prisoners or refugees

The trigger for official US involvement in the Vietnam War was an attack on 2 August 1964 by North Vietnamese forces on the destroyer USS *Maddox* in the Gulf of Tonkin. Five days later US Congress approved the Gulf of Tonkin Resolution, giving President Lyndon B. Johnson sweeping powers to support South Vietnam in opposing 'communist aggression' from the North. Johnson announced: 'The world must never forget that aggression unchallenged is aggression unleashed. We in the United States have not forgotten. That is why we have answered aggression with action.'

This action ended more than a decade later, during one eventful week in April 1975. On 23 April President Gerald Ford announced that US involvement in the war was over, to the dismay of the South Vietnamese and the delight of the Northern forces, who redoubled their efforts to reach the South Vietnamese capital, Saigon (now Ho Chi Minh City). On 29 April, as the North Vietnamese closed in on Saigon, the US began a massive helicopter evacuation, airlifting some 1,000 American personnel and troops and some 6,000 South Vietnamese from the city.

The official last day of the war was 30 April. The last US troops to be evacuated were 11 members of the US Marine Corps, who were lifted from the roof of the US Embassy in Saigon just before the embassy was sacked by a mass of South Vietnamese enraged at being abandoned. North Vietnamese tanks smashed through the gates of the presidential palace and, in the absence of President Nguyen Van Thieu who had resigned on 21 April and fled to Taiwan, General Duong Van Minh officially surrendered on behalf of South Vietnam. The war was at an end, and the very thing the Americans had fought to prevent occurred the following year with the proclamation of the Socialist Republic of Vietnam.

**DID YOU KNOW?**

● One of the reasons for US involvement in the Vietnam War was fear of the 'domino effect'. US politicians felt that communism should be contained and that if one Far Eastern state fell to this oppressive ideology others would follow like falling dominoes, creating the threat of worldwide communism

**Opposite top** A CIA employee (probably O.B. Harnage) helps Vietnamese evacuees onto an Air America helicopter from the top of 22 Gia Long Street, half a mile from the US Embassy (29 April 1975)
**Opposite bottom** A North Vietnamese tank rolls into a compound during the fall of Saigon (30 April 1975)

On 1 January 1999 several member-states of the European Union launched a new electronic currency, the Euro. On 1 January 2002 Euro coins and notes became legal tender and for the 12 states in the 'Eurozone' the first months of 2002 marked the last of their traditional currencies.

## Last Days of CURRENCIES

**Below** A customer pays with Euro notes for groceries bought at the Rialto outdoor market in Venice, Italy, where prices are marked in both Euros and Lire (January 2002)

**Opposite** A huge sculpture of the Euro symbol, constructed by German designer Ottmar Hoerl, is illuminated in front of the European Central Bank headquarters in Frankfurt, Germany (December 2001)

The British have agonized for years over whether or not to give up the pound and join a pan-European currency, but in fact Britain gave up its traditional currency long before the introduction of the Euro. The traditional British pound was made up of 20 shillings, each worth 12 pence, and the last day of this currency was 14 February 1971, the day before Decimalization Day. On 15 February decimal currency was introduced, with 100 'new pence' to the pound. A decade later 'new pence' were considered well enough established to drop the word 'new' and 1981 was the last year that coins were minted with this demarcation.

**1810** British coins are minted at the Tower of London for the last time before the Royal Mint moves to new premises nearby

**1889** The USA issues its last 3 cent coins

**1933** Gold coins circulate in the USA for the last time. The following year the USA comes off the gold standard and the Gold Reserve Act stipulates that gold is no longer legal tender

**1971** The last day of the British pound, shillings and pence is 14 FEBRUARY. The following day is dubbed D-Day, or Decimalization Day, when the new decimal currency is introduced

TIMELINE: LAST DAYS OF CURRENCIES

During the 1980s Continental Europe began discussing the idea of a pan-European currency and, after experimenting with the ECU (European Currency Unit) in 1987, it was decided to call the new currency the Euro. The Euro was launched as an electronic currency in 11 countries on 1 January 1999 and three years later it was launched as legal tender in the 12 countries that made up the so-called Eurozone (Greece had joined since 1999). There was a transition period during which both new and old currencies were legal tender, but with change given only in Euros, so that by 1 March 2002 the Euro was the only currency in use in the Eurozone.

And so the first two months of 2002 saw the last day of 12 European currencies. First to go was the Dutch guilder, whose last day in circulation was 28 January, followed by the Irish punt, on 9 February, and the French franc on 17 February. The last day of the remaining Eurozone currencies was 28 February, which saw the last of the Austrian schilling, the Belgian franc, the Finnish markka, the German mark, the Greek drachma, the Italian lire, the Luxembourg franc, the Portuguese escudo and the Spanish peseta.

**DID YOU KNOW?**

● Britain's decimalization in 1971 was overseen by the chairman of the Decimal Currency Board, Lord Fiske (Britain). Among the new coins were halfpence pieces that were so small that newspaper cartoonist Osbert Lancaster (England) referred to them as 'Lord Fiske's flies', implying that they were as fiddly as trouser buttons

● As well as in the Eurozone, the Euro was also introduced in 2002 in Andorra, Monaco, San Marino, the Vatican and French overseas territories including Martinique and Guadalupe in the Caribbean and Réunion in the Indian Ocean

**1981** British coins are minted as 'new pence' for the last time; henceforward they are minted as pence

**1999** The Euro is launched as an electronic currency

**2002** The Euro is launched as legal tender on I JANUARY. The last day of the Dutch guilder is 28 JANUARY, the Irish punt 9 FEBRUARY and the French franc 17 FEBRUARY. The last day of the remaining Eurozone currencies is 28 FEBRUARY

**The Last Day of**

# MORSE CODE

The last day of Morse Code as the official medium of international navigational communication and distress signals was 31 January 1999, before it was replaced on 1 February by an automated satellite alert system known as the Global Marine Distress and Safety System (GMDSS).

TIMELINE: MORSE CODE

**1791** Samuel Finley Breese Morse is born on 27 APRIL in Charlestown, Massachusetts, USA

**1826** Morse co-founds and becomes first president of the American National Academy of Design in New York

**1832** While returning to New York on board the packet ship *Sully*, Morse conceives the idea of an electromagnetic telegraph

**1837** Morse demonstrates his magnetic telegraph to Congress

**1838** Morse files a patent for his telegraph and the Morse Alphabet, later known as Morse Code (patent granted 1840)

**1844** The first telegraph transmission in Morse Code is made on 24 MAY, with the message: 'What hath God wrought?'

**1872** Morse's last day is 2 APRIL, when he dies in New York, aged 80

**1998** Britain's Royal Navy trains wireless operators in Morse Code for the last time, although Morse Code is retained for signalling by lamp

**1999** The official last day of Morse Code for distress signals at sea is 31 JANUARY, before satellite signalling comes into force on 1 FEBRUARY. On 12 JULY Globe Wireless (USA) sends what the company claims is America's last commercial Morse code transmission, an echo of the past: 'What hath God wrought?'

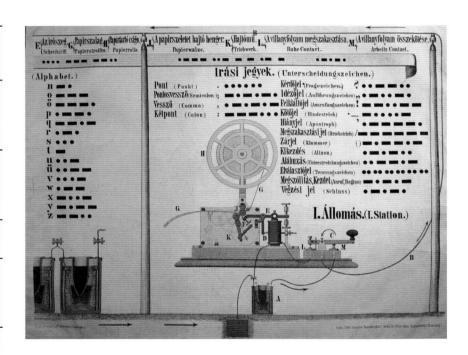

Morse Code, named after its inventor Samuel Morse (USA), represents letters and numbers by a series of dots and dashes, and is extremely versatile because it can be transmitted not only as sound (as originally intended) but also as flashes of light.

For 91 years Morse Code proved its worth as the official language for distress signals at sea, after the internationally recognized signal 'SOS' was agreed upon specifically because it was easy to remember, to transmit and to read in Morse Code: /... - - - .../. The SOS signal came into force on 1 July 1908 (the idea that it stood for 'Save Our Souls' was imposed later) and was used most famously on the night of 14/15 April 1912 by radio operators on board the *Titanic*. But technology moves on and the code that brought succour to thousands of mariners was rendered obsolete by the advent of satellite communications, which made voice transmissions clear and reliable, including that other internationally recognized distress signal, 'Mayday'.

The final nail in the coffin for Morse Code as the official international language of navigation was the introduction of the Global Marine Distress and Safety System (GMDSS), a push-button system that sends an automated distress signal by radio beacon and satellite. From 1 February 1999, when

**DID YOU KNOW?**

● The Morse V for victory – signalled by dot, dot, dot, dash – was used as the call sign for Allied broadcasts during the Second World War, which is said to be how the opening of Beethoven's Fifth Symphony became the world's most instantly recognized piece of music

● Before making what Globe Wireless (USA) claims was America's last commercial Morse Code transmission, company radio operator Tim Gorman (USA) relayed a last telegram to the White House, transmitted in Morse Code from a ship in San Francisco Bay. Gorman said: 'The message was 95 words, and it took me six or eight minutes to copy it. Then I just transmitted it to the White House via e-mail'

the system officially replaced Morse Code transmissions, all shipping of over 300 tonnes was required to carry GMDSS, while smaller vessels had until 2005 to comply. On that day the editorial of *The Times* newspaper (Britain) mourned the passing of an era by saying: 'So Morse lovers sign off today with 73s (best wishes) and 88s (love and kisses). But the rest is not quite silence. Like the paddle, Morse is part of maritime history. Like the paddle, it still has a purpose when modern systems fail.'

**Opposite** Illustration from a Hungarian educational poster showing the Morse Code alphabet and punctuation (19th century)
**Above** David Sarnoff (USA), the radio operator who picked up the *Titanic*'s distress signal, as a young operator in Nantucket Island

Our current Gregorian calendar originated in a calendar devised for the Romans and named after Julius Caesar. But the Julian calendar proved inaccurate, and after one and a half millennia it was adjusted by decree of Pope Gregory XIII, after whom the new, more accurate version is named.

**The Last Day of**

# THE JULIAN CALENDAR

**Opposite** The Assyrian Orthodox Christmas, still observed according to the Julian calendar, is celebrated here by Father Adda at St Matthew's Monastery on Mount Maqloub, Iraq (25 December 2003 according to the Julian calendar, 7 January 2004 according to the Gregorian)

Like ours, the Julian calendar had 12 months, 365 days and a leap year every 4th year to account for the extra 6 hours (or one quarter of a day) that it takes the earth to orbit the sun. But what the Romans had not realized is that the orbit actually takes an extra 6 hours, 11 minutes and 14 seconds. By the 16th century those 674 seconds per year had added up to 14 days, as a result of which the spring equinox was occurring on 11 March instead of 25 March as it had done in Roman times. More importantly for a medieval society in fear of God, it meant that religious festivals were being celebrated on the wrong day.

In order to redress the balance, the 19th Ecumenical Council of the Church of Rome, under Pope Gregory XIII (Italy), decreed in 1582 that 10 days would be suppressed in order to return the equinox to 21 March as it had been at the time of the Council of Nice. To prevent the problem recurring, the Council also decreed that, in future, century years would be leap years only if they were divisible by 400. The revised calendar became known as the Gregorian calendar after the Pope who instituted it.

For those (mainly Roman Catholic) countries that obeyed the papal decree, 4 October 1582 was the last day of the Julian calendar and it was followed by 15 October. But many (mainly Protestant) countries did not immediately comply and for hundreds of years the date differed between countries using the old and new calendars. By the time Britain and its colonies made the change in 1752 an 11th day had accrued, and when parliament announced that 14 September would follow 2 September riots broke out, with people demanding 'give us back our 11 days'. The last Western country to adopt the Gregorian calendar was Greece, in 1923.

**46BC** The Julian calendar is devised by Sosigenes (Egypt) for Julius Caesar (Roman) and instituted the following year, **45BC**

**1582 AD** Pope Gregory XIII (Italy) declares that a new calendar will replace the Julian calendar and, in those countries that obey the papal decree, 4 OCTOBER is the last day of the Julian calendar; it is followed by 15 OCTOBER. Those countries are: France, Italy, Luxembourg, Portugal, Spain, Belgium and parts of Germany

**1752** Britain and its colonies, including America, Canada and Australia, adopt the Gregorian calendar, and 2 SEPTEMBER is the last day of the Julian calendar in those places; it is followed by 14 SEPTEMBER

**1793** The last day of the Gregorian calendar in France comes on 4 OCTOBER; the following day France officially adopts the Revolutionary calendar, with dates calculated from 22 SEPTEMBER 1792 *See also: The Last Day of the French Revolutionary Calendar, page 89*

**TIMELINE: CALENDAR LAST DAYS**

**1805** The last day of the French Revolutionary calendar is 31 DECEMBER: Napoleon orders a return to the Gregorian calendar the following day, 1 JANUARY **1806**

**1873** Last day of the Julian calendar in Japan

**1875** Last day of the Julian calendar in Egypt

**1912** Last day of the Julian calendar in China

**1918** Lenin declares that the USSR will adopt the Gregorian calendar, and 1 FEBRUARY is the last day of the Julian calendar in the USSR, where it immediately becomes 14 FEBRUARY in the Gregorian

**1923** Greece is the last Western country to adopt the Gregorian calendar

The Last Day of

People still dispute what day was really the last of the second millennium. There is an argument that it should have been celebrated at the *end* of the year 2000, but modern society likes to see the zeroes roll over, and so, rightly or wrongly, the world partied on 31 December 1999.

# The Last Day of THE SECOND MILLENNIUM

## DID YOU KNOW?

● To celebrate its status as the first country to witness the last of the old millennium and the first of the new (according to the clock), the Republic of Kiribati gave Caroline Island, its easternmost point, the new name of Millennium Island. However, Kiribati was not the first place to witness the new millennium according to the sun: the first sunrise of the third millennium took place on uninhabited Young Island, one of New Zealand's Antarctic Balleny Islands. The first inhabited place to see sunrise was Pitt Island, one of New Zealand's Chatham Islands

**Right** An idyllic beach in Falealupo, Samoa, the last place on earth to witness the last of the old millennium according to the sun (*see: Timeline 08.02 GMT*)
**Opposite top** Fireworks explode above the Washington Monument as hundreds of thousands of Americans celebrate the arrival of the new millennium in Washington, DC

Rock musician Prince (USA, b. Prince Roger Nelson) had been singing about it since 1982: 'Tonight I'm gonna party like it's 1999.' But others argued that the last day of the second millennium should be celebrated a year later, their reasoning being that the calendar ran from 1BC to 1AD with no year 0, which meant that two millennia had not elapsed since the birth of Christ until the end, rather than the beginning, of the year 2000.

Despite these protestations, it was clear that most people were going to celebrate on 31 December 1999, but there was still the matter of timing to consider, with the millennium ending at times varying from 14 hours ahead of GMT in the East to 12 hours behind in the West. Again, there were arguments, some people claiming that the millennium officially ended in all places across the globe at midnight GMT (supported by Article V of the 1884

### DID YOU KNOW?

● Several nations and religions observe their own calendar in parallel with the Gregorian calendar accepted by most of the world. The Chinese are in the second half of their fifth millennium, the Gregorian year 2000 being the Chinese year 4698, while Orthodox Jews are in the second half of their sixth millennium, the Gregorian year 2000 being the Jewish year 5760. For Muslims, 2000 was the year 1420, and for Buddhists it was the year 2543

International Meridian Conference); others that it ended at sunset or midnight local time. Some partied twice, once at local time and once at GMT; many simply partied all day, just to make sure.

The first places on earth to witness the last of the old millennium were those of the Line Islands belonging to the Republic of Kiribati in the west Pacific, 14 hours ahead of GMT (those of the Line Islands not belonging to Kiribati are 10 hours behind). The last place to witness the last of the old millennium was the Ebon Atoll, part of the Republic of the Marshall Islands, 12 hours behind GMT. Because of the position of the dateline, the remainder of the Marshall Islands are 12 hours ahead of GMT, so the same sunrise that was the first of the new millennium in the main group of the Marshall Islands was the last of the old in the Ebon Atoll.

**TIMELINE: MILLENNIUM COUNTDOWN**

**GMT +14 hours** Those of the Line Islands belonging to Kiribati are the first places on earth to see the last of the old millennium according to the clock

**GMT +13 to +12 hours** New Zealand, many Pacific islands and parts of Asia see the last of the old millennium according to the clock

**16:05GMT** The first inhabited place to witness the first of the new millennium according to the sun is Mount Hapeka, Pitt Island, one of New Zealand's Chatham Islands, where the sun rises at 04:49 local time, 12 hours 45 minutes ahead of GMT

**GMT +11 to +5 hours** Most of Asia sees the last of the old millennium according to the clock

**GMT +10 to +8 hours** Australia sees the last of the old millennium according to the clock

**GMT +5 to +2 hours** The Middle East and parts of Africa see the last of the old millennium according to the clock

**GMT +2 to +0 hours** Mainland Europe, the British Isles, Scandinavia and most of Africa see the last of the old millennium according to the clock

**GMT -3 to -5 hours** South America sees the last of the old millennium according to the clock

**GMT -5 to -10 hours** Most of the USA and Canada see the last of the old millennium according to the clock

**08:02GMT** The last place to witness the last of the old millenium according to the sun is Falealupo, Samoa, where the sun sets at 19:02 local time, 11 hours behind GMT

**GMT -12 hours** The Ebon Atoll is the last place on earth to see the last of the old millennnium according to the clock

# LAST BUT NOT LEAST...

## The Last Day of the Third Reich

The Third Reich did not end with the death of Adolf Hitler (Germany) or even with the end of the Second World War. Before committing suicide, Hitler decreed that his successor should be Admiral Karl Dönitz (Germany), who thus became the last Führer on the death of Hitler. Germany surrendered on 7 May 1945 (ratified on 8 May), but the last day of the Third Reich came two weeks later with the capture and removal from power of Dönitz by the Allies on the night of 21/22 May.

**Left** Adolf Hitler (left) with Admiral Karl Dönitz (centre) and General Hermann Göring (right) (c.1944)

## Saddam Hussein's Last Day of Freedom

Whatever the rights and wrongs of the war in Iraq, the world is a better place without Saddam Hussein, whose last day of freedom was Saturday 13 December 2003. Having spent eight months on the run since the fall of Baghdad in April 2003, he was captured by US forces in a tiny cellar at a farmhouse close to his home town of Tikrit. After extracting information from a member of Saddam's clan, US troops had launched Operation Red Dawn and made their way to Al-Dawr, south of Tikrit, where they cordoned off an area around a rural farmhouse and discovered a 'spider hole', or cellar, beneath a hut close to the farmhouse. The former Iraqi dictator was found inside the narrow hole, which was 2–2.5 metres deep, wide enough to lie down in and concealed with a rug, bricks and dirt, According to a US military spokesman, Saddam, though armed with a pistol, offered no resistance when arrested and emerged from his hiding place 'very much bewildered'. After his identity had been verified by DNA tests, his capture was announced to the world with the words: 'Ladies and gentlemen, we got him. The tyrant is a prisoner.'

## The Last Day of the World

Believers in the prophecies of the 16th-century physician and astrologer Nostradamus (France, b. Michel de Notredame) made the most of 3 July 1999 because interpretations of his ambiguous and convoluted prophecies suggested that 4 July would be the last day of the world. Experts also suggested that Nostradamus might have meant 24 July or 28 July. But for those who woke up on 29 July thinking that Nostradamus was wrong and that they were safe, there is bad news.

Closer examination reveals that Nostradamus predicted not the end of the world, but the beginning of a 27-year long world war, saying: 'In the year 1999 and seven months, From the sky will come a great King of Terror.' Given that Nostradamus died some 20 years before the introduction of the Gregorian calendar – which moved the beginning of the year from March to January – 'seven months' (in French 'sept mois') is more likely to mean September than July. And given that he made his predictions more than 400 years ago, a small two-year error is forgivable. In September 2001 terror did indeed descend from the sky, prompting the Western world to begin waging a 'war on terror' with no foreseeable end, so Nostradamus may have been right after all.

## The Last Day of Room 101

Room 101 was immortalized in *Nineteen Eighty-Four*, the last novel by George Orwell (England, properly Eric Arthur Blair), as the torture chamber where enemies of the state were taken for aversion therapy by being made to face their worst fears. The original Room 101, from which Orwell took his inspiration, was an office at Broadcasting House, London, where he worked during the Second World War as a correspondent for the BBC. The office had its last day in autumn 2003, during the centenary year of Orwell's birth, when it was demolished during the refurbishment of Broadcasting House – but not before sculptor Rachel Whiteread (England) had worked her trademark magic by casting the interior of the room in concrete. Whiteread's cast temporarily stood next to the cast of Michelangelo's *David* in the Victoria & Albert Museum (V&A), London, England.

**Below** Rachel Whiteread's *Untitled (Room 101)* in the Cast Court of the V&A, London, England (2003)

## The Last Day of the French Revolutionary Calendar

The French Revolutionary calendar, devised by Gilbert Romme (France), was imposed by law on 5 October 1793, with dates calculated from 22 September 1792, the autumnal equinox of the year the Republic was proclaimed. The Revolutionary year had 12 months, named by the poet Fabre d'Eglantine (France), the last of which was Fructidor, the month of fruits. Each month was divided into three *décades* of 10 days each; the days were simply named after their number in the sequence, the last day of each *décade* being *Decadi* ('the 10th day'), which was a day of rest. The Revolutionary calendar proved impractical and, in 1805, Napoleon ordered that from 1 January 1806 France would reinstate the Gregorian calendar, making the last day of the Revolutionary calendar 10 Nivôse ('the month of snow') in the year XIV.

*See also: The Last Day of the Julian Calendar, page 84*

# Chapter Three

# Personal Lasts

Frank Sinatra, a.k.a. 'The Voice', was a showbiz colossus – singer, actor, film star, American icon and, inevitably, serial husband. His triumphs were many and his lasts are various, ranging from the last use of his original surname, Sinestro, in 1945, to his last day, 15 May 1998.

# THE MANY LASTS OF FRANK SINATRA

## TIMELINE: FRANK SINATRA'S LASTS

**1945** Uses the surname Sinestro for the last time

**1948** Birth of his last child, Christina (Tina) on 20 JUNE

**1953** Wins his first and last Oscar, for his supporting role in *From Here to Eternity*

**1964** Nearly the last of Sinatra: almost drowns in Hawaii while directing war film *None But The Brave*

**1971** The 'last of Sinatra': announces his retirement from showbiz and takes his 'last bow' after a gala performance in Los Angeles, USA, in MARCH, but returns two years later with the album *Ol' Blue Eyes is Back*

**1976** Marries his fourth and last wife, Barbara Marx, ex-wife of Zeppo

**1983** Makes his last film appearance, in *Cannonball Run II*

**1993–94** Records his last two albums, *Duets* and *Duets II*, and performs his last concerts

**1998** His last day is 15 MAY, when he dies, aged 82

Frank Sinatra (USA) was born Frank Sinestro on 12 December 1915. The last time he was known by that name was 1945, when his mother had his birth certificate altered to Francis Albert Sinatra after the family decided to Americanize its surname. A self-taught singer, he first came to public notice in 1935 on the radio show *Major Bowes and his Original Amateur Hour*, and was soon recording professionally.

The first two 'lasts of Frank Sinatra' came relatively early in his career when, in 1970, he swore he would never again perform in Las Vegas and then, in March 1971, when he announced his retirement from showbiz at the age of 56. Two years later he was back, refreshed and even more popular than before. During this lay-off his marriage to Mia Farrow (USA) foundered and, three years after his comeback, he married his fourth and last wife, Barbara Marx (USA), ex-wife of Marx brother Zeppo.

Sinatra's last film appearance was in *Cannonball Run II* in 1983, a poor sequel to the original film about the illegal US coast-to-coast car race, but he continued performing and recording music until 1994. His ailing health became evident when he collapsed in 1994 at a concert in Richmond, Virginia, while singing 'My Way', though he was well enough to wave to the audience as he was carried off. He recorded his last two albums, *Duets* and *Duets II* in 1993 and 1994, though these albums were not duets in the true sense: Sinatra sang alone and his 'co-singers', ranging from Tony Bennett and Liza Minnelli to Bono and Gloria Estefan, were recorded via digital telephone lines and dubbed alongside his voice.

### DID YOU KNOW?

● Frank Sinatra almost had his last day in 1964 when he came close to drowning on location in Hawaii while directing the war film *None But The Brave* – fortunately he was rescued from the surf by one of the actors. There is a suitable sense of theatricality about the fact that Sinatra, whose original name Sinestro derives from the Latin for 'left', was rescued by Brad Dexter (USA), whose name in Latin means 'right'

● Sinatra's third wife, Mia Farrow, was also a serial spouse – her last husband, after Sinatra and conductor-composer André Previn (USA), was the film director Woody Allen (USA)

**Above** Frank Sinatra and his fourth and last wife, Barbara, cut the cake at their wedding in Palm Springs, California (11 July 1976)
**Left** Frank Sinatra in a recording studio during the 1950s

Van Gogh is one of the world's most instantly recognizable painters, having produced more than 700 drawings and 800 paintings in a tragically short career of only nine years. In July 1890 he shot himself at or near the scene of his last painting, *Wheat Field under Threatening Skies with Crows*.

**Personal Lasts**

# ARTISTS' LAST PAINTINGS

## Van Gogh's last painting

'As a painter I shall never signify anything of importance. I feel it absolutely.' History has disproved this harsh assessment of his own work by Vincent van Gogh (Netherlands), but it is indicative of the despair and torment that blighted his life and eventually drove him to end it. In a more defiant mood, van Gogh wrote: 'The time will come when people will see that [my paintings] are worth more than the price of the paint', but within a year depression had set in again and in 1889, after cutting off one of his ears in remorse at threatening Paul Gauguin (France) with a razor, van Gogh committed himself to a mental asylum at St-Rémy, France. By May 1890 things seemed to have improved again and van Gogh went to live in Auvers-sur-Oise under the supervision of Dr Paul Gachet (France).

While in Auvers, van Gogh completed one painting a day until July, when he painted the ominous and foreboding *Wheat Field under Threatening Skies*

**DID YOU KNOW?**

• Van Gogh's prolific output increased rather than diminished towards the end of his life. In the 15-month period before his committal to St-Rémy, van Gogh painted more than 200 pictures, including some of his most famous works – *Sunflowers*, *The Bridge* and *The Chair and the Pipe*. After moving from St-Rémy to Auvers-sur-Oise on 21 May 1890, he painted one picture a day for his last 67 days before he shot himself

• On 15 May 1990, at an auction at Christie's, New York, Ryoei Saito (Japan) bought van Gogh's *Portrait of Dr Gachet* for a world record $75,000,000

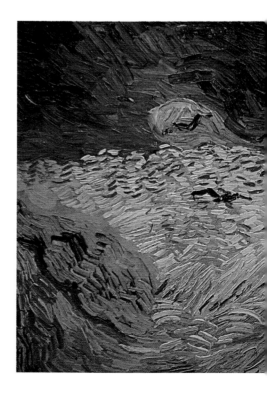

Right Charcoal portrait by Paul Gachet of Vincent van Gogh on his deathbed (29 July 1890)

Below Van Gogh's last painting, *Wheat Field under Threatening Skies with Crows*

*with Crows*. This last painting contrasts van Gogh's characteristic vivid hues, in the green and gold of the wheat field, with the less typical heavy colours of the sky darkening from blue to black. The eye is carried from vibrant gold of the field to threatening sky by the flight of crows, traditional symbols of discord and strife.

In a self-contradictory letter, van Gogh wrote of the paintings made at Auvers that he was trying to express 'sadness and extreme loneliness', but also 'the health and restorative forces that I see in the country'. *Wheat Field* encapsulates both and would be a moving painting even without the knowledge that it was his last. On Sunday 27 July he suddenly left lunch with the Gachets as if to continue work on the painting, and shot himself in or near the wheat field of the title. He then walked unsteadily back to his lodgings, where he died of his wounds two days later, having told his brother Theo: 'Don't weep. What I have done was best for all of us. This sadness will never end.'

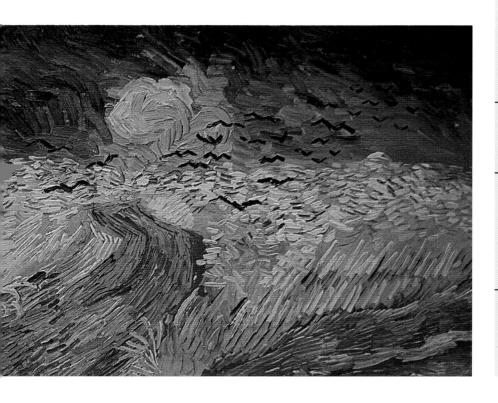

and Aeneas. He paints his last watercolours at Margate and Deal, England, later the same year

**1851** Turner leaves his sickbed to make his last drawing: the face of a drowned girl whose body he had seen, from his window, being recovered by the police from the River Thames. His last day is 19 DECEMBER, when he dies, aged **76**

**1882** Éduoard Manet completes his last major work, *Un Bar aux Folies-Bergères*. He dies the following year

**1890** Vincent van Gogh (Netherlands) shoots himself at or near the scene of his last painting, *Wheat Field under Threatening Skies with Crows*. His last day is 29 JULY; he is **37**

**1906** Paul Cézanne (France) dies, aged 67, on 22 OCTOBER after completing his last major work, *Le Jardinier*

**1926** Claude Monet (France), the last of the Impressionists, dies, aged 86, on 5 DECEMBER, while working on a monumental series of paintings inspired by the water garden at his home in Giverny, France. Among the last elements to be completed is *The Roses*, painted from 1925–26

**1951** Henri Matisse (France) completes his last major work, the decoration of the Chapelle du Rosaire in Vence, France, which he describes as: '...the culmination of a life of work and the coming into flower of an enormous, sincere and difficult effort.' His last day is 3 NOVEMBER **1954**

**1970** Mark Rothko (USA) is found dead in his studio on 25 FEBRUARY, having recently completed his last major work, the De Menil Chapel in Houston, Texas

**1973** Pablo Picasso (Spain) dies of a heart attack on 8 APRIL, still working at the age of 91 after an output of 300 sculptures, 140,000 paintings and drawings and 100,000 engravings, having promised 100 of his latest works to the Avignon Festival, France

**1983** Salvador Dalí paints his last picture, *The Swallow's Tail*. His last day is 23 JANUARY **1989**

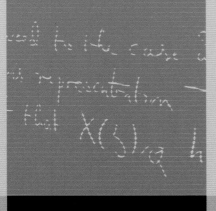

Pierre de Fermat is famous among mathematicians for founding or co-inventing various mathematical principles and methods whose significance few ordinary people understand. He is also famous throughout the world for his so-called Last Theorem, which remained unproven until 1994.

**Personal Lasts**

# FERMAT'S LAST THEOREM

### DID YOU KNOW?

● **What attracted Andrew Wiles to Fermat's Last Theorem was its deceptive simplicity. Remembering his first encounter with the theorem, he said: 'It looked so simple and yet all the great mathematicians in history couldn't solve it. Here was a problem that I, a 10-year-old, could understand and I knew from that moment that I would never let it go. I had to solve it'**

● **Newspapers reporting Wiles original flawed proof in 1993 included: *The Guardian* (Britain), which announced: 'The Number's Up for Maths' Last Riddle'; *Le Monde* (France), whose front page read: 'Le théorèm de Fermat enfin résolu'; and *The New York Times* (USA), whose front page carried the headline: 'At Last, Shout of "Eureka!" In Age-Old Math Mystery'**

The 17th-century mathematician Pierre de Fermat (France) had an enormous influence on modern mathematics, founding number theory, laying the groundwork for what would become differential calculus and analytic geometry and, with Blaise Pascal (France), founding probability theory. Fermat communicated his discoveries by means of letters to his friends, containing his results, but often without proofs. Other people later proved all his results bar one, which became the most famous unsolved problem in mathematics, and was known as Fermat's Last Theorem.

There are many integer (whole-number) solutions to the equation $x^2 + y^2 = z^2$, but, c.1637, Fermat wrote that there is no integer solution of $x^n + y^n = z^n$ if n is greater than 2. He also wrote that there was not enough room to include the proof of the theorem, setting a hare running that mathematicians were to chase for 358 years.

In 1963, at the age of 10, Andrew Wiles (England–USA) read about Fermat's Last Theorem in a library book and made it his life's ambition to prove what no mathematician before him had been able to prove. Thirty years later, on 23 June 1993, he announced his proof at the Isaac Newton Institute, Cambridge, England, turning to his audience after chalking up the

**Right** Pierre de Fermat

| **1601** Pierre de Fermat is born on 17 AUGUST in Beaumont-de-Lomagne, France, the son of a leather merchant | **c.1637** Fermat writes what will become known as his Last Theorem | **1665** Fermat's last day is 12 JANUARY, when he dies, aged 63, in Toulouse, France | **1727–83** Leonhard Euler (Switzerland) proves many of Fermat's discoveries relating to number theory | **1908** Paul Wolfskehl (Germany) dies, leaving 100,000 marks to whoever proves Fermat's Last Theorem *See also: The Last Bequest of Paul Wolfskehl, page 178* | **1953** Andrew Wiles is born on 11 APRIL in Cambridge, England |
|---|---|---|---|---|---|

**TIMELINE: FERMAT'S LAST THEOREM**

solution and saying: 'I think I'll stop there.' Unfortunately, he was not able to stop there because referees verifying his proof discovered a flaw, and for 14 months it appeared that he, like scores of mathematicians before him, had failed. But Wiles managed to repair his proof when, on 19 September 1994, he had what he calls 'this incredible revelation … It was so indescribably beautiful; it was so simple and elegant … It was the most important moment of my working life. Nothing I ever do again will mean as much.' Fermat's Last Theroem was proved at last.

**Below** Mathematician Andrew Wiles, who proved Fermat's Last Theorem

| **1963** Wiles reads about Fermat's Last Theorem in a book borrowed from his local library in Milton Road, Cambridge, England | **1986** Wiles dedicates his time purely to proving Fermat's Last Theorem | **1993** After seven years' intense work, Wiles announces his proof of Fermat's Last Theorem on 23 JUNE at the Isaac Newton Institute, Cambridge, England. He submits his proof to the journal *Inventiones Mathematicae* for verification by referees, one of whom detects a flaw | **1994** Wiles repairs his proof and Fermat's Last Theorem is at last truly solved | **1995** Wiles' absolute proof is published in *Annals of Mathematics*, marking the end of the mystery after 358 years |

Among the contenders for the world's greatest architect are Sir Christopher Wren, whose last building, St Paul's Cathedral, was completed in 1711, and Frank Lloyd Wright, whose last building, New York's Guggenheim Museum, was completed in 1959, the year of his death.

# ARCHITECTS' LAST BUILDINGS

TIMELINE: ARCHITECTS' LAST BUILDINGS

**1580** The Teatro Olimpico in Vicenza, Italy, the last building designed by Andrea Palladio (Italy), is begun in this, the year of his death. It is completed by Vincenzo Scamozzi (Italy), who also completes a number of Palladio's other unfinished buildings

**1711** British Parliament declares St Paul's Cathedral to be complete. It is the last building designed by Christopher Wren to be completed by the architect

**1873** Sir George Gilbert Scott (England) completes his last major building, the Foreign Office, London, England

**1909** Charles Rennie Mackintosh (Scotland) completes his last major building, the library wing of Glasgow School of Art, Scotland. His last architectural project is 78, Derngate, Northampton, England, in 1917

**1926** Antoni Gaudí (Spain) dies before completing his most celebrated work, the Sagrada Familia church in Barcelona, Spain, begun in 1884. His last major designs to be completed are the Casa Batlló (1905–07) and Casa Milá (1905–10), both in Barcelona

**1958** Sir Giles Gilbert Scott (England) completes his last major building, the Guildhall Building, London, England

**1959** The last building to be completed by Frank Lloyd Wright, the Guggenheim Museum in New York, opens in October, six months after his death (see: page 100)

## Christopher Wren's last building

Sir Christopher Wren is without doubt England's greatest architect, and examples of his work still adorn London, Oxford and Cambridge nearly 300 years after his death. The last house he designed was Marlborough House (between 1709 and 1710) on Pall Mall, London, for the Duchess of Marlborough, and the last of his works to be completed was the Chapel of the Royal Naval College in Greenwich, London, finished in 1742, fully 19 years after his death. But his undoubted masterpiece, and the last major building to be completed by the architect himself, was St Paul's Cathedral, London.

Wren was appointed Surveyor to the cathedral in 1663, but three years later it burned to the ground during the Great Fire of London and so, instead of repairing an ancient cathedral, he found himself building a new one. The clergy rejected Wren's first two designs and in 1674 he produced a third, with a clause allowing him to make 'ornamental' variations – Wren would take full advantage of this clause to create something closer to the rejected second design than the one that had been accepted.

The foundation stone of the new cathedral was laid on 21 June 1675. The quire was opened 22 years later, in December 1697, but the dome was yet to be built. More than a decade later, with Wren too old and frail to lay the last stone, his son Christopher was hauled to the top of the dome to perform the honour. Wren's son records the date of this act as 1710, but it was 1711 before parliament declared the new cathedral complete, 36 years after it had been started. Twelve years later Wren died at the age of 91 and was buried in the crypt of his great creation, beneath a tombstone with the inscription: *Lector, si monumentum requiris circumspice* – 'Reader, if you seek a monument, look around you.'

**1961** Walter Gropius (Germany–USA) completes his last major solo-designed building, the US Embassy in Athens, Greece. His last major building designed in collaboration with members of his firm TAC (The Architects' Collaborative) is the Rosenthal China Factory in Selb, Germany, in 1965

**1963** Le Corbusier (France, b. Charles Eduoard Jeanneret in Switzerland) completes his last major building, the Carpenter Center for the Visual Arts at Harvard University, Cambridge, Massachusetts, USA

**1968** Ludwig Mies van der Rohe (Germany–USA) completes his last major building, the National Gallery, Berlin, Germany

**DID YOU KNOW?**

● Christopher Wren commissioned Sir James Thornhill (England) to paint the interior of the famous dome at St Paul's. One day, Thornhill stepped back to get a better perspective on his work and came so close to the edge of the scaffold that his assistant dared not shout out a warning for fear the shock would make Thornhill fall. Instead he began to smear the paint Thornhill had just been working on, making the artist jump forward in anger and thus saving him from almost certain death

**Left and opposite** Before and after – one of Sir Christopher Wren's drawings for St Paul's Cathedral, London, and a modern view of the completed building

# Frank Lloyd Wright's last building

Frank Lloyd Wright (USA) is regularly described as 'America's greatest architect' – sometimes, but not always, with the qualification 'to date'. Global recognition came relatively late in his career, during his 60s, but when it did he made it count with several large and significant commissions. His last major design was the Marin County Civic Center, California, completed posthumously in 1969 by Taliesin Associates, but the last to be (almost) completed by the architect himself was the Guggenheim Museum in New York, which opened in October 1959, six months after Wright's death on 9 April that year at the age of 89.

The museum was financed by Solomon R. Guggenheim (USA) as a new home for his Museum of Non-Objective Painting, but it was Guggenheim's associate Hilla Rebay von Ehrenweisen (Germany–USA, b. France) who chose Wright to be the architect. In 1943 she wrote to him: 'I need a fighter, a lover of space, an originator, a tester and a wise man … I want a temple of spirit, a monument!' Wright was impressed by this approach and by her definition of Non-Objective Painting, writing back wittily that he was '…eager to build to objectify the non-objective point of view'.

As with Wren's cathedral, building the Guggenheim was not a simple process. Over 16 years Wright submitted six sets of plans and no less than 749 drawings, describing the building he was trying to create as 'one extended expansive well-proportioned floor space from bottom to top … gloriously lit from above'. Finally, the plans were approved and in 1956 construction began – the result, with its spiral ramp rising 28 metres towards the domed skylight, is an almost perfect embodiment of Wright's description. And like Wren's cathedral, this building stands as a monument to the genius of its architect.

**Below** Frank Lloyd Wright's earthquake-proof Imperial Hotel in Tokyo, Japan
**Opposite top and bottom** Wright's Guggenheim Museum, seen from without (1959) and within (1961)

Two names dominate the world of classical music: Mozart, the child prodigy who became an adult prodigy, and Beethoven, often named as the greatest composer of any era. Mozart's last work was his unfinished Requiem Mass, and Beethoven's last symphony was his Ninth, the 'Choral'.

# LASTS OF CLASSICAL MUSIC

## DID YOU KNOW?

● Not only did Mozart have an undisputed genius for creating music, he also had a phenomenal memory for recalling it. At the age of 14 he visited the Sistine Chapel in Rome, Italy, where he heard *Miserere*, a setting of Psalm 50 by Gregorio Allegri (Italy) and, after a single hearing, was able to write down the score from memory

● Schubert's *Unfinished Symphony* was not curtailed because of his death, nor was it his last. It was his eighth symphony of nine and was presented to the Musikverein of Graz, Austria, in 1822, but did not receive its first performance until 1865, fully 37 years after Schubert's death

● For many years, Gustav Mahler (Czechoslovakia–Austria) put off beginning a tenth symphony for superstitious reasons, because Beethoven, Schubert and Bruckner all died having completed nine symphonies. Eventually, in 1910, Mahler began his tenth, but died the following year, leaving it unfinished

**Above right** Unattributed engraving of Wolfgang Amadeus Mozart on his deathbed
**Opposite** Portrait of Ludwig van Beethoven with a lyre, by Willibrord Joseph Mähler (c.1840)

## Mozart's last work

Wolfgang Amadeus Mozart (Austria) produced work in prolific quantity as well as of prodigious quality. While the argument may continue as to whether he or Beethoven is the greater composer, there is no doubt that music flowed more naturally from Mozart who, unlike Beethoven, made few revisions or corrections once his music was committed to paper. Like Beethoven, Mozart wrote sublime symphonies but the pinnacle of Mozart's achievement lay not in symphonies, but in his 22 operas and 27 piano concertos.

Having begun composing at the age of six and graduated to his first piano concerto at 11, Mozart's output continued unabated until his death in 1791 at the age of 35. His greatest works came in the last decade of his life, during which he composed six of the world's great operas and three great symphonies that have been described as 'the crowning glories of 18th-century instrumental music'. The three symphonies, Nos 39, 40 and, his last, No.41, were written in a single inspired year, 1788, immediately after the death of his father. The last of his operas was *The Magic Flute*, and his 27th and last

TIMELINE :: CLASSICAL LASTS

**1750** Johann Sebastian Bach (Germany) dies of a stroke, aged 65, on 28 JULY, before completing his last work, a series of fugues known collectively as *The Art of Fugue*

**1752** George Frideric (Georg Friedrich) Handel (Germany–England) premieres his last oratorio, *Jephtha*. He becomes blind after an unsuccessful cataract operation that year; his last day is 14 APRIL 1759, when he dies, aged 74

**1788** Wolfgang Amadeus Mozart (Austria) composes his last symphony, No.41

**1791** Mozart composes his last opera, *The Magic Flute*, and last piano concerto (27th) K595 in B flat major. He dies, aged 35, on 5 DECEMBER leaving his last work, the Requiem Mass, unfinished

**1801** Joseph Haydn (Austria) completes his last major work, *The Seasons*. His last day is 31 MAY 1809, when he dies, aged 77

**1824** Ludwig van Beethoven premieres his Ninth and last symphony, the 'Choral', on 7 MAY. He completes his last composition of all, the String Quartet Op.135, in 1826. His last day is 26 MARCH 1827, when he dies, aged 56
*See also: Pallbearers, page 254*

**1828** Franz Schubert (Austria) dies, aged 31, on 19 NOVEMBER after completing his last major work, *String Quintet*, and writing songs later published as *Schwanengesang*. He is buried next to Beethoven, at whose funeral he had been a pallbearer
*See also: Pallbearers, page 254*

**1846** Felix Mendelssohn (Germany) completes his last work, *Elijah*. His last day is 4 NOVEMBER 1847, when he dies, aged 38

**1882** Richard Wagner (Germany) premieres his last work, the opera *Parsifal*, and travels to Venice for the winter, where he dies of a heart attack, aged 69, on 13 FEBRUARY

**1893** Peter Ilich (Pyotr Ilyich) Tchaikovsky (Russia) dies, aged 53, on 6 NOVEMBER after completing his sixth

*continued...*

piano concerto was K595 in B flat major – both were composed in 1791, the year that he died.

Mozart's last work of all was his unfinished setting of the Requiem Mass, which had been commissioned anonymously by a 'mysterious stranger' whom history has since revealed to be Count Walsegg (Austria). Walsegg was known for commissioning music that he would then claim to have composed himself – not the case with Mozart's last work, which is known universally as Mozart's Requiem. The Requiem was unfinished when Mozart died on 5 December 1791, in circumstances that have fuelled conspiracy theories ever since that he was poisoned.

## Beethoven's last symphony

The true value of the music of Ludwig van Beethoven (Germany) lies not only in the surviving works but also in the way that he revolutionized the conventions of his day and influenced so much of what was to follow. The core of his achievement lay in his 32 piano sonatas, 16 string quartets,

...continued

and last symphony, *Pathétique*. Giuseppe Verdi (Italy) completes his last major work, the opera *Falstaff*, at the age of 80. His last day is 27 JANUARY 1901, when he dies, aged 87

**1904** Antonin Dvořák (Czechoslovakia) dies, aged 62, on 1 MAY after completing his last work, the opera *Armida*

**1907** Edvard Grieg (Norway) dies, aged 64, on 4 SEPTEMBER before completing his last work, the opera *Olav Trygvason*

**1911** Gustav Mahler (Austria) dies, aged 50, on 18 MAY, in Vienna, Austria, before completing his tenth and last symphony

**1917** Claude Debussy (France) completes his last work, *Violin Sonata*. His last day is 25 MARCH 1918, when he dies, aged 55, in Paris

**1924** Jean Sibelius (Finland) composes his seventh and last symphony. He composes his last major work, the tone poem *Tapiola*, in 1926 and then goes into retirement. His last day is 20 SEPTEMBER 1957, when he dies, aged 91

**1933** Edward Elgar (England) makes preliminary sketches for his unfinished last work, the Third Symphony. His last day is 23 FEBRUARY 1934, when he dies, aged 76

**1945** Belá Bartók (Hungary) dies, aged 64, in New York on 26 SEPTEMBER before completing his last work, a concerto for viola

**1974** Dmitri (Dmitry) Shostakovich (Russia) completes his 15th and last symphony. His last day is 9 AUGUST 1975, when he dies, aged 68

**1976** Benjamin Britten (England) dies, aged 63, on 4 DECEMBER after completing his last work, *Welcome Ode*

nine symphonies and six concertos. Beethoven's first published work was for piano and when his output began to diminish towards the end of his career the piano was the first instrument for which he stopped writing: he composed his last piano sonata (Op.111) in 1822 and his last piano masterpiece, the *Diabelli Variations* (Op.120), in 1823. His last composition of all was a string quartet (Op.135), in 1826.

Beethoven's symphonies have been described as 'one of the pillars of Western art', and reached their culmination with Symphony No.9, the 'Choral'. In 1817, three years after completing Symphony No.8 and by then almost totally deaf, Beethoven made his first sketches for the 'Choral', which received its first performance on 7 May 1824 to critical acclaim that has never diminished. It had long been Beethoven's ambition to set to music Schiller's 'Ode to Joy', and he achieved his ambition with the stupendous choral finale of this, his last symphony.

The Ninth was not intended to be the last. Beethoven had accepted a commission of £100 from the London Philharmonic Society to compose a tenth symphony, but it was not to be: in 1827, just three years after the premiere of the Ninth, Beethoven died of pneumonia. Among the various last words attributed to the great composer tortured by deafness are: 'I shall hear in heaven.'

**DID YOU KNOW?**

● The motto of the finale of Beethoven's final string quartet (Op.135), written in 1826, was particularly apt for this, his last composition: 'Must it be? – It must be!' He contracted pneumonia later the same year and died just months later in 1827

● The title track of rock band Rainbow's 1981 album *Difficult to Cure* is a guitar rendition by Ritchie Blackmore (England) of Beethoven's setting of the 'Ode to Joy', the choral finale of the Ninth symphony. Beethoven's Ninth also formed the basis of the soundtrack to the 1988 film *Die Hard*

**Below** A steel monument honouring Jean Sibelius (*see: Timeline 1924*) stands in Sibelius Park, Helsinki, Finland. The monument was designed by Eila Hitunen in 1967

**Opposite** Beethoven's grave in Vienna, Austria

The Beatles had no less than 17 UK No.1 singles, of which 13 also made it to the top of the US charts. Their last transatlantic No.1 was 'Get Back' in 1969 and their last in the UK was 'Ballad of John and Yoko' later the same year. Their last original album was *Let It Be*, released in 1970.

# LASTS OF POP MUSIC

**TIMELINE: POP LASTS**

**1959** The last day of Buddy Holly (USA, b. Charles Hardin Holley), who is killed in a plane crash on 3 FEBRUARY, aged 22. His last Top 20 single, 'It Really Doesn't Matter Any More', is released posthumously later the same year

**1969** The Beatles have their last UK No.1: 'Ballad of John and Yoko' and their last USA No.1: 'Get Back' from *Let It Be*. Elvis Presley (USA) records his last US No.1 single, 'Suspicious Minds'

**1970** The Beatles release their last album, *Let It Be*. Jimi Hendrix (USA) plays his last concert tour, including the Isle of Wight Festival, England, and continental Europe. His last day is 18 SEPTEMBER when he dies, aged 27, allegedly of a drug overdose, in his girlfriend's flat in London, England. The last album approved by Hendrix is *The Cry of Love*, released in 1971

**1971** The Doors (USA) record *L.A. Woman*, their last album as a foursome. The last day of singer Jim Morrison (USA) is 3 JULY, when he allegedly dies, aged 27, in Paris, France (there are rumours that his death is faked). The remaining members of the band reunite in 1978 to record *An American Prayer*, setting music to poems recorded by Morrison in 1970

**1973** Elvis Presley records his ninth and last No.1 album, *Aloha From Hawaii By Satellite*. His last day is 16 AUGUST 1977, when he dies, aged 42, in his mansion at Graceland after swallowing large quantities of at least 14 prescription drugs

## Beatles' lasts

'We're more popular than Christ now. I don't know which will go first, rock and roll or Christianity.' Most people did not go as far as John Lennon (England) in their assessment of the Beatles' success, but a new word was coined to describe the phenomenon: Beatlemania. The fact that their songs are still played, parodied, quoted and covered 40 years later makes it surprising to learn that their reign lasted just six years, from their first UK No.1 single in 1963 ('From Me to You') to their last in 1969.

The last member of the group to join was Ringo Starr (England, b. Richard Starkey), when in 1962 he replaced Pete Best (England) on drums. For most of the rest of the decade the Beatles were listing firsts, not lasts, until 1968 when they began recording what would be their last album, *Let It Be* (released in 1970 after the band had split up). Their last recording session as a foursome took place on the roof of the Apple Records headquarters in Savile Row, London, on 30 January 1969, when they recorded a live version of 'Get Back' as part of a film for the *Let It Be* album. (It was not the last session for Paul, George and Ringo, who reunited in 1995 to add their contributions to a demo of the late John Lennon singing 'Free as a Bird'.)

Later in 1969 'Get Back' became the Beatles' last No.1 single in the USA, but not in Britain, where the subsequent release of 'Ballad of John and Yoko' became their last UK No.1 later the same year. In 1969, announcing the end of the band that had defined the decade, John Lennon said: 'I'd like to say thank you very much on behalf of the group and myself and I hope we passed the audition.'

**DID YOU KNOW?**

● The Beatles appeared on the cover of the Rolling Stones album *Their Satanic Majesties Request*. The Stones' album cover was designed in 1967 by pop artist Michael Cooper (England), who earlier the same year had photographed the sleeve for the Beatles' *Sgt. Pepper's Lonely Hearts Club Band*. The *Sgt. Pepper*'s sleeve featured a doll wearing a shirt saying 'Welcome the Rolling Stones', and Cooper reciprocated by hiding pictures of the Fab Four in the undergrowth of the *Satanic Majesties*' sleeve

**1977** T. Rex (England) release their last album, *Dandy in the Underworld*, and play their last concert, in Portsmouth, England. The last day of their lead singer Marc Bolan (England, b. Mark Feld) is 16 SEPTEMBER, before he is killed, aged 29, in a car crash when the Mini driven by his girlfriend, Gloria Jones (USA), hits a tree in the early hours of 17 SEPTEMBER

**1979** AC/DC (Australia) release *Highway To Hell*, their last album with Bon Scott (Australia, b. Ronald Belford Scott in Scotland) before his death, aged 33, from alcohol abuse on 19 FEBRUARY **1980** in London, England

**1980** John Lennon releases his last single, 'Just Like Starting Over', and, with Yoko Ono (Japan), his last album, *Double Fantasy*. His last day is 8 DECEMBER when, aged 40, he is shot by Mark Chapman (USA). *Uprising* is the last album to be released by Bob Marley (Jamaica, b. Nesta Robert Marley) during his lifetime. His last day is 11 MAY **1981**, when he dies of cancer, aged 36. His last No.1 album is the posthumously released *Legend* in **1984**

**1982** *Midnight Love* is the last album to be released by Marvin Gaye (USA) during his lifetime, and contains his last Top 10 hit, 'Sexual Healing'. His last day is 1 APRIL **1984**, when he is shot by his father in an argument

**1991** Queen (Britain) release *Innuendo*, their last album with Freddie Mercury (Britain, b. Faroukh Bulsara in Zanzibar) before his death from AIDS on 24 NOVEMBER, aged 45. Vocals recorded by Mercury in 1991 are later used for the posthumous album *Made in Heaven* (released in **1995**)

**1993** Nirvana (USA) release their last album, *In Utero*. The last day of singer/guitarist Kurt Cobain (USA) is 5 APRIL **1994**, when he shoots himself, aged 27

**1997** INXS (Australia) release their last album, *Elegantly Wasted*. The last day of singer Michael Hutchence (Australia) is 22 NOVEMBER, when he inelegantly kills himself in a hotel room, aged 37

**Above** John Lennon and Yoko Ono pictured during filming of the promotional film for 'The Ballad of John and Yoko' (1969)

**Below** The Beatles on the roof of the Apple Records headquarters in London, during their last recording session as a foursome (30 January 1969)

Among the world's best-known novelists are Charles Dickens, the most published novelist of all time, and Ernest Hemingway, whose distinctive characterization gave rise to the term 'Hemingway hero'. Their last novels were *The Mystery of Edwin Drood* and *The Garden of Eden* respectively.

**Personal Lasts**

# AUTHORS' LAST NOVELS

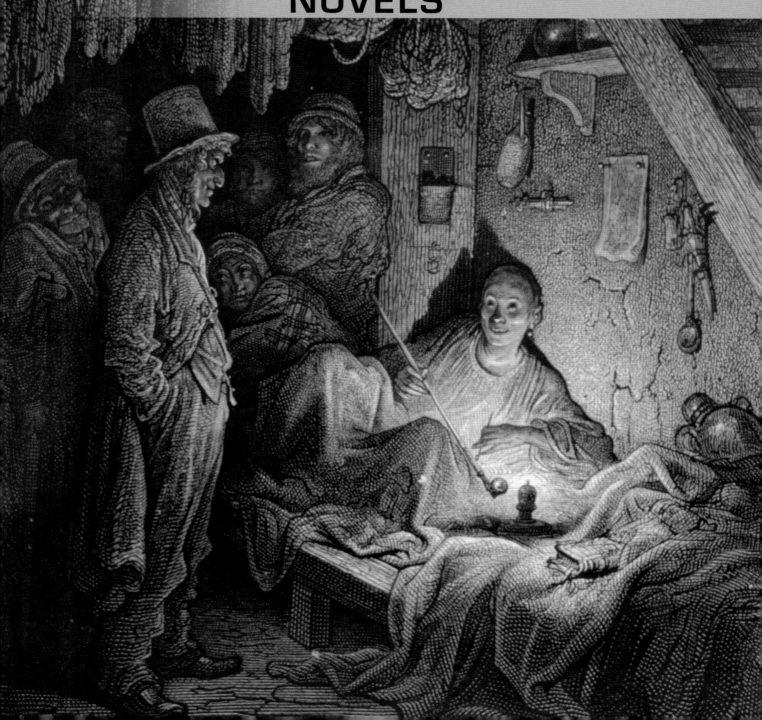

# Charles Dickens' last novel

As well as being a prolific writer, Charles Dickens (England) was also an energetic reader of his work. By 1869 Dickens was exhausted and ill health forced him to take a break from reading; he did, however, agree a contract for what was to be his last novel, *The Mystery of Edwin Drood*. Publishers Chapman & Hall paid him an advance of £7,500, but Dickens was so worried about his health that he insisted on the inclusion of a clause to say that a proportion of the advance would be repaid if he failed to complete the novel through death or disablement.

Publication of *Edwin Drood* began in monthly instalments, and sales of the first instalment were reported to have 'far outstripped every one of its predecessors'. The story centred on two orphans, Edwin Drood and Rosa Bud, whose widower fathers, before their deaths, had betrothed the two children to be married. Edwin and Rosa realize they are incompatible and break off the engagement, but not before admirers of Rosa have plotted villainy against Edwin, who disappears in mysterious circumstances before he and Rosa can announce their decision.

The last page Dickens wrote was a description of his beloved Rochester, England, which appears in the novel as Cloisterham, and he died leaving the mystery of Edwin Drood unsolved – there were no notes or plan to indicate whether Edwin had been murdered or whether he was living in disguise as one of the other characters and would later reveal himself. Dickens' last words were somewhat more prosaic than his last description of Rochester. After he collapsed with a stroke on 8 June, his sister-in-law was struggling to carry him to the sofa and he murmured: 'On the ground.' He said nothing else before his death the following evening.

## DID YOU KNOW?

● A doctor was present at all of Charles Dickens' last readings and instructed Dickens' son Charley: 'If you see your father falter in the least, you must run and catch him and bring him to me, or, by heaven, he'll die before them all.' During the 'Final Farewell Reading' at St James' Hall, Piccadilly, on 15 March 1870, Dickens' pulse rose from 72 to 124 and after a standing ovation he announced: 'From these garish lights I now vanish for ever more, with a heartfelt, grateful, respectful, affectionate farewell'

**Opposite** 'The Lascar's Room', a scene from *The Mystery of Edwin Drood*, engraved by A. Doms after the original by Gustave Doré (1872)
**Above** Charles Dickens at his last reading (1870)

**TIMELINE: AUTHORS' LAST NOVELS**

**1616** Miguel de Cervantes (Spain) completes his last novel, the romantic adventure *The Travels of Persiles and Sigismunda* (pub. 1617). He writes the introduction, in which he bids farewell to life, just four days before his death in Madrid on 23 APRIL, aged 68

**1832** Walter Scott (Scotland), the second most published novelist of all time after Charles Dickens, completes his last novel, *Castle Dangerous*, published as the last part of the collection *Tales of My Landlord* in this the year of his death

**1868** Alexandre Dumas (France, a.k.a. Dumas père), the third most published novelist of all time, completes his last historical novel, *The White and the Blue*. He dies, aged 67, on 5 DECEMBER 1870, before completing his last play, *Joseph Balsamo*, which is completed and produced in 1878 by his son, Alexandre Dumas fils

**1870** In MARCH Charles Dickens (England) gives his last public reading. He suffers a stroke on 8 JUNE and dies, aged 58, the following day before completing his last novel, *The Mystery of Edwin Drood*

**1880** Fyodor Dostoevsky (Russia) completes his last novel, *The Brothers Karamazov*. He dies the following year

**1894** Robert Louis Stevenson (Scotland) dies, aged 44, on 3 DECEMBER of a brain haemorrhage before completing his last two works, *Weir of Hermiston* (published 1896) and *St Ives*, completed by A.T. Quiller-Couch (England) and published in 1897

**1899** Leo Tolstoy (Russia) completes his last major novel, *Resurrection*, for which he is excommunicated in 1901. His last day is 21 NOVEMBER 1910, when he dies, aged 82

**1905** Jules Verne (France) dies, aged 77, on 24 MARCH after completing his last novel, *Invasion of the Sea*

**1910** Mark Twain (USA, pseudonym of Samuel Langhorne Clemens) dies, aged 74, on 21 APRIL, leaving several uncompleted manuscripts. His last work to date to be published is *The Mysterious Stranger* in 1916

*continued…*

## Ernest Hemingway's last novel

Ernest Hemingway (USA) was one of America's greatest and most influential novelists, winning the Pulitzer Prize in 1953 for *The Old Man and the Sea*, and the Nobel Prize for Literature the following year. He cheated death more than once in his all-action lifestyle and twice read his own obituary, but in the end, despite the success and acclaim, he could not escape from himself.

Hemingway's last day came when he shot himself in the mouth at home in Ketchum, Idaho, USA, in the early hours of 2 July 1961, leaving no suicide note. The shot woke his fourth and last wife, Mary, who issued a statement saying that he had killed himself accidentally while cleaning the gun. However, history was repeating itself – Hemingway's father had also shot himself, a traumatic incident that appeared in several of Hemingway's stories.

Three of his books were published after his death: the autobiographical

*A Moveable Feast* (1964), describing his life in Paris, France, during the 1920s; his last complete novel, *Islands in the Stream* (1970), which has been described as 'an excrutiating novel best ignored'; and his last, unfinished novel *The Garden of Eden*, which in 1986 became his last work to be published. *The Garden of Eden*, on which Hemingway worked intermittently from 1946 until 1961, was an immediate bestseller, but provoked mixed reactions from critics. Set on the Côte d'Azur during the 1920s, it tells the story of American writer David Bourne, his wife, Catherine, and the dangerous liaisons they engage in when they both fall in love with the same woman. *Publisher's Weekly* wrote that this was not a 'bona fide Hemingway novel', but *Time* magazine described it as: 'A lean, sensuous narrative ... taut, chic, and strangely contemporary', citing it as a fine example of Hemingway 'doing what nobody did better'.

## DID YOU KNOW?

● When former riverboat pilot Samuel Langhorne Clemens began writing novels, he chose the pseudonym Mark Twain (*see: Timeline 1910*) from a boatman's call indicating a depth of two fathoms – 'by the mark, two' was usually shortened to 'mark twain'

● Margaret Mitchell's novel *Gone With the Wind* embodied several firsts and lasts – not only was it both her first and last novel, but she reportedly wrote the first chapter second and the last chapter first. Her last day was 16 August 1949, when she died after being hit by a car

● Today, the Stevenson family is most often remembered for the novels of Robert Louis, including *Kidnapped* and *Treasure Island*, but in their time four generations of the family were more famous for their engineering feats, including building nearly all of Scotland's lighthouses. The novelist of the family once said: 'I might write books until 1900 and not serve humanity so well'

**Left** Ernest Hemingway sits at his typewriter and considers his work (1944)
**Above** Frontispiece illustration of author Mark Twain from *A Tramp Abroad* (also known as *Innocents Abroad*), showing memories of foreign travel swirling around him as he tries to write (1869)

The plays of William Shakespeare are the world's most performed, most widely read and most filmed. Shakespeare wrote at least 37 plays as well as penning 154 sonnets and several longer poems. The last of the plays written by him alone was *The Tempest*, completed in 1611.

# SHAKESPEARE'S LAST PLAY

The plays of William Shakespeare (England) are often grouped into categories: tragedies, comedies, historical plays and the 'Late Romances', or 'Last Plays'. As a group, the four Last Plays (*Pericles*, *The Winter's Tale*, *Cymbeline* and *The Tempest*) are distinctly different in tone to Shakespeare's earlier work, reflecting the maturity of his outlook as he prepared to leave London and retire to Stratford. The last of the four, *The Tempest*, was written for the 1611–12 season at the Blackfriars and Globe Theatres, but was not printed until the First Folio of 1623.

*The Tempest* tells the story of the magician Prospero, Duke of Milan, who has been exiled on a lonely island with his daughter Miranda after being ousted from his throne by his brother Antonio. Through magic, Prospero makes their exile bearable and eventually engineers a reconciliation with

**1613** *King Henry VIII* is produced as the last play usually credited to Shakespeare (although written with John Fletcher, England) to receive its first performance. John Webster's *Two Noble Kinsmen*, the last play to which Shakespeare contributed, is first performed

**1616** Shakespeare's last day is 23 APRIL, when he dies, aged 51, at home in Stratford-upon-Avon. He is buried two days later in the church where he had been baptized 52 years earlier

**1670** Shakespeare's last direct descendant (a granddaughter) dies

### DID YOU KNOW?

● Shakespeare's last day is popularly thought also to have been his first. The exact date of his birth is not certain, but he was baptized on 26 April 1564 and tradition has it that he was born three days earlier, on St George's Day. He died 52 years later, on St George's Day 1616

● One of the world's greatest and most persistent conspiracy theories is that Shakespeare did not write his own plays. Several candidates for authorship have been put forward, one of the most plausible being playwright Christopher Marlowe (England), who supposedly died in 1593 after being stabbed in a pub brawl. The Marlowe Society contends that the brawl was a ruse to enable Marlowe, a spy for Queen Elizabeth I, to escape arrest and persecution, and that he lived out his life in exile, selling his plays to Shakespeare's company to be produced under Shakespeare's name

Antonio, as well as his own restoration to his throne. The last lines of the epilogue, spoken by Prospero, are particularly apt for a man seeking to retire from his life's work: 'As you from crimes would pardon'd be, Let your indulgence set me free.'

However, debate still continues as to which play should be classified as Shakespeare's last. He also collaborated on at least two plays with John Fletcher (England), his successor as playwright for his theatre company, the King's Men. These plays were the historical *King Henry VIII*, which is usually included in Shakespeare's oeuvre and was first performed in 1613, making it the last of his plays to receive its first performance, and *The Two Noble Kinsmen* (also 1613), which is sometimes cited as Shakespeare's last play, but was written mainly by John Webster (England), to whom it is usually attributed.

**Opposite** Simon Keenlyside (left) as Prospero, Cyndia Sieden (right) as Ariel and Christine Rice (middle) as Miranda in the Royal Opera production of *The Tempest* at the Royal Opera House, London (February 2004)

**Above** William Shakespeare (unattributed portrait, 1598)

Marilyn Monroe was already a Hollywood icon before her last film, *The Misfits*. By contrast, Bruce Lee died before the release of *Enter the Dragon*, the film that brought him international mainstream recognition; Lee's son, Brandon, suffered a similar fate with his last film, *The Crow*.

# ACTORS' LAST FILMS

It shouts and sings with life... explodes with love!

Seven Arts Productions presents

CLARK         MARILYN
**Gable Monroe**          MONTGOMERY **Clift**
in the **John Huston** production of **the Misfits**
Co-starring
**Thelma Ritter  Eli Wallach**  Screenplay by **Arthur Miller**  Produced by **Frank E. Taylor**  Directed by **John Huston**

**TIMELINE: LAST FILMS**

**1941** Greta Garbo (Sweden–USA, b. Greta Lovisa Gustafsson) retires from the screen after scathing reviews of her last film, *Two-Faced Woman*. Her last day is 15 APRIL **1990**, when she dies, aged **84**

**1955** James Dean (USA) completes his third and last film, *Giant*, released in 1956 after his death, aged 24, in a car crash on 30 SEPTEMBER **1955**

**1956** Grace Kelly (USA) completes her last dramatic role, in *The Swan*, before retiring from the screen to marry Prince Rainier III of Monaco later this year. *High Society* is sometimes named as her last film because it was released last, although completed earlier the same year. She is later lured out of retirement to narrate the documentary film *The Children of Theatre Street*, her last screen contribution. Her last day is 14 SEPTEMBER **1982**, when she dies, aged **52**

*continued...*

## Marilyn Monroe's last film

'A legend in his or her own lifetime' is a woefully overused phrase, but it was true of Marilyn Monroe (USA, b. Norma Jean Baker). The rags to riches story of Hollywood's biggest star had already made her a legend long before her last film, *The Misfits*, which was a box office flop when it was released in 1961, but soon achieved cult status after the death of its female lead the following year. *The Misfits* has been described as 'more of a mausoleum than a movie', being not only Monroe's last film but also that of Clark Gable (USA), who died before it was completed.

The Misfits is a bleak, despairing story of three drifters who hunt horses to sell for pet food, and was written by Monroe's third and last husband, Arthur Miller (USA). Miller created the role of Roslyn Taber especially for Monroe, but her performance was marred by her emotional state – author and actress argued constantly on set, and January 1961 saw the last day of their marriage.

In 1962, the year after the release of *The Misfits*, Monroe began work on another film, *Something's Got To Give*, but was fired in June for persistent absence. The title of the film proved prophetic: something did give, and in the early hours of 5 August 1962 Marilyn Monroe was found dead in her bedroom with an empty bottle of sleeping pills beside her. Rumours that she was murdered have persisted ever since – her sleeping problems were well known and that in itself would provide perfect cover for anyone bent on foul play. John Huston (USA), director of *The Misfits*, said later: 'Her great enemy was sleeplessness. Only God knows why she feared it so much.'

**Above** 'It shouts and sings with life … explodes with love!' Poster for *The Misfits* (1961)
**Opposite** Marilyn Monroe and Clark Gable on location during the filming of *The Misfits* (1960)

**DID YOU KNOW?**

● In its obituary, *The Times* newspaper said of Marilyn Monroe: 'Her career was not so much a Hollywood legend as *the* Hollywood legend: the poor orphan who became one of the most sought after and highly paid women in the world; the hopeful Hollywood unknown who became the most potent star-attraction in the American cinema; the uneducated beauty who married one of America's leading intellectuals'

# The last films of Bruce and Brandon Lee

Bruce Lee (China, b. Lee Jun Fan in USA) was almost single-handedly responsible for transforming martial arts films from a minority art form into a mainstream film genre. The last film that he completed was also his most famous – *Enter the Dragon*, in which Lee's character, in order to expose an opium-smuggling racket, infiltrates a group of martial artists who are travelling to Hong Kong for a tournament. But Lee did not live to see the phenomenal success of the film, or to enjoy his resulting fame.

On 20 July 1973, just a month before the premiere of *Enter the Dragon*, he took a painkiller to ease a headache, fell asleep and never woke up. The autopsy reported that he had died of a cerebral oedema (brain swelling) brought on by an allergic reaction to the painkiller, but conspiracy theories have thrived ever since that he was murdered by a Chinese gang or that he had succumbed to 'the curse of the dragon'. His last film of all was *Game of Death*, which he had started filming in 1972, but had put on hold to make *Enter the Dragon*; it was completed posthumously using a stand-in and released in 1978.

It seems that the curse, if it existed, extended to Lee's son, Brandon, who also died an early death before completing *his* last film, *The Crow*, which was also completed using a stand-in. On the night of 30 March 1993 Brandon Lee was fatally shot by a stunt pistol fired by fellow actor Michael Massee. The official investigation concluded that the tip of a dummy bullet used in an earlier scene had been lodged in the chamber of the gun and was propelled out of the barrel by the blank round being used that night. (Dummy bullets give the appearance of real bullets for close-ups, while blanks provide noise and flash for action shots.) As with his father, conspiracy theories have thrived ever since that Brandon's death was not an accident.

**Opposite** Bruce Lee in his last film, *Game of Death* (released 1978)

**Below** Brandon Lee in his last film, *The Crow* (1993)

**1960** Clark Gable (USA) dies, aged 59, on 16 NOVEMBER during the making of his last film, *The Misfits* (released 1961)

**1961** Marilyn Monroe completes her last film, *The Misfits*. Her last day is 4/5 AUGUST 1962, when she dies, aged 36

**1973** Brigitte Bardot (France, b. Camille Javal) completes her last film, *If Don Juan Were a Woman*. Bruce Lee (USA) dies, aged 32, on 20 JULY. The last film made during his lifetime is *Enter the Dragon*. His last film of all is *Game of Death*, released posthumously in 1978

**1976** John Wayne (USA, b. Marion Michael Morrison) completes his last film, *The Shootist*. His last day is 11 JUNE 1979, when he dies, aged 72

**1979** Marlene Dietrich (Germany–USA) stars in her last dramatic role, in *Just a Gigolo*. In 1984 she tells the story of her life in the documentary *Marlene*. Her last day is 6 MAY 1992, when she dies, aged 90

**1984** Richard Burton (Wales, b. Richard Walter Jenkins) dies, aged 58, on 5 AUGUST after playing his last role, in *Nineteen Eighty-Four*, which is released later the same year

**1985** Laurence Olivier (England) completes his last dramatic role, in *Wild Geese II*. He makes his last screen appearance in Derek Jarman's documentary drama *War Requiem*. His last day is 11 JULY 1989, when he dies, aged 82

**1989** Audrey Hepburn (Belgium, b. Edda Van Heemstra Hepburn-Ruston) completes her last film, *Always*. Her last day is 20 JANUARY 1993, when she dies, aged 63

**1993** Brandon Lee (USA) dies, aged 28, on 30 MARCH while making *The Crow* (released 1994), after being shot by a supposedly harmless stunt pistol

**1994** Katharine Hepburn (USA) completes her last film, *Love Affair*. Her last day is 29 JUNE 2003, when she dies, aged 96

*See also: Last Car Journeys, page 236; Pallbearers, page 254*

Alfred Hitchcock was the acclaimed master of suspense and, although he never won an Oscar as Best Director, his talent was recognized by the Academy when he won a lifetime achievement award in 1979, the year before he died. His last film, released in 1976, was *Family Plot*.

# DIRECTORS' LAST FILMS

## Alfred Hitchcock's last film

The career of Alfred Hitchcock (England–USA) is neatly divided into two parts, one based in England and one in America. His last film before he emigrated to the USA in 1939 was *The Lady Vanishes* (1938) and his first in America was *Rebecca* (1940), which won an Oscar for Best Film. Hitchcock was naturalized in 1955 and made his most famous films, including *North by Northwest* (1959) and *Psycho* (1960), as an American citizen. His last completed film, released in 1976, was *Family Plot*, and his last unfinished screenplay was for a film with the working title *The Short Night*.

    *Family Plot* is more significant for being Hitchcock's last film than for its intrinsic qualities, and is certainly no artistic swansong: critic Paul Duncan

**TIMELINE: DIRECTORS' LAST FILMS**

**1947** Ill health forces Sergei Eisenstein (Russia) to cease work on his last, unfinished film, *Ivan the Terrible Part III/The Battles of Ivan*. His last completed film is *Ivan the Terrible Part II/The Boyars' Plot*, completed in 1946, but suppressed until 1958. His last day is 11 FEBRUARY 1948, when he dies, aged 59, of a heart attack

**1966** John Ford (USA) completes his last film, *Seven Women*. His last day is 31 AUGUST 1973, when he dies, aged 78

**1967** Charlie Chaplin (England) directs his last film, *The Countess from Hong Kong*. His last acting role is in *A King in New York* (1957). He is knighted in 1975 and his last day is 25 DECEMBER 1977, when he dies, aged 88

**1973** Orson Welles (USA) completes his last feature film as director, *F for Fake*. His last day is 10 OCTOBER 1985, when he dies, aged 70. His last dramatic role as an actor is in *Someone to Love*, released in 1987. Several archive films directed by or including performances by Welles are released posthumously

## DID YOU KNOW?

• Hitchcock once said: 'The most horrible sound in the world is of a hand smacking the bottom of a ketchup bottle, only because, as a result of that smacking, some ugly, dark-red goo oozes from the neck of the bottle and lays itself over some innocent French fried potatoes'

• As well as directing films, Alfred Hitchcock also produced and hosted his own television series for a decade. He clearly enjoyed working on the small screen, saying: 'Television has brought murder back into the home – where it belongs'

described it as 'an enjoyable, lightweight movie that never fulfils its potential'. Based on the novel *The Rainbird Pattern* by Victor Canning, the plot follows psychic Blanche Tyler and her boyfriend George Lumley as they attempt to track down Eddie Shoebridge, heir to a fortune, for a finder's fee. But Shoebridge has his own criminal agenda, which is foiled by Blanche and George, who eventually discover the evidence needed to expose him.

*The Short Night* was to have been based on the story of spy George Blake (Britain, b. Netherlands), but failing health forced Hitchcock to stop work on this, his last screenplay. He was awarded an Oscar for Lifetime Achievement at the 1979 Academy Awards and knighted in the 1980 New Year's Honours list, but did not live long to bask in his glory: he died in hospital on the morning of 29 April that same year.

**Opposite** Alfred Hitchcock holding a magnifying glass on the set of his television show, *Alfred Hitchcock Presents* (May 1956)

**Below** Barbara Harris and Bruce Dern in Alfred Hitchcock's last film, *Family Plot* (1976)

**1975** Hitchcock wraps his last film, *Family Plot*, on 18 AUGUST. It receives its first screening on 21 MARCH 1976 at the Los Angeles International Film Festival. His last day is 29 APRIL 1980, when he dies, aged 80

**1977** Luis Buñuel (Spain) completes his last film, *That Obscure Object of Desire*. He dies, aged 83, on 29 JULY 1983 shortly after the publication of his autobiography, *My Last Sigh*

**1980** François Truffaut (France) completes his last film, *Confidentially Yours*. His last day is 21 OCTOBER 1984, when he dies, aged 52

**1984** Ingmar Bergman (Sweden) completes *After the Rehearsal*, his last feature film before retiring from cinema, although he continues to write novels and screenplays and to direct television drama. David Lean (England) completes his last film, *A Passage to India*

**1987** Federico Fellini (Italy) completes his last film, *Intervista*. His last day is 31 OCTOBER 1993, when he dies, aged 73

**1993** Derek Jarman (England) completes his last two films, *Blue* and *Wittgenstein* (the latter shot in just two weeks). His last day is 19 FEBRUARY 1994, when he dies, aged 52

**1995** After recovering from a stroke, Michelangelo Antonioni (Italy) completes his last film, *Beyond the Clouds*, co-directed by Wim Wenders (Germany)

**1999** Stanley Kubrick (USA) completes his last film, *Eyes Wide Shut*, which he describes as 'my best film ever'. The film receives its first screening at Warner Brothers' headquarters on 2 MARCH. Kubrick dies in his sleep, aged 70, in the early hours of 7 MARCH

As many as 14 murders have been attributed to 19th-century serial killer Jack the Ripper, whose real identity remains unknown, but it is generally accepted that only five were actually committed by him. His last known victim, discovered on 9 November 1888, was Mary Jane Kelly.

**Personal Lasts**

# JACK THE RIPPER'S LAST VICTIM

Much has been written about Jack the Ripper, but little is known for certain, and it has even been suggested that 'Jack' was actually a woman. Between August and November 1888 five prostitutes were found murdered and mutilated within one square mile in Whitechapel in the East End of London, England – a series of crimes that became known as the Whitechapel Murders. After the discovery of the second victim, Annie Chapman (England), police received a taunting letter signed 'Jack the Ripper'. There is some doubt as to whether this was actually written by the murderer, but the nickname stuck and it still provokes speculation more than a century later as to the identity it hides.

Although several more murders would be attributed to Jack the Ripper in the wake of the Whitechapel Murders, the last victim for whose death he or she is known beyond all reasonable doubt to be responsible was Mary Jane Kelly (Ireland) who, like many other East End prostitutes, lived in fear of the Ripper. Kelly had been planning to leave London, intending to return only when the killer had been caught, but on the morning of 9 November 1888 her body, disembowelled and partially dismembered, was discovered by her rent collector.

Only the previous day Sir Charles Warren (Wales) had performed his last act as Metropolitan Police Commissioner, taking responsibility for the failure of his force to catch the Ripper by handing in his resignation. This most notorious of serial killers was never caught – it seems that after this last murder s/he simply stopped killing, possibly living as late as the 1950s and then taking the true identity of Jack the Ripper with him or her to the grave.

7 AUGUST **The body of Martha Turner (England, a.k.a. Martha Tabram),** sometimes cited as the first victim of Jack the Ripper, is found at George Yard Buildings (now Gunthorpe Street), London

31 AUGUST **Mary Anne Nichols (England, a.k.a. Polly Nichols),** the first victim usually attributed to Jack the Ripper, is found in Buck's Row (now Durward Street) with her throat cut

8 SEPTEMBER **The body of Annie Chapman (England)** is discovered in Hanbury Street. Her last words to her lodging-house-keeper are reported as: 'Don't let my doss, I'll soon be back with the money. See what a fine new bonnet I've got!' (These words are also sometimes attributed to Polly Nichols)

30 SEPTEMBER **The body of Elizabeth Stride (Britain, b. Sweden)** is found in Berner Street (now Henriques Street); it appears that the Ripper has been interrupted before he can carry out his usual mutilation

## DID YOU KNOW?

● Among those suggested by so-called 'Ripperologists' as suspects for the true identity of Jack the Ripper are: the Duke of Clarence, eldest son of King Edward VII; the painter Walter Sickert (Britain, b. Germany), who appeared obsessed with the murders; Severin Klosowski (Poland),

who was hanged in 1903 for poisoning his wife; Dr Pedachenko (Russia), a surgeon allegedly sent to Britain by the tsarist secret police to test the British police system; and a barrister called Druitt (Britain), whose body was found floating in the Thames shortly after the last murder

**Opposite** A modern view of Artillery Passage, one of the many alleyways in the Whitechapel area terrorized by Jack the Ripper

**Below** Illustration showing police discovering the body of one of Jack the Ripper's victims (1888)

1 OCTOBER The body of Catherine Eddowes (England) is found in Mitre Square, the Ripper's second victim of the night of 30 SEPTEMBER/ 1 OCTOBER

8 NOVEMBER **Mary Jane Kelly** (Ireland, sometimes recorded as Marie Jeanette Kelly) takes her last client back to her room in Miller's Court, off Dorset Street (now Duval Street). Sir Charles Warren (Wales) performs his last act as Metropolitan Police Commissioner, handing in his resignation

9 NOVEMBER **The** mutilated body of Kelly, Jack the Ripper's last known victim, is discovered by her rent collector

**Personal Lasts**

Napoleon was forced to abdicate as emperor of France in 1814, but he returned to power less than a year later. His second and last reign was to be a short one – later becoming known as the 'Hundred Days' – and ended with defeat in his last battle, at Waterloo, Belgium.

# NAPOLEON'S LAST BATTLE

When Napoleon Bonaparte (France) returned to power in France, the rest of Europe united against him. Napoleon immediately advanced into Belgium, hoping to wipe out the Prussian and Anglo–Dutch Armies before they could join forces, which they managed to do only just in time. On Sunday, 18 June 1815 Napoleon confronted the Anglo–Dutch Army, under the command of Arthur Wellesley, 1st Duke of Wellington (Ireland), at Waterloo, some 12 miles south of Brussels. After a diversionary attack on Château d'Hougoumont, on Wellington's right flank, Napoleon launched an unsuccessful attack on the Allies' centre. Wellington

later recalled: 'The French came on in the old style – and we drove them off in the old style.'

After a lull, Napoleon's Marshal Ney (France) made the error that would cost Napoleon the battle, control of Europe, his crown and his freedom, breaking all the rules of field combat by launching an impetuous, unsupported cavalry attack against intact squares of Allied infantry. Ney did succeed in capturing the fortified farmhouse of La Haye Sainte, but Napoleon now compounded Ney's original error by prevaricating for half an hour before committing his reserves. During this time the Prussian Army arrived, under the command of Gebbard Leberecht von Blücher (Prussia, now Germany), having fought off subsidiary French forces at Wavre earlier in the day.

Now it was do or die for both sides. Napoleon urged his Imperial Guard forward, shouting: 'A Bruxelles, mes enfants, à Bruxelles', but it was too late. The French advance faltered in the face of a surprise manoeuvre by the British 52nd Rifles. Wellington capitalized by ordering a general advance and, supported by Blücher's army, succeeded in routing the French. Afterwards, Wellington acknowledged just how close it had been: 'It was a damn near thing – the nearest run thing you ever saw in your life.'

**Below** *Cuirassiers Charging the Highlanders at the Battle of Waterloo on 18th June 1815*, by Felix Philippoteaux (1874)

**Above right** Referring to the story of Robinson Crusoe, this engraving of Napoleon in exile on the island of St Helena is entitled *The New Robinson of St Helena* (1815)

TIMELINE: NAPOLEONIC LASTS

**1797** Napoleon Bonaparte (France) forces Austria to sign the Treaty of Campo Formio, marking the last day of the first stage of the French Revolutionary Wars, known as the War of the First Coalition

**1805** The defeat of the French fleet by Horatio Nelson (England) at the Battle of Trafalgar, Spain, marks the last of Napoleon's ambitions to invade Britain

**1808** The defeat of the French army by the Duke of Wellington (Ireland) at the Battle of Vimeiro, Portugal, marks the last of the French occupation of Portugal

**1813** The defeat of the French army by Wellington at the Battle of Vitoria, Spain, marks the last of the French occupation of Spain

**1814** The last day of Napoleon's first period as emperor of France comes when he is forced to abdicate

**1815** Napoleon's last battle is fought at Waterloo, Belgium, on 18 JUNE. The last day of Napoleon's second period of power (the 'Hundred Days') is 22 JUNE, when he abdicates and surrenders to the British

**1821** Napoleon's last day is 5 MAY, when he dies, aged 51, in exile on the British island of St Helena

Towards the end of America's so-called Indian Wars, Chiefs Sitting Bull and Crazy Horse defeated General Custer at the Battle of Little Big Horn, which included Custer's famous Last Stand. The battle was the last Native American victory in a war whose ultimate outcome was inevitable.

# CUSTER'S LAST STAND

General George Armstrong Custer (USA) has been variously described as an American cavalry hero and a vainglorious fool. Having served with distinction as a Union brigadier general in the American Civil War, he was given command of the 7th Cavalry in the so-called Indian Wars against the Native American tribes of the Great Plains, where his actions at the Battle of Little Big Horn, whether through misinformation, miscalculation or lack of support, led to the deaths of himself and one-third of his men.

On 25 June 1876, Custer was leading his cavalrymen into Dakota Territory as part of a campaign against an alliance of Sioux and Cheyenne led by Chiefs Sitting Bull and Crazy Horse (both America). When Custer's scouts reported a Native American encampment in the valley of the Little Big Horn River (in present-day Montana), he either underestimated or was misinformed about the

### DID YOU KNOW?

● As well as the Last Stand at the end of his life, Custer had a less famous last at the start of his military career – he graduated from West Point as part of the Class of 1861, in last place

**Left** General George Armstrong Custer in military uniform (c. 1864)
**Opposite top** The graves of Custer and his men who were killed at the Battle of Little Big Horn. The site forms part of the Custer Battlefield National Monument (1975)
**Opposite bottom** Sioux and Cheyenne leaving the battlefield after their victory over Custer and the US 7th Cavalry at the Battle of Little Big Horn

size of the enemy force and decided to attack immediately without waiting for reinforcements. He divided his own forces to make a three-pronged attack with a mere 647 men against more than 2,000 Native American braves.

Custer and his unit of some 265 men found themselves surrounded and were forced to make a stand, now famous as Custer's last, in which he and the entire unit were killed. The Sioux and Cheyenne continued fighting the remaining cavalry (who some historians criticize for failing to support Custer's stand) until the following day, eventually winning a short-lived victory, and their last – a day later still, on 27 June, they were driven onto a reservation by General Alfred H. Terry (USA). On 29 December 1890 the Native Americans were finally defeated in the last battle of the Indian Wars, and the last to date on American soil, the massacre at Wounded Knee.

*See also: The Last Face on Mount Rushmore, page 36;*
*The Last Battle on British/American Soil, page 148*

**c.1834** Sitting Bull is born Tatanka Iyotake near Grand River, South Dakota

**1839** George Armstrong Custer is born in New Rumley, Ohio

**c.1849** Crazy Horse is born Ta-Sunko-Witko in South Dakota

**1861** Custer graduates from West Point

**1861–65** Custer serves with distinction in the American Civil War

**1866** Custer takes command of the 7th Cavalry in the so-called Indian Wars

**1874** Custer leads an expedition that discovers gold in the Black Hills, land sacred to the Sioux and the Cheyenne. The resulting gold rush escalates the conflict

**1876** Custer's Last Stand: he is killed, aged 36, on 25 JUNE at the Battle of Little Big Horn. His detractors claim that Custer acted impetuously, while his supporters blame the other two units involved for not riding to his rescue

**1877** Crazy Horse surrenders and dies on 5 SEPTEMBER in custody at Fort Robinson, Nebraska

**1881** Sitting Bull surrenders

**1885** Sitting Bull appears in Buffalo Bill Cody's Wild West Show

**1890** Sitting Bull's last day is 15 DECEMBER, when he is killed during the suppression of the Native American Ghost Dance religious movement. The massacre of Native Americans at Wounded Knee on 29 DECEMBER, part of the same suppression, marks the last day of the Indian Wars

TIMELINE: SITTING BULL, CUSTER AND CRAZY HORSE

Christ's Last Supper has a huge significance for the Christian religion, providing the basis for the celebration of Holy Communion, but it has also taken on a separate significance in the secular world as the subject of one of the world's most celebrated paintings.

**Personal Lasts**

# LAST SUPPERS

**TIMELINE: THE LAST SUPPER**

**c.30AD** Christ celebrates his last supper with his disciples

**1494–97** Leonardo da Vinci paints his *Last Supper* at the convent of Santa Maria delle Grazie, Milan, Italy

**1573** Veronese (Italy, b. Paolo Caliari) completes his *Feast in the House of Levi* and is brought before the Inquisition – who have mistaken it for a depiction of the Last Supper – to answer charges of trivializing religious subjects

**1594** Tintoretto (Italy, b. Jacopo Robusti) dies on 31 MAY after finishing his last work, *The Last Supper*

**1943** During the Second World War, Allied bombs destroy the convent of Santa Maria delle Grazie, except for the wall on which *The Last Supper* is painted

### DID YOU KNOW?

● The superstition that sitting 13 people at a dinner table is unlucky long predates Christ's Last Supper. It originates in Norse myth, which says that Loki, the god of mischief and destruction, intruded at a banquet in Valhalla, becoming the 13th guest, and that the sweet-natured god Balder was killed as a result. The superstition was reinforced by Christ's Last Supper with his 12 disciples, after which both he and Judas Iscariot met their demise. At one time in France, people called *quatorzièmes* were paid to attend a meal if a 14th person was required at the dinner table

# Christ's last supper

According to the Gospels, Jesus Christ ate his final meal with his disciples immediately before Judas betrayed him in the Garden of Gethsemane. Perhaps the most celebrated meal in history, this last meal has since become known as the Last Supper. Jesus had arranged to celebrate Passover with his disciples in the upper room of a house in Jerusalem, but the meal proved not to be a traditional Passover supper. Christ blessed the bread, broke it and gave it to the disciples, saying: 'Take, eat; this is my body. Do this in remembrance of me.' He then took a cup of wine (the cup has since become part of the legend of the Holy Grail), gave thanks and said: 'Drink of it, all of you; for this is my blood of the new Covenant, which is poured out for many

**Below** *The Last Supper* by Leonardo da Vinci

**1649** King Charles I (Britain) is executed on 30 JANUARY. For his last meal (breakfast, not supper) he is persuaded to eat some bread and drink some claret

**1977** Murderer Gary Gilmore (USA), subsequently the subject of the novel *The Executioner's Song* by Norman Mailer (USA) and of punk song '(Looking through) Gary Gilmore's Eyes', is the first convict in 10 years to be executed in the USA and the last to date to be executed by firing squad, when he dies, aged 36, on 17 JANUARY. His last meal comprises hamburger, eggs and potatoes. His last words before facing the firing squad are: 'Let's do it'

**1986** John William Rook is executed by lethal injection on 19 SEPTEMBER for murder. His last meal is a dozen hot dogs and a can of cola (opposite)

**1992** The execution of Rickey Ray Rector (USA) on 24 JANUARY by the State of Arkansas is championed by the state governor, who wants to be seen as tough on crime. The state of mind of the prisoner raises questions about whether he is fit to stand trial or to be executed: he does not finish his last meal, saying that he wants to keep the pecan pie 'for later'. Governor Clinton takes up office as president the following year

**1995** President Françoise Mitterrand (France) allegedly eats the delicacy ortolan at his last supper

**1997** Larry Wayne White (USA) is executed on 22 MAY in Houston, Texas, for the murder of a 72-year-old woman. His last meal is liver and fried onions, tomatoes, cottage cheese and a glass of water. He is one of the first condemned prisoners to be denied his last cigarette (*See also: Did You Know?, right*) AUGUST Diana, Princess of Wales, and Dodi Fayed eat their last supper, at the Ritz-Carlton Hotel in Paris, before setting out on their last car journey (*see: page 240*). Diana has scrambled eggs with wild mushrooms followed by fillet of sole tempura and asparagus tips; Dodi has roast turbot

for the forgiveness of sins.' For 2,000 years Christ's words and symbolic actions have been repeated in churches around the world as part of the celebration of Holy Communion, which is also known as the Eucharist, from the Greek 'to give thanks'.

Two of the four Gospels record Christ's last words, while on the cross, as: 'My God, My God, Why hast thou forsaken me?', but say that he cried out again before dying, while St John records his last words as: 'It is finished.'

## Leonardo da Vinci's *Last Supper*

Christ's Last Supper has been the subject of numerous paintings, none greater or more famous than that painted at the end of the 15th century by Leonardo da Vinci (Italy), on the wall of the refectory of the convent of Santa Maria delle Grazie in Milan, Italy. Da Vinci did not want to use the fresco technique usually employed for wall paintings and instead used tempera, which allowed him to work more slowly and carefully, and to make revisions. However, his mix did not work properly and soon after completion the paint began to flake. Despite this technical flaw, the artistry of the painting is unsurpassed and it is rightly considered one of the world's greatest works.

As well as using a revolutionary method of painting, Leonardo also revolutionized the arrangement of the scene. Traditionally, the disciples had been painted sitting in a row with Judas separated from the rest, but Leonardo created action and drama by placing all 12 disciples in groups on either side of Christ, who is isolated in stillness at the centre, his head framed by the window behind. Sublime use of perspective focusses all the attention on Christ, despite the activity going on around him, which includes Judas knocking over the salt with his elbow.

## President Mitterrand's last supper

Anticipating his imminent death from prostate cancer, President Françoise Mitterrand (France) is said to have organized a last supper on 31 December 1995, comprising four delicacies: Marennes oysters, foie gras, roast capon, and ortolan. In France it is illegal to hunt, buy or eat ortolan, a tiny bird also known as a bunting, but it is so highly prized a delicacy that the law is often ignored. The birds are prepared by the traditional method of blinding them so that they gorge themselves, drowning them in Cognac (though in 1873 French author Alexandre Dumas père specified vinegar) and then roasting them. Traditionally, each person eats only one ortolan, but at his last supper Mitterrand allegedly ate two – the second is said to be the last thing he ate before dying a week later.

### DID YOU KNOW?

● When George W. Bush (USA, now president) was governor of Texas, the state amended the law governing the last meals of condemned prisoners, who would be executed two hours after eating by a lethal injection of sodium thiopental, pancuronium bromide and potassium chloride. The state decreed that prisoners would no longer be allowed a last cigarette 'on health grounds'

Right *Ortolan Bunting,* by John Gould and H.C. Richter (1873)

Below The last supper of John William Rook (*see: Timeline 1986*), executed at the age of 31 by the State of North Carolina, USA, for murder (photograph by Celia Shapiro)

**2001** Timothy McVeigh (USA), the Oklahoma Bomber, is executed in Indiana on 11 JUNE. His last meal is two pints of mint choc-chip ice cream

**2004** In response to a question from *The Observer* newspaper (Britain), singer and actress Marianne Faithfull (Engand) says: 'I expect each meal to be my last ... My last meal would be a salad, and then pasta with white truffles.' Spoon-bending psychic Uri Geller (Israel) answers: '...hummus, tahini, pitta bread, olives from the Holy Land, dates and figs. I don't believe in the end of life; these foods would give me the energy I need to pass through to the next'

129

# LAST BUT NOT LEAST...

## Billy the Kid's Last Victim

Billy the Kid (USA, b. Henry McCarty, later alias William H. Bonney) was an outlaw whose death changed his reputation from that of unprincipled killer to folk hero. Legend has it that 'the Kid' first killed at the age of 12 and that by the time he himself was killed he had murdered 21 men, one for each year of his life, but in fact he is only confirmed as killing five men. By either count his last victim was Robert W. Ollinger (USA), a warden at Messilla Jail, New Mexico. Billy shot Ollinger and escaped on 28 April 1881, before being tracked down and shot on 14 July in Fort Sumner, New Mexico, by his former friend, lawman Pat Garrett (USA).

**Above** Billy the Kid meets his end at the hands of Sheriff Pat Garrett, in a woodcut from *Beadle's Half Dime Library* (1881)

## Thomas Edison's Last Patent

Thomas Alva Edison (USA) was the most prolific inventor of all time, with 1,093 US patents to his name as well as many other foreign patents. In 1871 he established an industrial research laboratory that is often described as the world's first R&D (research and development) laboratory. In 1876 he moved this laboratory to Menlo Park, New Jersey, after which he became known as the Wizard of Menlo Park for his inventive genius. Edison filed what was to be his last patent, for a 'Holder for Article to be Electroplated', on 9 January 1931 and died on 18 October that year, aged 84. The patent for the 'Holder' was granted posthumously on 16 May 1933 as US Patent No. 1,908,380.

## Michelangelo's *Last Judgement*

One of the most famous works by the sculptor, painter and poet Michelangelo (Italy, b. Michelangelo di Lodovico Buonarroti) is the ceiling of the Sistine Chapel in the Vatican, Rome, which he painted from 1508 to 1512. Later, in 1536, he returned to the chapel to paint a fresco on the altar wall depicting the Last Judgement, which he completed in 1541.

Feeling that his employer, the Pope, had fleeced him, Michelangelo included himself in the painting in the guise of the flayed St Bartholomew. Michelangelo's last painting was the fresco *The Crucifixion of St Peter* in the Vatican Chapel, which he completed in 1550 at the age of 75.

## The James Gang's Last Train Robbery

Jesse James (USA) is a legendary outlaw celebrated in ballads, pulp fiction and Hollywood movies, but the reality was not so romantic. James fought with a band of pro-Confederate guerrillas during the American Civil War and, after the war, formed a criminal gang with his brother Frank. For 15 years the James Gang carried out robberies on banks and trains. The last train robbery carried out by the gang took place on the Chicago & Alton Railroad at Blue Cut, Glendale, Missouri, on 7 September 1881, when they stole $1,500, as well as gold and jewels, from the passengers. In that year a bounty of $5,000 was put on Jesse's head, which prompted gang member Robert Ford (USA) to turn traitor and he subsequently shot Jesse for the reward, killing him on 3 April 1882.

## Alistair Cooke's Last *Letter from America*

Journalist Alistair Cooke (England–USA) was BBC foreign affairs correspondent specializing in US affairs before emigrating in 1937 and becoming a US citizen in 1941. From 1945 until 2004 he broadcast his weekly BBC radio programme *Letter From America*, the BBC's longest-running speech programme to date. Though he didn't know it, Friday 20 February 2004 was to be his last *Letter*, because ill health forced the 95-year-old broadcaster to miss his programme on 27 February. One missed deadline was one too many, and at the beginning of the following week Cooke followed the advice of his doctors by announcing his retirement. He died just weeks later, on 29 March, aged 95.

A comment made during an interview in 1999 epitomizes his view of his own work and of transatlantic relationships: 'I just think it's a great privilege for anyone who knows both countries well to be able to watch two different kinds of human beings.'

**Right** Alistair Cooke broadcasting for the BBC (1 February 1946)

# Chapter Four

# Last to Date

**The Last** 

# ASTEROID IMPACT

Scientists have shown that dinosaurs were rendered extinct by the catastrophic impact of an asteroid or comet some 65 million years ago. But that was not the last space object to hit Earth – lesser impacts happen relatively often, the last significant one to date being in 1930.

Asteroids are rocky, comets are icy, and meteorites are the small pieces left after a smaller object known as a meteoroid has burned up as a meteor (streak of light) in the outer atmosphere. But whatever the technical differences between them, the result of any sizeable object from space colliding with Earth is devastating. The idea that such impacts should be taken seriously gained scientific credence when physicist Luis Alvarez (USA) showed that the dinosaurs were destroyed by an asteroid or comet, and reached fever pitch in 1994 when scientists watched Comet Shoemaker-Levy 9 smash into Jupiter, causing chaos over an area as large as Earth.

The most famous recent Earth impact took place at 07:17 on 30 June 1908, when a meteorite 50 metres in diameter exploded in the sky over the unpopulated region of Tunguska, Siberia. Although it did not strike Earth, seismic vibrations were recorded up to 600 miles away and, at half that distance, eyewitnesses reported hearing 'deafening bangs' and seeing a ball of fire in the sky, followed by a 'pillar of fire' on the horizon.

The last significant confirmed impact to date took place at 08:00 on 13 August 1930, when an asteroid or comet exploded in the sky over Rio Curach, Brazil. Interviews with eyewitnesses formed the basis of a report by Catholic missionary Father Fidele d'Alviano (Italy) in the papal newspaper *L'Osservatore Romano* (Italy). A summary of this report, published in the magazine *New Scientist*, describes how: 'The sun suddenly turned blood red and everything was plunged into darkness. A fine white ash rained down, followed by an ear-piercing whistle. Finally, three balls of fire streaked across the sky and exploded, creating earthquake-like shocks.' Astronomer Mark Bailey (Britain) who rediscovered Father d'Alviano's report in the 1990s estimates from the full description that the explosion was about one-tenth as powerful as that at Tunguska.

**DID YOU KNOW?**

● Luis Alvarez, the physicist who, with his geologist son Walter, deduced that an asteroid or comet impact wiped out the dinosaurs, was a man of many talents. He invented a radar guidance system during the Second World War for landing aircraft in poor visibility, won the 1968 Nobel Prize for Physics for his work on subatomic particles, founded two companies to make optical devices, and applied his scientific talents to unravelling the mysteries of the pyramids and the assassination of Kennedy. His last day was 1 September 1988, when he died, aged 77

## DID YOU KNOW?

● An eyewitness 25 miles from the epicentre of the Tunguska impact said: 'The sky was split in two ... high above the forest the whole northern part of the sky appeared covered with fire. I felt a great heat, as if my shirt had caught fire ... At that moment there was a bang in the sky, and a mighty crash ... I was thrown 20 feet ... and lost consciousness for a moment ... The crash was followed by a noise like stones falling from the sky, or guns firing. The earth trembled... At the moment when the sky opened, a hot wind ... blew past the huts from the north'

**1954** Mrs Hewlett Hodges (USA) is struck on the hip by a 4kg meteorite that crashes through the roof of her home in Sylacauga, Alabama, USA, on 30 NOVEMBER

**1980** Physicist Luis Alvarez (USA) posits the theory that the dinosaurs were wiped out by an asteroid or comet impact, a theory later given credence by the discovery of an impact crater in the Yucatán peninsula

**2004** On 13 JANUARY scientists come within minutes of alerting US President George W. Bush to the fact that they think asteroid 2004 AS1 has a one-in-four chance of hitting Earth, but further analysis reveals that it is not on a collision course

**Above** A painting of the Tunguska impact, created by W.K. Hartmann from eyewitness accounts

**Left** The southern swamp at the epicentre of the Tunguska impact, taken on an expedition to the site (1930)

The six planets closest to the sun are visible with the naked eye and have been known since antiquity. The invention of the telescope led to the discovery between 1781 and 1930 of three more planets and, on 14 November 2003, to what some people have hailed as a 10th planet, Sedna.

# PLANET TO BE DISCOVERED

TIMELINE: PLANETS

**Antiquity** Most of the planets of the solar system are visible with the naked eye (the so-called Evening Star is not a star, but the planet Venus) and have been observed since ancient times

**1781** Uranus is discovered on 13 MARCH by Sir William Herschel (Germany–Britain), and is the first planet to be found using a telescope

**1846** Neptune is discovered on 23 SEPTEMBER by Johann Galle (Germany). It is the last planet to date to be discovered in our solar system if one accepts the argument that Pluto and, by extension, Sedna are not planets

**1930** Pluto is discovered on 18 FEBRUARY by Clyde Tombaugh (USA), working at the Lowell Observatory in Arizona, USA (established by Lowell in 1894 as the Flagstaff Observatory). It is the last planet to date to be discovered in our solar system if one classifies Pluto, but not Sedna, as a planet

**2003** A team of three astronomers discovers an object known initially as 2003 VB12, 'the coldest, most distant object known to orbit the sun' and the largest since the discovery of Pluto. The team names the object Sedna, but says that according to its own criteria neither Sedna nor Pluto is a planet

The first planet to be discovered using a telescope was Uranus, found by Sir William Herschel (Germany–Britain) in 1781. Its orbit was not regular and astronomers surmised that the cause must be the gravitational pull of another, undiscovered, planet. They were correct, but Neptune, the eighth and by some definitions the last planet to date, was not discovered until 1846, by Johann Galle (Germany).

However, the existence of Neptune did not fully explain the orbital irregularities of Uranus, and Neptune's orbit was also irregular, so the search continued for yet another planet. In 1915, based on observations of Uranus

and Neptune, astronomer Percival Lowell (USA) predicted the position of a ninth planet that he called Planet X. On 18 February 1930, using a 'blink comparator' that he had invented to enable him to make a systematic photographic search, Clyde Tombaugh (USA) discovered what is generally accepted to be the last planet to date – Pluto – just six degrees from where Lowell had predicted it would be. Some scientists have since claimed, however, that the orbital perturbations of Uranus and Neptune were spurious and that the discovery of Pluto was by coincidence rather than calculation.

Many astronomers argue that Pluto should not be classified as a planet, and the same arguments will apply to the discovery of what might or might not be the 10th and last planet to date to be discovered in our solar system. On 15 March 2004 NASA announced the discovery of 'the coldest, most distant object known to orbit the sun', three times as far away as Pluto. The discovery was made on 14 November 2003 at the Palomar Observatory, California, USA, by a team comprising Mike Brown of Caltech, Chad Trujillo of the Gemini Observatory and David Rabinowitz of Yale University (all USA), who named it Sedna, after the Inuit goddess of the sea.

**DID YOU KNOW?**

● With the exception of Sedna, Pluto exerts the weakest gravitational force of any of the planets in our solar system – a person weighing 10st (63.5kg) on Earth would weigh 1st 10lb (10.8kg) on Earth's moon and just 7lb (3kg) on Pluto. The same person would weigh 25st 5lb (161kg) on Jupiter, which exerts the strongest gravitational force

● Sedna is so far from the centre of the solar system that, according to Caltech scientists, a person standing on its surface could block out the entire sun with the head of a pin held at arm's length. Sedna's orbit is closer to being an oval than a circle, and is so distant that it takes 10,500 Earth years to orbit the sun

**Opposite** Astronomer Percival Lowell using the 24-inch Clark telescope to study the planets

**Above** An artist's impression of Sedna at the outer edge of the solar system – the sun is so distant that it appears as a bright star rather than the familiar ball of fire seen from earth. The artist gives Sedna a moon, whose existence has been hypothesized, but not yet proved

One-fifth of the world's population watched in 1969 as Neil Armstrong became the first human to walk on the surface of the moon. Far fewer were watching three years later, as Gene Cernan stepped back into the lunar module to leave the moon at the end of humanity's last visit to date.

## 138 **The Last** MAN ON THE MOON

**TIMELINE: MANNED MOON LANDINGS**

**1969** Apollo 11 (USA) makes the first manned moon landing, on 20 JULY. Neil Armstrong and Edwin 'Buzz' Aldrin walk on the moon, Michael Collins orbits in the command module. Apollo 12 (USA) lands on the moon on 20 NOVEMBER. Charles Conrad and Alan L. Bean walk on the moon, Richard F. Gordon orbits in the command module

**1970** Apollo 13 (USA) moon landing abandoned after an oxygen tank explodes. Successfully returns to Earth on 17 APRIL

**1971** Apollo 14 (USA) lands on the moon on 5 FEBRUARY. Alan B. Shepard, Jr and Edgar D. Mitchell walk on the moon, Stuart Rossa orbits in the command module. Apollo 15 (USA) lands on the moon on 30 JULY. David R. Scott and James B. Irwin drive on the moon, in the lunar rover; Alfred Worden orbits in the command module

**1972** Apollo 16 (USA) lands on the moon on 20 APRIL. John W. Young and Charles M. Duke, Jr walk on the moon, Thomas Mattingley orbits in the command module. Apollo 17 (USA) makes the sixth and last manned moon landing to date, on 11 DECEMBER, and departs on 14 DECEMBER. Eugene A. Cernan and Harrison H. Schmitt walk on the moon, Ronald Evans orbits in the command module

'Here man completed his first explorations of the moon. May the spirit of peace in which we came be reflected in the lives of all mankind.' These were the sentiments expressed on a plaque left on the lunar surface by the crew of Apollo 17, the last human mission to date to visit the moon.

In 1961 US President John F. Kennedy swore that by the end of the decade America would land a man on the moon. It was a bold claim, but (unless the conspiracy theorists are to be believed) it was achieved on 20 July 1969, five months inside Kennedy's deadline. But once the goal had been achieved America began to lose interest. At $400 million dollars a trip, travelling to the moon began to look like an expensive indulgence, and manned exploration was to last just three years. On 7 December 1972 Apollo 17 left Earth to begin NASA's last manned mission to the planet's nearest neighbour, and on 11 December a lunar module touched down on the moon for the last time.

Three days later, after the longest stay of any Apollo landing, mission commander Eugene A. Cernan (USA) stepped off the surface as the last man to date to stand on the moon. He followed fellow astronaut Harrison H. Schmitt (USA) into the lunar module and prepared to blast off for their rendezvous with Ronald Evans (USA) in the orbiting command module. Cernan's counterpart to Armstrong's 'one small step' speech was to say to those watching on earth: 'We leave as we came and, God willing, as we shall return – with peace and hope for all mankind.' He then added, more prosaically: 'Okay, let's get this mother out of here.'

**DID YOU KNOW?**

● The last golf shots to date to be played on the moon were struck in February 1971 by astronaut Alan B. Shepard Jr, who hit two balls using an improvised club made with an iron head and a makeshift shaft. His bulky spacesuit meant that he could not adopt the proper stance, so he hit both balls with a one-handed swing. After Apollo 14's return to Earth, the Royal & Ancient Golf Club (Scotland) sent Shepard a telegram reading: 'Warmest congratulations to all of you on your great achievement and safe return. Please refer to the Rules of Golf section on etiquette, paragraph 6, quote – before leaving a bunker a player should carefully fill up all holes made by him therein, unquote'

**Left** Gene Cernan (left, the last man on the moon) and Ronald Evans in the Apollo 17 command module. Cernan was mission commander and Evans the command module pilot
**Below** The last man on the moon – Gene Cernan on the lunar surface during mankind's last visit to Earth's nearest neighbour

To date, four US presidents have been assassinated while in office. Abraham Lincoln was shot by John Wilkes Booth, James Garfield by Charles Guiteau and William McKinley by Leon Czolgosz. The last US president to be assassinated was John F. Kennedy, on 22 November 1963.

**Lasts of the** # US PRESIDENCY

**TIMELINE: LASTS OF THE US PRESIDENCY**

**1841** William Henry Harrison serves as the last president to have been born a British subject (until the Declaration of Independence in 1776, all Americans were British subjects; Harrison was born in 1773). His presidency lasts just one month before he dies of pneumonia

**1857** James Buchanan, expecting the southern states to secede from the Union, announces: 'I am the last president of the United States.' He is, of course, proved wrong

**1868** Andrew Johnson becomes the first president to be impeached, and the last before Bill Clinton in 1998. Johnson is acquitted by one vote (a two-thirds majority is required for conviction). (In 1974 Richard Nixon avoids impeachment by resigning)

**1893** Grover Cleveland is elected for the second time to become the first president, and the last to date, to serve two non-consecutive terms

**1913–21** Woodrow Wilson serves as the last president to be elected by men only (in 1920 Congress pass the 19th amendment, extending the vote to women)

**1933–45** Franklin D. Roosevelt serves as the last president to serve more than two terms (in 1947 Congress pass the 22nd amendment, ratified in 1951, barring future presidents from serving more than two terms)

**1963** John F. Kennedy becomes the last president to date to be assassinated

## The last presidential assassination

John Fitzgerald Kennedy (USA) was a young, dynamic president with high ideals. He announced in his Inaugural Address on 20 January 1961 that he would fight 'against the common enemies of man: tyranny, poverty, disease and war itself', but he also warned that the USA would 'oppose any foe to assure the survival and success of liberty'. Most famous outside America for his handling of the Bay of Pigs invasion and the Cuban Missile Crisis and for launching the space race, at home Kennedy tried to introduce comprehensive civil rights reforms, many of which were stalled by Congress.

Favourite to win a second term in the 1964 presidential election, Kennedy was assassinated while driving through the streets of Dallas, Texas. Just after 12.30pm on 22 November 1963, Kennedy sat next to his wife, Jackie, in an open car as the presidential motorcade drove through the cheering crowds. Shots rang out and, after some confusion, the police escorted the car to Parkland Hospital, where 25 minutes later Kennedy was pronounced dead from bullet wounds to the neck and head.

**Below** John Wilkes Booth preparing to assassinate President Abraham Lincoln on the balcony of Ford's Theater, Washington, DC, 15 April 1865

**Opposite** John F. Kennedy and his wife, Jackie, in the open-topped presidential limousine

Police later arrested ex-US Marine Lee Harvey Oswald (USA), a pro-Cuban campaigner who had defected to the USSR in 1959 and since returned to the USA, and charged him with Kennedy's murder. Oswald never admitted to the crime and two days later, before he could be brought to trial, he himself was assassinated by strip-club owner Jack Ruby (USA, properly Jack Rubenstein), who in turn died before serving his sentence. Rumours have persisted ever since that Oswald and Ruby were part of a wider conspiracy, though Ruby always insisted that he had acted alone, saying: 'I did it for Jackie Kennedy.' Ruby's lawyer announced: 'I think, as millions of other Americans think, that he should be given the Congressional Medal of Honor.'

**1974** Gerald Ford becomes the last unelected president to date (depending on one's definition of elected, see 2000) when he succeeds to the presidency on the resignation of Richard Nixon, who becomes the last president to date to resign. (Ford was not elected vice president either: he had succeeded to that post in 1973 on the resignation of Spiro Agnew)

**1981** Ronald Reagan is the last president to date to be shot, on 30 MARCH, by disc jockey John Hinckley III

**1998** Bill Clinton becomes the second president, and the last to date, to be impeached. He is formally impeached in DECEMBER, and stands trial in JANUARY 1999; like Johnson (1968), he is acquitted

**2000** George W. Bush becomes the last unelected president to date (depending on one's definition of elected, see 1974), when he is awarded the presidency by the US Supreme Court rather than by a clear electoral victory

## DID YOU KNOW?

● There are some uncanny historic parallels between Abraham Lincoln, the first president to be assassinated, and John F. Kennedy, the last to date to be assassinated. Lincoln was elected to Congress in 1846, Kennedy in 1946; Lincoln was elected president in 1860, Kennedy in 1960. Both presidents were shot on a Friday, both were shot in the head and both were succeeded by men named Johnson – Lincoln's successor, Andrew Johnson, was born in 1808 and Kennedy's successor, Lyndon B. Johnson, in 1908. Lincoln's assassin, John Wilkes Booth, was born in 1839; Lee Harvey Oswald in 1939 – both were themselves assassinated before their trials. Lincoln was shot at Ford's Theater; Kennedy was shot in a 'Lincoln' car made by Ford

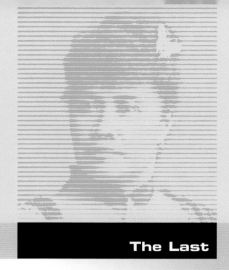

In 1776 thirteen former British colonies declared themselves 'free and independent states' and formed the United States of America. Since then 37 other states have joined them, the 50th and last to date being Hawaii, as celebrated in the title of the television series *Hawaii Five-O*.

## The Last STATE TO JOIN THE UNION

**H**awaii, the only state of the Union to have once been an independent monarchy, is a Pacific archipelago of some 20 volcanic islands, of which the largest are Hawaii, Maui and Oahu. The official relationship between the USA and this former Polynesian kingdom dates back to 1851, when King Kamehameha III placed his kingdom under US protection after rivalry between Britain, France and the USA over control of the islands. Although at first Hawaii remained an independent kingdom, US

**Below** Surfers at Ehukai Beach, Oahu, Hawaii (1996)
**Opposite** Queen Liliuokalani of Hawaii (1887)

influence gradually increased, particularly with the Reciprocity Treaty of 1887 by which Hawaii was granted duty-free export of sugar in exchange for ceding Pearl Harbor to the USA, which subsequently established a naval base there.

Then, in 1893, a force led by nine Americans, two Britons and two Germans, assisted by US marines, overthrew Queen Liliuokalani, the last monarch of Hawaii, and on 16 January 1894 established a republic. (A century later the US government officially apologized for the part its predecessors played in the uprising, which took place while the kingdom was supposedly under the protection of the USA.) Sanford B. Dole became the first and last president of the republic and, just four and a half years later, on 7 July 1898, his government agreed to annexe Hawaii to the USA. Annexation officially took place on 12 August and two years after that, on 14 June 1900, the islands were granted full territorial status as a strategically important outpost of the USA.

After Pearl Harbor proved to be of such vital importance during the Second World War, pressure grew for full member status of the USA and on 21 August 1959 Hawaii became America's 50th state and the last to date. It will remain the last unless and until another American Dependent Territory is granted full statehood; these territories include Puerto Rico, the Virgin Islands, American Samoa, Guam and the Northern Mariana Islands.

**DID YOU KNOW?**

● As well as being chronologically the last two states to join the Union, Alaska and Hawaii also contain three of the USA's four geographical lasts: America's last point north is Point Barrow, Alaska; the last point west is Cape Wrangell, Attu Island, Alaska; and the last point south is Ka Lae, Hawaii. The last point east is West Quoddy Head, Maine

TIMELINE: STATES OF THE UNION LASTS

**1733** The last of the colonies that will later become the original 13 states is founded and named Georgia, after King George II of Great Britain

**1790** Rhode Island is the last of the original 13 states to ratify the US constitution

**1861** Tennessee is the last state to secede from the USA and join the Confederacy during the American Civil War

**1867** Alaska is the last state to be purchased from a foreign country (from Russia, for $7,200,000), but is not officially admitted to the Union until 1959

**1870** Georgia is the last Confederate state to be readmitted to the USA after the American Civil War

**1959** JANUARY, Alaska becomes the 49th state of the Union. AUGUST, Hawaii becomes the 50th and last state of the Union to date

*See also: Lasts of Royalty, page 24*

**The Last** WAR BETWEEN USA & BRITAIN

American independence from Britain was ratified in 1783, but that did not bring everlasting peace between the two countries. The last war to date between the two nations was the War of 1812; the last battle of that war was the Battle of New Orleans, which ended on 8 January 1815.

## DID YOU KNOW?

● Until the War of 1812 the official home of the US president was grey, the colour of the Virginia sandstone used to build it, and was known as the Executive Mansion. When the damage inflicted by British forces in August 1814 was repaired after the war the mansion was painted white to hide the smoke damage, since when it has been known as the White House

● The last war to date between Spain and the USA was the Spanish–American War of 1898, known in Spain as 'The Disaster of 1898', in which Spain lost Cuba, Puerto Rico, Guam and the Philippines, the last remnants of its once-mighty empire, to the USA

Although there have been more recent grievances, such as boundary disputes between the USA and the British colony of Canada, the last full-scale war between the USA and Britain was sparked off by poor Anglo–American relations during the Napoleonic wars between Britain and France. The USA claimed the right to neutrality and the free movement of shipping during the war, but the British naval blockade of Europe prevented this, a matter exacerbated by the fact that American sailors were being press-ganged into Britain's Royal Navy. As a result, on 18 June 1812 US Congress declared war on Britain.

As well as neutrality, American aims included the conquest of Canada, and it was along this border that most of the fighting took place. In April 1813 the Americans sacked York (now Toronto) and in August the following year the British occupied Washington, DC, and avenged the sacking of York by setting fire to the presidential mansion later known as the White House (*see Did You Know?*). That same month, peace talks began in Ghent (now part of Belgium) and the Treaty of Ghent was signed on 24 December 1814, bringing an end to what became known as the War of 1812. However, news of the treaty did not reach New York until 11 February 1815, and the treaty was not ratified until 15 February, with the result that the last battle between the two nations took place after the peace treaty had been signed. The British decided to attack from the south, and General Sir Edward Pakenham (Britain) landed near the mouth of the Mississippi and advanced towards New Orleans. Fighting took place sporadically from December 1814 until, on 8 January 1815, the British made their final assault and were soundly defeated by American forces led by Major General Andrew Jackson (USA), who later became the seventh president of the United States.

**Left** Major General Andrew Jackson with his troops defending New Orleans against British forces during the War of 1812
**Right** The British sail up the Chesapeake to sack the new US capital at Washington, DC

**1812** JUNE, US Congress declares war on Britain

**1813** USA destroys the (then British) city of York, Canada (now Toronto)

**1814** AUGUST, British forces capture Washington, DC, and, in retaliation for the destruction of York, set fire to the presidential mansion (now the White House, *see Did You Know?*). On 24 DECEMBER the Treaty of Ghent is signed

**1815** News of the Treaty of Ghent is slow to reach the combatants, and on 8 JANUARY the USA defeats Britain in the Battle of New Orleans, the last battle to date between the two nations. The treaty is ratified on 15 FEBRUARY, officially the last day of the war

**1846** The last border conflict between the USA and Britain, over claims to what is now the state of Oregon, is settled by the Oregon Treaty of 15 JUNE, ceding to the USA all land south of the 49th parallel with the exception of Vancouver Island, Canada

TIMELINE: WAR OF 1812

Invasions are a historical commonplace for nations that share a continent with other nations, but for some countries the idea of invasion is, fortunately, an antiquated concept. The last invasion of mainland Britain to date took place in 1797, of the USA in 1846 and of Canada in 1871.

# INVASIONS

For most western European and Scandinavian nations, the last invasion to date took place during the Second World War. Sadly, for many Eastern European, Middle and Far Eastern nations, and many in the less developed world, the last invasion to date is even more recent. But for a fortunate few the last invasion to date of their nation's mainland was more than a century ago.

The last invasion to date of the British mainland took place in 1797, during the Revolutionary Wars waged by France against countries hostile to the Revolution. On 23 February a party of 1,200 Frenchmen, mainly criminals released from gaol for the purpose, were landed from four ships at Carregwastad Point, near Fishguard, Wales. The incursion lasted two days, before the commander of the invasion force, General Tate (Ireland–USA), surrendered to the combined forces of the local militia and the South Pembrokeshire Yeomanry, saying that he considered it 'unnecessary to attempt any military operations as they would only tend to bloodshed'. The details seem comical now, but at the time news of the invasion caused panic in London, where there was a run on the Bank of England that was enough to force Britain off the gold standard.

The last invasion to date of the USA took place in 1846 at the start of the US–Mexican War, when Mexican cavalry rode into Texas, which had

**TIMELINE: SOME LAST INVASIONS**

**1797** The last invasion to date of the British mainland takes place on 23 FEBRUARY during the French Revolutionary Wars when a party of French soldiers lands at Carregwastad Point, near Fishguard, Wales, but surrenders without a fight

**1846** The last invasion of mainland USA takes place at the start of the US–Mexican War (1846–48), when Mexican cavalry enter the disputed territory of Texas

**1871** The last invasion of Canada is an incursion in OCTOBER, the last of a series of raids by Irish–American Fenians

**1940** The Channel Islands are the only part of the British Isles to suffer invasion during the Second World War. Guernsey is occupied by Germany on 30 JUNE and Jersey on 1 JULY. The islands are liberated without a fight in MAY **1945**

**1944** The last confirmed 'invasion' to date of Australian soil takes place when a Japanese military reconnaissance party lands the fishing vessel *Hiyoshi Maru* on the Australian west coast and spends several hours ashore on 19 and 20 JANUARY

**1982** On 19 MARCH Argentine scrap merchants land without permission and raise the Argentine flag on South Georgia, part of the British crown colony of the Falkland Islands. A full military invasion follows on 2 APRIL, the last invasion of British soil to date. British forces recapture the Falkland Islands on 14 JUNE
*See also: Port Stanley, page 150*

**DID YOU KNOW?**

● It is said that while the Frenchmen engaged in the last invasion of the British mainland were preparing to do battle with the local militia and the South Pembrokeshire Yeomanry (*see: Timeline 1797*), they mistook the traditional red flannel dresses worn by a group of local Welsh women for the famous red jackets of the British Infantry, whom they assumed had arrived in support, and immediately surrendered without a fight

**Right** Climbers ascend Mount Snowdon, Wales, accompanied by women wearing the traditional Welsh national costume (*see Did You Know?*)

declared itself an independent republic in 1836 and had become a member state of the USA in 1845. The USA fiercely defended its newest state and as a result of the war also gained New Mexico and California from Mexico.

The last invasion to date of Canada was an incursion in October 1871 by members of the Irish–American Fenian Brotherhood, who made several cross-border raids in 1866 and 1870–71 aimed at provoking a rebellion against the government; all the raids were repelled by Canadian militiamen.

**Above** Mexican battery at Monterey captured by General Zachary Taylor's troops in 1846, during the US–Mexican War

As with invasions, some countries have been more fortunate than others in the length of time since a battle has been fought on their sovereign soil. The last battle to date on English soil was in 1685, on mainland British soil in 1746, and on mainland American soil in 1890.

**The Last**

# BATTLE ON BRITISH/ AMERICAN SOIL

## Sedgemoor, the last battle to date on English soil

Having left no legitimate heir, British King Charles II was succeeded by his brother, James II, who was deeply unpopular because he was a Roman Catholic. Within months of the succession, James Scott, Duke of Monmouth (England), the eldest illegitimate son of Charles II, returned from exile in the Netherlands to claim the throne in what became known as the Monmouth Rebellion.

On the night of 5 July 1685 Monmouth's rebel army camped at Bridgwater and the royalists, under the command of the Earl of Feversham (France), camped three miles away at Sedgemoor. Knowing that he could not win a pitched battle, Monmouth decided to risk a night attack, but in the small hours of 6 July the rebels were discovered, losing first the element of surprise and then their momentum as they failed to cross a drainage ditch protecting the royalist camp. At dawn, Feversham ordered flanking attacks on the rebel line, which broke and fled – the last battle to date on English soil had been won and lost, and the Monmouth Rebellion had been crushed.

### Culloden, the last battle to date on mainland British soil

The unpopularity of James II led to his deposition from the throne and the settlement of the succession to the British crown on the Electors of Hanover (Germany) in order to prevent the restoration of James II's heirs by his supporters, the Jacobites. The first Jacobite Rebellion was raised in Scotland in 1715 and 30 years later Charles Edward Stuart, a.k.a. Bonnie Prince Charlie (Britain, b. Italy), landed in Scotland to reignite the Jacobite cause. The Hanoverian King George II dispatched an army under the command of his third son, the

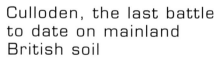

**TIMELINE: SOME LAST BATTLES**

**1685** During the Monmouth Rebellion, the Duke of Monmouth (England) is defeated at the Battle of Sedgemoor on 6 JULY, the last battle to date on English soil. Monmouth's last day comes just over a week later, when he is beheaded for treason on 15 JULY

**1746** During the second Jacobite Rebellion, Bonnie Prince Charlie (Britain, b. Italy) is defeated at the Battle of Culloden, Scotland, on 16 APRIL, the last battle to date on mainland British soil

**1890** In the last battle of the so-called Indian Wars, the American cavalry is victorious at the Battle of Wounded Knee, the last battle to date on mainland American soil

**1982** In the last series of battles of the Falklands War, British forces are victorious in retaking Port Stanley on 14 JUNE, the last battles to date on British sovereign soil.

Duke of Cumberland, to suppress the uprising and the opposing forces met for the last time on 16 April 1746 near Culloden, Scotland. The battle began with a cannonade that decimated the already inferior Jacobite numbers. The Jacobites nonetheless launched a charge, but a flanking attack from concealed royalist detachments put Bonnie Prince Charlie in such danger that he withdrew from the field and the leaderless Jacobites were routed – the last battle to date on mainland British soil was over in less than an hour.

**Above** *The Battle of Culloden 1746*, coloured engraving by Laurie and Whittle (1797)
**Opposite** Portrait of James Scott, Duke of Monmouth, in the robes of the Order of the Garter, by Sir Peter Lely

## Wounded Knee, the last battle to date on mainland American soil

America's so-called 'Indian Wars' between Native Americans and white settlers lasted nearly 270 years, from 1622 until 1890. The last 30 years of the Indian Wars, during which the US Cavalry fought the Sioux and the Cheyenne, became known as the Sioux Wars and culminated on

**Below** The widow of a Sioux warrior sits beneath a burial platform and mourns for her slain husband shortly after the massacre at Wounded Knee (published in *Harper's Weekly*, 1891)

29 December 1890 in the Battle of Wounded Knee.

On 28 December Chief Big Foot (America) and a group of Sioux were returning to the Pine Ridge Reservation when they were intercepted by cavalrymen and taken to a camp at Wounded Knee Creek, South Dakota. The following day Colonel James Forsyth (USA) of the Seventh Cavalry arrived and told the Sioux to hand over their weapons. During the ensuing argument a shot was fired, which precipitated a short, bloody massacre that killed 25 cavalrymen and 200 Sioux men, women and children, including Chief Big Foot, the last Native American Chief to die in battle. Often referred to not as the Battle but as the Massacre of Wounded Knee, this was the last 'battle' of the Indian Wars, and the last to date on mainland American soil.

*See also: Custer's Last Stand, page 124*

## Port Stanley, the last series of battles to date on British sovereign soil

In 1982 Argentinian forces invaded the British crown colony of the Falkland Islands in the South Atlantic. Britain immediately sent a task force to retake the islands, culminating in the battle for the capital, Port Stanley, from 11–14 June. This involved breaking a ring of Argentine defences in six separate engagements at Mount Longdon, Two Sisters, Mount Harriet, Tumbledown Mountain, Wireless Ridge and Mount William. Fierce attacks against these well-defended positions finally broke Argentine resistance and the invaders began retreating into Port Stanley itself, where, according to one press report, 'white flags began to blossom like flowers' and the Argentinians capitulated without further action. In London, British Prime Minister Margaret Thatcher told parliament that victory had been 'boldly planned, bravely executed and brilliantly accomplished'.

**Below** A Royal Marine stands amidst helmets abandoned by Argentine soldiers after they had surrendered to the British at the conclusion of the Falklands War (1982)

For centuries the Tower of London was notorious as a place where many prisoners were taken, but from which few were set free. The last prisoner to be executed at the Tower was the German spy Josef Jakobs, and the last person to be imprisoned there was Rudolf Hess, both in 1941.

**The Last** PRISONER IN THE TOWER OF LONDON

| | | | | | |
|---|---|---|---|---|---|
| **1660** The Tower of London is used as a royal residence for the last time | **1810** For the last time, coins are minted at the Tower of London before the Royal Mint moves to new premises nearby | **1834** The last of the animals comprising the Royal Menagerie is moved from the Tower to the recently opened Zoological Gardens in Regent's Park, now better known as London Zoo | **1941** Josef Jakobs (Germany) is the last person to be executed at the Tower of London, shot as a spy on 14 AUGUST. **Rudolf Hess** (Germany) is held in the Tower of London, the last person to date to be imprisoned there | **1966** onwards Hess is the last remaining prisoner in Spandau Prison, Germany | **1987** Hess dies at Spandau, which is demolished soon afterwards |

**■ TIMELINE: LASTS OF THE TOWER OF LONDON**

Officially still a royal palace, the Tower of London has at various times been used as a fortress, an armoury, an observatory, as the Royal Mint and as the home of the Royal Menagerie and the Crown Jewels. More famously, it has also been a prison and site of execution. The first prisoner to be held in the Tower, in 1101, was Ralf Flambard (England, also the first to escape), and the last to leave, in 1941, was Rudolf Hess (Germany, b. Egypt).

Flambard and Hess survived their visits to the Tower, but in the intervening 840 years many prisoners did not. The last prisoner of the Tower to be executed was Josef Jakobs (Germany), a Second World War spy who parachuted into Britain wearing civilian clothes and carrying an identity card naming him as James Rymer. Jakobs was held at the Tower, court martialled, found guilty of spying – a capital offence under the code of war – and shot at 07:12 on 14 August 1941.

That same year the Tower welcomed its last prisoner to date, Rudolf Hess, who, early in the Second World War, had been Hitler's deputy as leader of the Nazi party. In May 1941 Hess flew alone to Britain and parachuted into Eaglesham, Scotland, to broker a peace deal, demonstrating a division in the German leadership that prompted British Prime Minister Winston Churchill to announce: 'The maggot is in the apple.' But Hess did not have the backing of his country and instead found himself imprisoned for the rest of the war, spending some of that time at the Tower of London. In 1946, at the Nuremberg Trials, Hess was convicted of war crimes and spent the remaining years of his life in Spandau Prison, Germany, where he died, as Spandau's last prisoner, in 1987.

**DID YOU KNOW?**

● There are rumours that the man who flew to Britain, was imprisoned in the Tower of London and subsequently spent the rest of his days in Spandau Prison was not the real Rudolf Hess, but an impostor

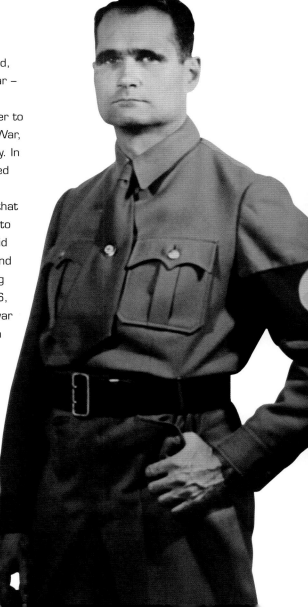

**Left** The Tower of London
**Right** Rudolf Hess, photographed in 1934

Since the first Pope, the apostle St Peter, was crucified upside down c.64AD, no less than 33 Popes have died in violent circumstances. Pope John Paul II almost joined that number in 1981 when he was shot in an assassination attempt by escaped murderer Mehmet Ali Agça.

**Lasts of** THE PAPACY

# The last Pope to be shot

Statistically, being Pope is not a very safe job. Thankfully, for most of the 20th century it seemed that executions and assassinations of the head of the Roman Catholic Church were a thing of the past, but on 13 May 1981 Pope John Paul II (Poland, b. Karol Jozef Wojtyla) was shot as he blessed the crowds in St Peter's Square, Rome.

The Pope was being driven through a crowd of some 20,000 people in the open-topped 'Popemobile' to perform his weekly blessing when 23-year-old

**Opposite** Pope John Paul II collapses in the 'popemobile' after being shot by Mehmet Ali Agça (13 May 1981)
**Below** Pope John Paul II meets his would-be assassin on a Christmas visit to Rebibbia Prison, Rome, and forgives Agça his crime (27 December 1983)

**TIMELINE: PAPAL LASTS**

**1154** Adrian, or Hadrian, IV (England, b. Nicolas Breakspear) is the first Englishman, and the last to date, to be elected Pope

**1370** Gregory XI (France, b. Pierre Roger de Beaufort) is the last French-man to date to be elected Pope

**1522** Adrian or Hadrian VI (Netherlands, b. Adrian Dedel) is the last Dutchman to date to be elected Pope, and the last non-Italian-born Pope for 456 years

**1978** John Paul II (Poland, b. Karol Jozef Wojtyla) is the last Pole to date to be elected Pope

**1981** John Paul II is the last Pope to date to be shot, in an assassination attempt by Mehmet Ali Agça (Turkey)

Mehmet Ali Agça (Turkey) fired several shots from a Browning 9mm pistol. Four bullets hit John Paul II, two of them lodging in his lower intestine, the others hitting his left hand and right arm. Two bystanders were also hit. While police surrounded Agça to prevent the crowd lynching him, the Pope was driven away at high speed and underwent a five-hour operation to remove the bullets, after which he made a full recovery.

Subsequent investigation showed that Agça had arrived in Rome under a false identity, having escaped from a Turkish jail where he was being held for the murder of a newspaper editor. Police found a letter in Agça's room giving the bizarre reason for his assassination attempt: 'To demonstrate to the world the imperialistic crimes of the Soviet Union and the United States.' Agça claimed to be protesting about the Soviet invasion of Afghanistan and US interference in El Salvador (although the reasons he gave later changed), but his letter did not explain what connection he thought the Pope might have with the government of those two countries. The inevitable theories that Agça was part of a wider conspiracy have never been proved.

**DID YOU KNOW?**

● Adrian IV, the last English Pope, is said to have issued a controversial Papal Bull granting English King Henry II lordship over Ireland in order to reform the Irish church, but some scholars question the authenticity of the Bull, claiming it to be a forgery. Henry II gave his son John the title King of Ireland in 1177

The two parts of *The Godfather* provided three Oscar lasts – Vito Corleone is the last role to date to produce two Oscar winners, Marlon Brando is the last actor to date to refuse an Oscar, and *The Godfather Part II* is the last sequel to date to win an Oscar for Best Picture.

# OSCAR-WINNING MOVIE SEQUEL

Setting aside the *The Lord of the Rings*, which was originally conceived as a trilogy and whose parts are therefore not sequels in the conventional sense, *The Godfather Part II* is the only sequel so far to have won an Oscar for Best Picture, and is therefore by definition the last to date.

The original *The Godfather*, directed by Francis Ford Coppola (USA) and winner of three Oscars, including Best Picture, is the gangster movie against which all others are measured. Adapted by Coppola and Mario Puzo (USA) from Puzo's novel, it is a New York gangland saga that unfolds as the Corleone family, led by Vito Corleone, fights to retain power over rival Mafia families. Part II, also directed by Coppola, was even more successful, winning six Oscars in 1974, including the all-important Best Picture. This was both a sequel and a prequel, incorporating a prelude showing how Vito Corleone, played as a young man by Robert de Niro (USA), arrived in the USA from Sicily, and then picking up where the original left off to continue the saga with Vito's son Michael, played by Al Pacino (USA), now in charge.

Between them, the two parts of this epic saga also produced two other Oscar lasts. Vito Corleone is the last role to date to win two Oscars – one for Marlon Brando (USA) as Best Actor in the original film, and another for Robert de Niro as Best Supporting Actor in the sequel. But Brando, an active civil rights campaigner, did not collect what would have been his second Oscar. Instead, he became the last actor to date to refuse the award, in protest at the nation's treatment of Native Americans.

**DID YOU KNOW?**

● In an interview in 1980, George C. Scott (USA), the first actor to refuse an Oscar, said of Marlon Brando's Oscar refusal two years after his own: 'Once I got the nomination [for *Patton*] I made it perfectly clear should I win, I would not accept it. I didn't do what Marlon did. I didn't wait until I won the * * * * * * * thing and then tell them to jam it up their * * * * – which I think is rude'

**Opposite top** Robert de Niro as Vito Corleone in *The Godfather Part II*
**Opposite bottom** At the 1973 Academy Awards, Sacheen Littlefeather refuses the Academy Award for Best Actor on behalf of Marlon Brando who won it for his role in *The Godfather*. She is carrying a letter from Brando in which he explains that he is refusing the award in protest at the nation's treatment of the Native Americans (27 March 1973)

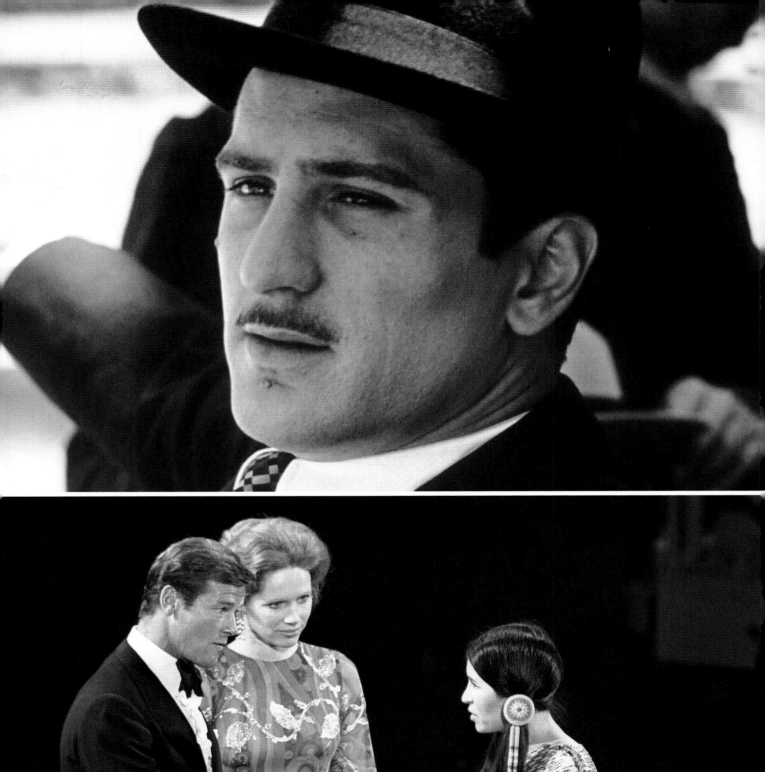

# WIMBLEDON

The Wimbledon Championships were established in 1877 by what was then the All England Croquet & Lawn Tennis Club, but England has not provided any singles champions since the last British men's champion to date, Fred Perry, in 1936, and the last ladies', Virginia Wade, in 1977.

## Men's singles title

In nearly 130 years of the competition, the Wimbledon men's singles title has to date been won by players representing a mere 13 nations. Of those nations, New Zealand has been waiting longest for a repeat performance – Tony Wilding was the last New Zealander to date to win the title, way back in 1913. The next longest wait has been for the nation that established the competition – Britain's last winner to date being Fred Perry (England, later USA), in 1936.

In 1934 Perry became the first British men's singles champion for 25 years, the last before him being Arthur Gore in 1909. Perry then went on to become the first player to win the men's singles three times in succession since the abolition of the Challenge Round (*see: Did You Know?*), and the last British player to date to hold the title. Sadly for British tennis, he emigrated to the USA the following year and turned professional, thus disqualifying himself from the Wimbledon Championships, which remained an amateur competition until 1968.

**Left** Fred Perry, the last British men's Wimbledon champion (photographed c.1934)
**Opposite** Virginia Wade, the last British ladies' Wimbledon champion, during the 1977 Ladies' final

**1967** The Championships are held as an amateur event for the last time, 1968 being the first Wimbledon Open Championships

**1973** Jan Kodes is the last Czech player to date to win the men's singles title

**1977** Virginia Wade beats Betty Stove (Netherlands) 4–6, 6–3, 6–1 to become the last British player to date to win the ladies' singles title

**1980 onwards** Players from Australia, Croatia, Germany, Holland, Sweden, Switzerland and USA have all won the men's singles title since 1980. Players from Australia, the Czech Republic, Germany, Russia, Spain, Switzerland and the USA have all won the ladies' singles title since 1980

**1985** The Championships are played using white tennis balls for the last time, before the introduction of yellow balls in 1986

**DID YOU KNOW?**

● Fred Perry was a supremely confident player, and was once heard to say: 'I'm glad I'm not playing me today, I feel so good'

● The trophies awarded for the men's and women's singles are the Challenge Cup and the Challenge Trophy respectively. The original meaning of a challenge cup was that all the other players would compete in a knock-out competition for the right to challenge the holder, who therefore effectively had a bye to the final. The last time the Wimbledon Championships included a 'Challenge Round' was 1921, before the round was abolished for the 1922 competition

● Approximately 44,400 tennis balls are used each year – during the qualifying tournaments, in practice sessions and on court during the Championships

## Ladies' singles title

The ladies' singles title has to date been won by players from only 10 nations. Of those, the longest wait for another champion has been for France, whose only winner of the title – making her by definition the last to date – was Suzanne Lenglen. Lenglen won five consecutive titles from 1919–23 and went on to win a sixth in 1925 before turning professional the following year.

The next longest wait has been for Brazil, whose three wins to date all came from Maria Bueno, in 1959, 1960 and 1964. And the third longest wait has been for Britain, whose last winner to date was Virginia Wade (England) in 1977, the centenary of the Wimbledon Championships. It was Wade's 16th attempt at the title and she was beginning to despair of ever winning at Wimbledon, saying: 'Perhaps I worshipped it too much, and I didn't believe I was worthy of all those superstars whose spirits dwelt there.' But on 1 July 1977 she beat Betty Stove (Netherlands) to prove that she was worthy of those superstars.

# LAST BUT NOT LEAST...

## The Last Canadian Province to Date

On 31 March 1949 Newfoundland was the 10th and last province to date to become part of Canada. Newfoundland was established during the 16th century as the first English colony, although British sovereignty was not recognized until 1713, after the conclusion of Queen Anne's War.

The province achieved internal self-government in 1855, but fell into financial difficulties in the 1930s, which ultimately resulted in a close-run referendum in 1948 on whether to join what was then the Dominion of Canada: 78,323 people voted in favour and 71,334 voted against. And so Newfoundland became the last Canadian province to date by a margin of less than 5%.

## The Last British Prime Minister to Date to be Assassinated

Only one British prime minister to date has been assassinated, making the murder of Spencer Perceval (England) both a first and a last. Perceval, a Tory, was appointed prime minister in 1809 and proved to be an able leader with great potential. However, that potential was snuffed out on the afternoon of 11 May 1812, when Perceval walked through the lobby of the House of Commons, which was and still is open to the public, where he was shot by aggrieved businessman John Bellingham (England). Various reports suggest that Bellingham had either been interned in Russia, or that his business had been ruined by the war with France, or both, and that he had repeatedly failed to gain compensation from parliament, pushing him to the desperate measure of assassinating the Prime Minister. If he had hoped to further his cause by his actions, he was disappointed – just over one week later he was hanged for his crime. His last words were: 'I thank God for having enabled me to meet my fate with so much fortitude and resignation' – quite ironic given the lack of fortitude and resignation with which he met the fate of his business affairs.

**Left** British Prime Minister Spencer Perceval is assassinated

## Switzerland's and Sweden's Last Wars to Date

Today Switzerland is more famous than Sweden for its peaceful political stance and its neutrality in foreign affairs, but in fact Switzerland's last war to date is more recent than Sweden's. The last war to date in which Sweden was engaged was from 1813–14, when Jean-Baptiste Bernadotte (b. France, later King Karl XIV Johan of Sweden and Norway) led Sweden into war against Denmark. Bernadotte succeeded in wresting Norway from Danish control and securing the union of Norway with Sweden under the terms of the Treaty of Kiel. Sweden's policy of neutrality in foreign affairs was officially adopted later in the 19th century and the union with Norway was peacefully dissolved in 1905.

Meanwhile, the Swiss Confederation, as Switzerland is officially known, was reorganized in 1815, at which time the great powers of Europe officially recognized the country's 'Perpetual Neutrality'. But there was to be one more war – in 1845 seven cantons formed the *Sonderbund* ('separatist league') to resist the strengthening of the federal government, and in 1847 this league was defeated by federal troops in a brief civil war known as the War of the Sonderbund, the last war to date in Switzerland's history.

## The Last Swedish Prime Minister to Date to be Assassinated

Olof Palme (Sweden) joined his country's Social Democratic Labour Party in 1949 and became leader of the party's youth movement in 1955, rising to the post of prime minister in 1969 and almost immediately straining Swedish–US relations with his stance over the Vietnam War. He succeeded in carrying out major constitutional reforms, but lost power in 1976 over proposals to fund the welfare system through higher taxes. He returned to power in 1982 and was re-elected in 1985, but his career ended abruptly on the night of 28 February 1986 when he was shot by a lone gunman as he walked home with his wife through Stockholm after a visit to the cinema. Palme was hit in the chest and his wife in the back; both were rushed to hospital, where Palme died of his injuries. The identity of the assassin has never been established, and no organization has ever claimed responsibility.

**Above** A plaque commemorating Swedish Prime Minister Olof Palme, set into the Stockholm street where he was shot. On 10 September 2003 Swedish foreign minister Anna Lindh was killed while shopping in the same area of the city centre

# Chapter Five

# Last Requests and Bequests

**The Last Bequest of**

# JOHN HARVARD

In a tale of two cities with the same name, 17th-century preacher John Harvard studied at Cambridge University, England, and later emigrated to America where his last bequest went to a newly founded college in Cambridge, Massachusetts, now known as Harvard University.

**TIMELINE: JOHN HARVARD**

**1607** John Harvard is born in Southwark, London, the son of Robert Harvard, who owns a butcher's shop and the Queen's Head Inn. John is baptized at St Saviour's Church (now Southwark Cathedral)

**1632** Graduates with a BA from Emmanuel College, Cambridge

**1635** Awarded an MA by Emmanuel College, Cambridge. His mother dies, bequeathing him the Queen's Head Inn, a half share of a property on Tower Hill, and £250

**1636** The college that will become America's first university is founded on 28 OCTOBER in Newtowne, Massachusetts

**1637** Harvard's last surviving brother, Thomas, dies leaving him £100 and a silver bowl and chest. John and his wife, Anne, sell the inn and emigrate, arriving in Boston, Massachusetts, on 26 JUNE and settling in Charlestown, Massachusetts

**1638** John Harvard dies of consumption, leaving his library and half his fortune to the college founded two years earlier in Newtowne. Newtowne is renamed Cambridge College

**1639** Cambridge College is renamed Harvard College in honour of its major benefactor

**1907** Members of Harvard University pay for the reconstruction of the Harvard Chapel within Southwark Cathedral, London, England

In 1584 Sir Walter Mildmay, a staunch Puritan, founded Emmanuel College, Cambridge University, as a training college for Puritan church ministers. During the 1630s Puritanism was not in favour in England and a number of Emmanuel graduates emigrated to America seeking greater religious freedom. Many of those graduates settled in the Massachusetts Bay Colony and in 1638 Newtowne College, Massachusetts, was renamed Cambridge in honour of one of them, the preacher Thomas Shepherd (England–America).

Shepherd had been followed to America by another Emmanuel graduate and preacher, John Harvard (England–America), who in 1637 settled with his wife in Charlestown, Massachusetts. The year before Harvard arrived in America, the Great and General Court of the Massachusetts Bay Colony had voted to establish a college in Newtowne that would later become America's first university. The year *after* he arrived, Harvard died of consumption and left much of his wealth to this new educational institution. In his last will and testament he bequeathed his library of nearly 400 books, as well as half his fortune, amounting to £779, to the recently established college, which changed its name that same year (with the name of the town) from Newtowne College to Cambridge College. On 3 March 1639 Cambridge College changed its name again when it was renamed Harvard College in honour of its generous benefactor.

**Below** Harvard University during the early 19th century

**Opposite** Statue of John Harvard by Daniel Chester French (1884)

● The Puritan John Harvard would not have approved of the antics of one 19th-century Harvard professor, who murdered a colleague over a debt. Dr George Parkman disappeared in 1849 after lending money to his colleague Dr John White Webster. As security, Webster gave Parkman a mortgage on his personal effects, including a valuable collection of minerals, but Parkman discovered that Webster had used the same minerals as security for another loan and began pursuing Webster to collect the debt. A week after Parkman's disappearance, human body parts were found in a vault beneath Webster's laboratory and, having confessed, he was hanged for murder on 30 August, 1850. Harvard might have approved more of the actions of Parkman's widow, who raised money to support Webster's wife and children

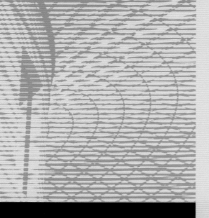

**The Last Bequest of**

# HANS SLOANE

Hans Sloane's last bequest is now far more famous than his connection with it. Sloane himself is more often remembered in the name of London's Sloane Square, but his last bequest was to form the basis of one of the world's great public institutions – the British Museum.

**Above** Undated portrait of Sir Hans Sloane
**Opposite** The Great Court of the British Museum, enclosed in 2000 under a new atrium designed by Sir Norman Foster

Sir Hans Sloane (Ireland) made his name and fortune as a doctor, being appointed to such eminent posts as physician-general to the British army and royal physician to Queen Anne, King George I and King George II. He was also a compulsive collector, amassing during his lifetime a collection of some 80,000 items of natural history, antiquities, books and curiosities. Sloane wanted to bequeath his collection to the nation, but he did not want to deprive his two daughters of part of their inheritance, a dilemma recorded in memoirs written by his friend Thomas Birch (Britain): 'And tho' the intrinsic value of it [the collection] was too much to be given away intirely from his own children, he left it to the public on such easy terms, as he thought would readily be complied with...'

These 'easy terms' were that the collection would be sold to the nation for a fraction of its value. A codicil to his last will and testament, dated 10 July 1749, directs that his trustees shall apply to 'his majesty [George II] or to parliament' for 'twenty thousand pounds of lawful money of great-Britain, unto my executors or the survivors of them, within twelve months after my decease, in consideration of the said collection or musaeum: It not being, as I apprehend or believe, a fourth of their real and intrinsic value...'

The King declined the offer, but parliament accepted on behalf of the nation and passed an Act establishing the British Museum and authorizing the organization of a lottery to raise funds to purchase, house and administer not only Sloane's bequest but also the Harleian Library, assembled by Robert and Edward Harley, 1st and 2nd Earls of Oxford, and the library of the Cotton family. In 1755 the trustees bought Montagu House in Bloomsbury, where the British Museum opened to the public on 15 January 1759 and on which site it remains today, although Montagu House has long since been replaced.

**DID YOU KNOW?**

● At least two other British institutions can trace their origins to Sloane's bequest. The original British Museum collections were regularly augmented with purchases and gifts and, despite the construction of new buildings, the museum soon outgrew the space available and so a decision was made to split the collections. The natural history collection was moved to South Kensington to become what is now the Natural History Museum, which opened in 1881, and, in 1998, the book collections moved to St Pancras to become part of the new British Library

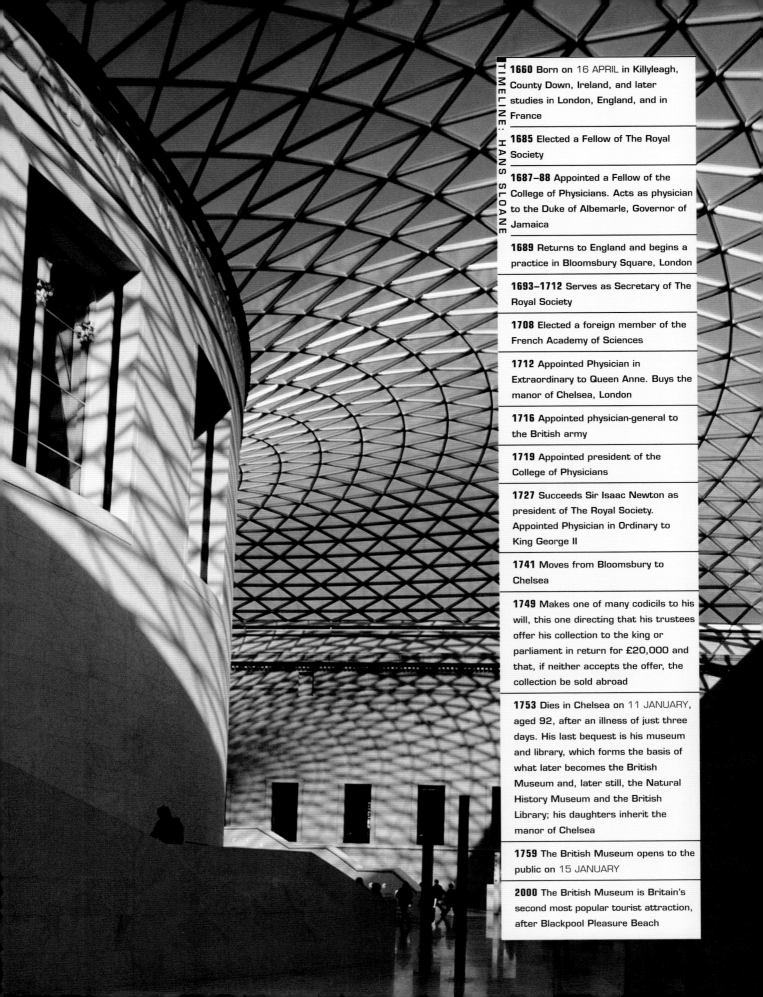

**1660** Born on 16 APRIL in Killyleagh, County Down, Ireland, and later studies in London, England, and in France

**1685** Elected a Fellow of The Royal Society

**1687–88** Appointed a Fellow of the College of Physicians. Acts as physician to the Duke of Albemarle, Governor of Jamaica

**1689** Returns to England and begins a practice in Bloomsbury Square, London

**1693–1712** Serves as Secretary of The Royal Society

**1708** Elected a foreign member of the French Academy of Sciences

**1712** Appointed Physician in Extraordinary to Queen Anne. Buys the manor of Chelsea, London

**1716** Appointed physician-general to the British army

**1719** Appointed president of the College of Physicians

**1727** Succeeds Sir Isaac Newton as president of The Royal Society. Appointed Physician in Ordinary to King George II

**1741** Moves from Bloomsbury to Chelsea

**1749** Makes one of many codicils to his will, this one directing that his trustees offer his collection to the king or parliament in return for £20,000 and that, if neither accepts the offer, the collection be sold abroad

**1753** Dies in Chelsea on 11 JANUARY, aged 92, after an illness of just three days. His last bequest is his museum and library, which forms the basis of what later becomes the British Museum and, later still, the Natural History Museum and the British Library; his daughters inherit the manor of Chelsea

**1759** The British Museum opens to the public on 15 JANUARY

**2000** The British Museum is Britain's second most popular tourist attraction, after Blackpool Pleasure Beach

## The Last Bequest of JAMES SMITHSON

The fact that the Smithsonian Institution is named after a man named Smithson is not surprising. What is surprising is that the illegitimate son of a French-born English aristocrat should leave more than 100,000 gold sovereigns to found an institution in a country he had never visited.

### DID YOU KNOW?

• The chemical compound zinc carbonate is also known as 'smithsonite', after this accomplished mineralogist

James Louis Macie Smithson (England) was born the illegitimate son of Elizabeth Macie and Sir Hugh Smithson Percy, 1st Duke of Northumberland, whose forbears played a colourful role in British history and two of whom appear in Shakespeare's *Henry IV Part I*. Because Smithson was illegitimate, society required him to use his mother's name, and so it was as James Macie that he was educated at Oxford University and later elected a Fellow of The Royal Society in 1787 in recognition of his eminence as a chemist and mineralogist. Only in 1801, on the death of his mother, did he begin using the name Smithson.

● Smithson did not specify in his will the reason for bequeathing such a large amount to a country he had never visited, but some historians suggest that it may have been a form of revenge on the attitudes of British society towards him as the illegitimate child of a nobleman. This hypothesis is supported by Smithson's comment that he hoped his name would 'live in the memory of man when the titles of the Northumberlands and the Percys are extinct and forgotten'

In 1826, at the age of 61, Smithson made his last will and testament, which came into force when he died three years later. He named his nephew as beneficiary of his entire estate, but with the caveat that, should his nephew die without an heir, the estate would pass 'to the United States of America, to found at Washington, under the name of the Smithsonian Institution, an Establishment for the increase and diffusion of knowledge among men'.

Smithson's nephew died without an heir in 1835 and the following year President Andrew Jackson (USA) announced to Congress news of the unexpected bequest. Two years later still, the 100,000 gold sovereigns were delivered to the US Mint, where they were valued at $508,318. It was eight years before Congress finally agreed on what form the institution should take, by which time another president was in office. On 10 August 1846 President James K. Polk signed the Act of Congress by which The Smithsonian Institution was established.

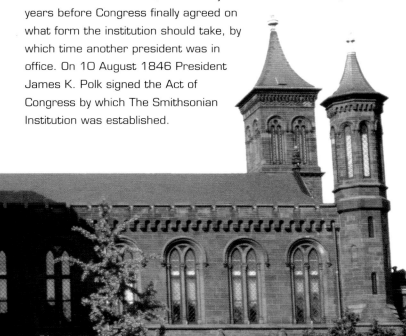

**TIMELINE: JAMES SMITHSON**

**1765** Born James Louis Macie in Paris, France, the illegitimate son of Elizabeth Macie and Sir Hugh Smithson Percy, 1st Duke of Northumberland, and later educated at Oxford University, England

**1787** Elected a Fellow of The Royal Society

**1801** Adopts Smithson as his surname on the death of his mother, keeping Macie as his third given name

**1826** Makes his last will and testament, naming his nephew as beneficiary

**1829** Dies in Genoa, Italy, on 27 JUNE aged 64, leaving his estate to his nephew

**1835** Smithson's nephew dies with no heir, so the estate passes to the USA to found the Smithsonian Institution

**1846** On 10 AUGUST The Smithsonian Institution is established by Act of Congress

**1904** Alexander Graham Bell (Scotland–USA) takes Smithson's remains from Italy to Washington, DC, where they are reinterred in a tomb in the Smithsonian Building

**Left** The administrative offices of the Smithsonian Institution, overlooking the Edith Haupt Gardens. The castellated building was completed in 1855 and originally housed the main research centre of the institution
**Above** Undated portrait of James Smithson

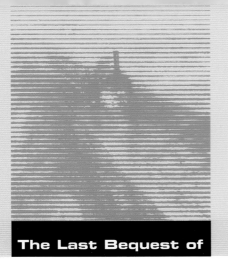

J.M.W. Turner was one of the great masters of landscape art, in both oil and watercolour. Turner's bequest to the British nation comprised some 300 oils and 19,000 watercolours, now permanently on display at Tate Britain, which also sponsors the Turner Prize for contemporary art.

# J.M.W. TURNER

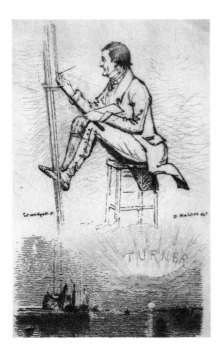

**Above** A 19th-century illustration of Turner at work above a detail from his painting *The Fighting Temeraire*. Turner called this painting 'My Darling' and refused to sell it

Joseph Mallord William Turner (England) is now universally acknowledged as a genius of landscape painting, but it was not always so. Perhaps appropriately for the man whose name is attached to the often controversial Turner Prize, while many of his contemporaries recognized his genius, many others among them misunderstood his work and ridiculed his methods. In 1844 *The Times* newspaper summed up the division with reference to his masterpiece, *Rain, Steam and Speed*: 'Whether Turner's pictures are dazzling unrealities, or realities seized upon a moment's glance, we leave his detractors and admirers to settle between them.'

When he died in 1851, Turner's will stated that his personal property should be sold and the proceeds used to found a charitable institution for 'Poor and Decayed Male Artists born in England and of English Parents only and lawful issue', and that any of his own works remaining in his studio should be bequeathed to the nation, to be kept together in a special gallery built for the purpose. But his family challenged the will and succeeded, on a technicality, in inheriting the property, preventing the foundation of the charitable institution and the purpose-built gallery.

However, by a decree of 1856, almost five years after his death, the nation inherited what has been known ever since as the Turner Bequest – nearly 300 oil paintings and some 30,000 sketches and watercolours, including 300 sketchbooks. The bequest was initially kept at the National Gallery in London, but in 1897 the entire bequest, apart from a few works that remain at the National Gallery, was moved to the new Tate Gallery (now Tate Britain), where it was housed in the Duveen Wing, which had been specially built for the purpose as Turner had wished.

| | | | | |
|---|---|---|---|---|
| **1775** Born Joseph Mallord William Turner on 23 APRIL in London, England. Later exhibits his first watercolours in the window of his father's barbershop in Covent Garden, London | **1789** Enters The Royal Academy at the age of 14 | **1790** Begins exhibiting at The Royal Academy and redefines the art of watercolour | **1796** Exhibits an oil painting at The Royal Academy for the first time | **1851** Dies on 19 DECEMBER in Chelsea, London, aged 76. His last will and testament includes a bequest to the nation of property and some 300 oil paintings and 19,000 watercolours. His family contests the will |

TIMELINE: J.M.W. TURNER

## DID YOU KNOW?

● Turner's last words are often reported as: 'The sun is God', a particularly apt sentiment for a painter who rendered light so gracefully. In fact, he made this remark some weeks before he died, and biographer James Hamilton (Britain) points out that: 'Remembering his own mortality, and the religious perceptions that had floated lightly in the background of his life over the past 20 years, he may equally have said: "The Son is God"'

**Below** Turner's masterpiece *Rain, Steam, and Speed* was almost certainly painted at Isambard Kingdom Brunel's Maidenhead Railway Bridge over the Thames in Berkshire, England

**1856** The works in Turner's studio are accepted by decree on behalf of the nation as the Turner Bequest

**1897** The National Gallery of British Art (later Tate Gallery) opens in London, financed primarily by sugar magnate Sir Henry Tate (England), with one wing financed by Sir Joseph Duveen (England) specifically to house the Turner Bequest

**1984** The Turner Prize for contemporary art is initiated

**1987** The Clore Gallery is opened as an extension to the Tate Gallery, purpose-built as a new home for the Turner Bequest

**The Last Bequest of**

# CHARLES DICKENS

The last will and testament of Charles Dickens was relatively ordinary except for the fact that it was the last will and testament of Charles Dickens. But when they relate to 'England's most popular author' and the world's most published novelist, even ordinary details are interesting.

## DID YOU KNOW?

● The inscription on Dickens' tombstone in Westminster Abbey reads:

To the Memory of
**CHARLES DICKENS**
(ENGLAND'S MOST POPULAR
AUTHOR)
Who died at his residence, Higham,
near Rochester, Kent,
**JUNE 9TH, 1870**
Aged 58 Years
HE WAS A SYMPATHISER WITH THE
POOR, THE SUFFERING, AND
THE OPPRESSED; AND
BY HIS DEATH, ONE OF ENGLAND'S
GREATEST WRITERS IS LOST
TO THE WORLD.

**Opposite** Undated photograph of Charles Dickens
**Opposite inset** Dickens' mistress, the actress Ellen Ternan, who was provided for in his will

I n 1869, at about the same time as he signed the contract for his last novel, *The Mystery of Edwin Drood*, Charles Dickens (England) made his last will and testament, which came into force after his death on 9 June 1870. His total estate proved to be worth £93,000, of which, surprisingly, only half came from his novels – the other half was made from his famous public readings.

Most of the estate was divided, conventionally enough, between his children, with the exception of several specific bequests. He left £1,000 to his lover, the young actress Ellen Ternan, a bequest that Dickens biographer Wolf Mankowitz describes as 'inexplicable', although he then goes on to explain it: 'It was not enough to provide for her permanently, but sufficient to advise the posthumous world of what had been so discreetly veiled while he lived.'

The greatest specific bequest outside those to his children was to his sister-in-law, Georgina, who received £8,000 as well as most of his jewellery and his private papers. Dickens' eldest son, Charley, inherited his father's library in addition to his share of the estate, and Dickens' estranged wife, Kate, received a small income for the rest of her life, the paucity of which Dickens explained (or attempted to excuse) in the will with the statement that since their separation 'all the great charges of a numerous and expensive family have devolved wholly upon myself'.

Dickens wanted to be buried quietly in a country churchyard, but the nation, led by *The Times* newspaper, demanded that his talent and popularity be recognized by burial in Poets' Corner at Westminster Abbey. The family agreed to this, but insisted that the funeral itself must be conducted according to the terms of Dickens' will: it must be private, and noone, in the words of the will, was to wear a 'scarf, cloak, black bow, long hatband or any other such revolting absurdity'.

**TIMELINE: CHARLES DICKENS**

| | | | | |
|---|---|---|---|---|
| **1812** Born Charles John Huffam Dickens on 7 FEBRUARY in Portsmouth, England, the son of a Royal Navy clerk | **1824** His father and family are imprisoned in Marshalsea debtors' prison, London, and Dickens is sent to work in a blacking factory at Hungerford Market, near what is now Charing Cross Station, London | **1827** Works as a solicitor's office boy | **1828** Begins a career as a journalist as House of Commons reporter for the *Morning Chronicle* newspaper, although he still nurses ambitions to be an actor | **1833** *Monthly Magazine* publishes a sketch by Dickens entitled 'Under the Poplar Walk', written under the pseudonym 'Boz', his younger brother's nickname. A collection of his sketches will be published in 1836 as *Sketches by Boz* |

**1836** The first instalment of *The Pickwick Papers*, which will be his first novel, is published. Marries Catherine Hogarth ('Kate'), the daughter of the editor of the *Evening Chronicle*, one of the newspapers he has been writing for

**1837–52** He and Kate have seven sons and three daughters

**1858** He and Kate separate

**1870** Makes his last public reading on 15 MARCH. **Dies on 9 JUNE** at Gadshill, near Rochester, England, of a stroke suffered the previous day, before completing his last novel, *The Mystery of Edwin Drood*. Against his wishes he is buried in Westminster Abbey
*See also: Authors' Last Novels, page 109*

Oliver Winchester made his fortune producing rifles and, when he died in 1880, his last bequest was not unusual: he left the entire fortune to his son William. William died in 1881 and the fortune passed to Oliver's daughter-in-law, to whom it proved more of a curse than a blessing.

## The Last Bequest of OLIVER WINCHESTER

**TIMELINE: THE WINCHESTER FAMILY**

**1810** Oliver Winchester is born in Boston, Massachusetts, and later runs a company making shirts in Baltimore, Maryland

**1856** Becomes principal shareholder in the Volcanic Repeating Arms Co.

**1860** Supervises the development of the first practicable repeating rifle (designed by Benjamin Tyler Henry)

**1866** Changes the name of his company to Winchester

Before he became involved in the gun-making business that literally made his name, Oliver Winchester (USA) was a shirt-maker, and in 1848 he invented and patented a method of cutting shirt patterns that proved so successful he was able to open a large-scale factory in New Haven, Connecticut. The success of the shirt business also left him with some spare cash, and he began investing in a local gun manufacturing business called the Volcanic Repeating Arms Company. He became the majority shareholder, reorganized the company, and in 1866 changed its name to the Winchester Repeating Arms Company.

**Below** 'Give him year 'round fun ... for years to come', undated (1950s) American advertisement for Winchester rifles
**Opposite** The Winchester Mystery House

## DID YOU KNOW?

● The Winchester-Henry rifle had such a reputation that, although it was not official government issue during the American Civil War, some 11,000 Union soldiers bought their own. It also had a reputation among Confederate soldiers, who called it 'the damned Yankee rifle you could load on Sunday and shoot all week'

By the time he died in 1880, Winchester was a multi-millionaire. He left his fortune to his son William, who did not live long to enjoy his legacy – he died the following year aged only 41, leaving everything to his wife, and Oliver's daughter-in-law, Sarah. And then the trouble began.

Distraught at the loss of her husband, Sarah consulted a medium who told her that the ghosts of those killed by Winchester rifles were taking their revenge, and that the only way to appease these restless spirits was to continuously build a house for them. Sarah moved to Santa Clara, California, and began building in 1884. She continued building until her death in September 1922, by which time she had spent an estimated $5 million extending the house to some 160 rooms covering an area of 6 acres, making it one of the largest homes in the USA. Her sprawling creation, the legacy of the man who made 'the gun that won the West', is now open to the public as the Winchester Mystery House.

Repeating Arms Co. Produces the Winchester 66 (designed by Nelson King, USA)

**1873** Produces the Winchester 73, which later becomes known as 'the gun that won the West' and the subject of the feature film *Winchester 73*, starring James Stewart (USA)

**1880** Dies in New Haven, Connecticut, leaving his entire fortune to his son William Wirt Winchester

**1881** William dies of tuberculosis on 7 MARCH, leaving the $20 million fortune to his wife, and Oliver's daughter-in-law, Sarah (née Pardee)

**1884** Sarah begins building what will later be known as the Winchester Mystery House, in Santa Clara, California

**1922** Sarah dies aged 85, having extended the house to some 160 rooms

**The Last Bequest of**

# ALFRED NOBEL

Alfred Nobel made his fortune from manufacturing explosives, but he wanted to be remembered for a more peaceful contribution to humanity. In his will, he left a large proportion of his estate for the endowment of the Nobel Foundation, which finances the annual Nobel Prizes.

**Above** Nobel Prize award ceremony at the Stockholm Concert Hall (10 December 2003)

Alfred Bernhard Nobel (Sweden) was one of a select band of people to have read their own obituary. In April 1888 he looked to see what the newspapers had written about his recently deceased brother Ludwig, and found that one paper had confused the brothers and mistakenly printed his, Alfred's, obituary instead. Referring to Alfred's expertise in explosives, the obituarist called him 'a merchant of death' and 'the dynamite king', making no mention of his philanthropic activities. As a result, Nobel decided to found the now world-famous Nobel Foundation.

When he died eight years later, on 10 December 1896, part of Alfred Nobel's last will and testament was a bequest of £2 million to establish and fund the foundation. Being suspicious of lawyers, Nobel did not employ professionals to draft the will or to specify the arrangements for awarding the prizes, something that nearly stymied the foundation before it had begun. Some of his relatives contested the will, and many Swedes felt that the prizes should be eligible only to Swedish citizens, but the objections were overruled and the first prizes were awarded, to men from Switzerland, France, Germany and the Netherlands, on 10 December 1901, the fifth anniversary of Nobel's death.

Nobel had willed prizes to be awarded to those who 'have conferred the greatest benefit to mankind' in the five categories of peace, literature, physics, physiology or medicine, and chemistry. In 1969 the Bank of Sweden inaugurated a sixth prize, the last Nobel Prize to date, naming it: 'The Bank of Sweden Prize in Economic Sciences in Memory of Alfred Nobel.'

**DID YOU KNOW?**

● The original name for Nobel's most famous invention, a stable form of the explosive nitroglycerine, was the literal and unimaginative 'Nobel's Safety Powder'. Later, Nobel registered the far more dynamic trademark 'Dynamite', taking his inspiration from the Greek *dynamis*, meaning power

**Right** Alfred Nobel, photographed in 1893, three years before his death

**1833** Alfred Nobel is born on 21 OCTOBER in Stockholm, Sweden, the son of an engineer, inventor and explosives expert

**1866** Invents dynamite

**1875** Invents gelignite

**1896** Dies of a brain haemorrhage, aged 63, on 10 DECEMBER in San Remo, Italy, his last bequest being the establishment of the Nobel Foundation. His estate includes the rights to 355 patents

**1901** The Nobel Foundation awards the first Nobel Prizes

**1969** The sixth and last Nobel Prize is created, inaugurated by the Bank of Sweden

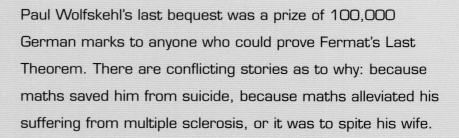

Paul Wolfskehl's last bequest was a prize of 100,000 German marks to anyone who could prove Fermat's Last Theorem. There are conflicting stories as to why: because maths saved him from suicide, because maths alleviated his suffering from multiple sclerosis, or it was to spite his wife.

# The Last Bequest of PAUL WOLFSKEHL

The details of the Wolfskehl Prize, bequeathed by mathematician Paul Wolfskehl (Germany), are well documented, but the reason why he made his bequest is uncertain. For many years the accepted story was that Fermat's Last Theorem had saved him from suicide – rejected by the woman of his dreams, he had set a time and a date to shoot himself, but on the appointed day he found he had a few hours to spare before his midnight deadline. He supposedly spent the time at the library, where he discovered a flaw in a paper by Ernst Kummer (Germany) relating to Fermat's Last Theorem, and spent all night correcting the gap in Kummer's work. Not only had he missed his appointment with death, but also the honour his proof brought him gave him a new reason for living.

This version of the story says that he altered his will in recognition of the theorem that had saved his life. However, recent research by Professor Klaus Barner (Germany) states that Wolfskehl turned from medicine to mathematics when he began suffering the first symptoms of multiple sclerosis, maths being something in which he could participate from a wheelchair, and that he may have offered the prize in recognition of the meaning that maths gave his life during his suffering. But Barner also suggests that after a wedding forced on him by his family, so that he would have a carer during his illness, his wife, Marie Frölich (Germany), made his life a misery and Wolfskehl altered his will in order to prevent her from inheriting his entire fortune.

The rules of the prize included the fact that the award would take place 'not earlier than two years after publication of the memoir to be crowned'. Almost 90 years after its inauguration, Andrew Wiles (England–USA) collected the Wolfskehl Prize, two years after his proof of Fermat's Last Theorem was published in *Annals of Mathematics*.

**Above** Paul Wolfskehl

**TIMELINE: THE WOLFSKEHL PRIZE**

| | | | | | |
|---|---|---|---|---|---|
| **1856** Paul Friedrich Wolfskehl is born on JUNE 30 in Darmstadt, Germany, the younger of two sons of Johanna Wolfskehl and banker Joseph Carl Theodor Wolfskehl | **1880** Wolfskehl qualifies as a doctor. At about this time he begins to exhibit symptoms of multiple sclerosis. Begins studying mathematics in Bonn | **1881–83** Continues his mathematics studies in Berlin, where he attends lectures by Ernst Kummer (Germany) | **1890** Wolfskehl is paralysed by multiple sclerosis | **1903** Marries Susanne Magarethe Marie Frölich (Germany) on 12 OCTOBER under pressure from his family to marry someone who will care for him | **1905** In JANUARY Wolfskehl alters his will, his last bequest being the Wolfskehl Prize |

## DID YOU KNOW?

● The offer of such a large prize has posed problems over the years for those burdened with the task of checking often-spurious entries. One official received a letter containing the first half of a purported proof and promising to send the second half on receipt of an advance of DM1,000. Another printed cards reading: 'Dear.... Thank you for your manuscript on the proof of Fermat's Last Theorem. The first mistake is on: Page.... Line.... This invalidates the proof' and instructed his students to fill in the blanks. Yet another replied by saying he was not competent to examine the proof and gave the name and address of an 'expert' who would do so – in fact the name and address of the last person to send him an attempted proof

| **1906** Wolfskehl dies, aged 50, on 13 SEPTEMBER in Darmstadt, leaving a bequest of 100,000 German marks to the first person to prove Fermat's Last Theorem | **1908** On 27 JUNE the German Royal Society of Science in Göttingen announces the inauguration of the prize | **1994** Andrew Wiles (England-USA) proves Fermat's Last Theorem *See also: Fermat's Last Theorem, page 96* | **1995** Wiles' proof is published in *Annals of Mathematics* | **1997** Wiles collects the Wolfskehl Prize, now worth DM75,000 (approximately $50,000, or £30,000), on 27 JUNE | **2007** The deadline set in Wolfskehl's will for proving Fermat's Last Theorem is 13 SEPTEMBER, **101 years** after Wolfskehl's death and not 13 SEPTEMBER 2006 as often cited |

Franz Kafka's last request was that all his papers be burned, including the unpublished manuscripts of *The Trial*, *The Castle* and *America*. Had this request been adhered to, the world would have been deprived not only of three great novels but also of the adjective 'Kafkaesque'.

## The Last Request of FRANZ KAFKA

Author Franz Kafka (b. Prague, now Czech Republic) once wrote: 'I have no literary interests, but I consist of literature, it is the only thing I am and can ever be.' For him, writing was not a matter of choice, it was something he was driven to do. Strange, then, that he should publish only seven short works during his lifetime and leave strict instructions that all his

**Below** A page from one of Kafka's works diaries, which begins: 'Aber jeden Tag soll zumindest eine Zeile gegen mich geriechtet werden wie man dei Fernrohre jetzt gegen den Kometen richtet…' (Every day one line at least shall be directed at myself, just as telescopes are now directed at the comet…) (Manuscript, 1910)

**Opposite** Graffiti in Prague, depicting Franz Kafka (undated)

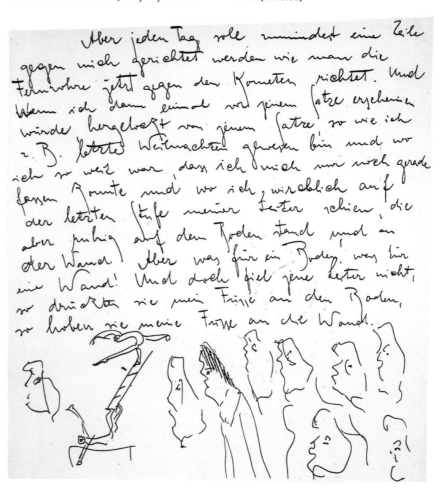

FRANZ
KAFKA
A JEHO ČTYŘI TVÁŘE
ENDY &
sgt. RUFFER

unpublished work, including his three novels, should be destroyed.

Kafka was a hypersensitive, tortured individual who, despite his undoubted literary genius, remained unsure of his own talent. In 1922 he wrote to his friend of 20 years, novelist, poet and dramatist Max Brod (b. Prague, now Czech Republic): 'Anxiety about subject matter is really neither more nor less than life itself coming to a halt. People don't usually suffocate for lack of air, but for lack of lung power.' Coming from someone who was to die of tuberculosis two years later, this is a very powerful image of artistic doubt.

Kafka's last request did not form part of an official last will and testament, but took the form of a pencilled note found in a drawer after his death in 1924. Kafka had made a list of his three novels and a number of stories and asked that Max Brod destroy the listed works 'unread and in their entirety'. Thankfully, Brod ignored these instructions and personally oversaw the publication of the works, giving rise to the irony that, having written about protagonists who had no power over their own destiny, Kafka himself proved to have none over his own.

Charles Millar was a Canadian lawyer and financier who had a wicked sense of humour. In his will he bequeathed a large amount of money and shares to various people as a posthumous experiment to discover just how far those people would go in betraying their principles for wealth.

# CHARLES MILLAR

## DID YOU KNOW?

● A synopsis of *Hamlet*, the play cited in Juan Potomachi's will (*see: Timeline 1955*), is contained in the play's most famous speech. 'To be or not to be: that is the question: whether 'tis nobler in the mind to suffer the slings and arrows of outrageous fortune...' is an anagram of 'In one of the Bard's best thought-of tragedies, our insistent hero, Hamlet, queries on two fronts about how life turns rotten'

From the value of his estate it is clear that Charles Vance Millar (Canada) was very successful in his career as a lawyer and financier, but he has become more famous since his death than he was in life because of the bizarre stipulations of his will. Millar, who died unmarried, left more than half a million dollars-worth of cash and shares in a posthumous psychological experiment to find out what people will do for money. The thought of the havoc his will would wreak must have sweetened his last moments.

Part of his extraordinary last bequest was to leave shares in a racetrack to a preacher and a judge, both of whom he knew to be wholly against gambling; both men accepted the bequest. In a similar test of moral stature, he left shares in a brewery to a group of churchmen whom he knew to be strongly opposed to alcohol; all except one accepted the bequest.

Strangest of all, he left $500,000 (sometimes recorded as $750,000) to whichever woman from Toronto, Canada, 'has given birth to the greatest number of children at the expiration of 10 years from my death'. The subsequent race to give birth became known as the Stork Derby, and it was tied by four women who shared the money, each having given birth to 9 children in those 10 years: Annie Smith, Kathleen Nagle, Lucy Timleck and Isabel MacLean. Two other women were disqualified: Pauline Clarke, who had given birth to 10 children, was disqualified because 5 of them were born out of wedlock, and Lillian Kenney, because several of her 12 children had died and she could not prove that they were not stillborn. Clarke and Kenney were each given a $12,500 consolation prize and the remainder of the prize money was divided between the other four.

**Left** Laurence Olivier as Hamlet holds Yorick's skull in his film of the play (1948)

**Opposite** A stork delivers the first baby of 1928, the year that Charles Millar died and initiated the 'Stork Derby'

**1856** The last bequest of poet Heinrich Heine (Germany) is to leave his entire estate to his wife on condition that she remarries. The reason Heine gives for this strange condition is 'so that there will be at least one man to regret my death'. Heine's last words are: 'God will pardon me ... that is His job'

**1928** Charles Millar's last bequest is to leave more than half a million dollars to discover just what people will do for money

**TIMELINE: HUMOROUS WILLS**

**1955** The last bequest of Juan Potomachi (Argentina) is the equivalent of some £30,000 left to his local theatre, Teatro Dramatico, on condition that they use his skull as a prop when performing *Hamlet*

**1972** The last request of Harold West (Britain), who believed in vampires, is that: 'My doctor is to drive a steel stake through my heart to make sure that I am properly dead'

**1975** The last request of Edward Horley (England) is that his solicitors cut a lemon in two and send one half to the tax inspector and the other to the tax collector, both with the message: 'Now squeeze this'

**1983** The last request of Tony Gribble (Britain) is that his ashes be placed in an egg timer 'so that I can continue to be of use after my death'

**The Last Request of**

The fortunes of novelist F. Scott Fitzgerald rose and fell from one extreme to another, both in life and in his posthumous reputation. His last requests regarding his funeral reflected these changes, being altered at the last minute from a grand exit to 'the cheapest funeral'.

# F. SCOTT FITZGERALD

I n his most famous novel, *The Great Gatsby*, F. Scott Fitzgerald (USA) wrote: 'In his blue gardens, men and girls came and went like moths among the whisperings and the champagne and the stars.' The same could be said of the author's fortunes. With the publication of his first novel, *This Side of Paradise*, Fitzgerald became not only the youngest novelist Scribner's had ever published but also 'the spokesman of the Jazz Age'. His career reached its zenith with *The Great Gatsby* in 1925, a decade in which he lived the life of one of his playboy characters, but by the time of his death in 1940 he had plumbed the depths of debt and alcoholism and was critically dismissed in many quarters as 'the darling of a fatuous decade'.

**Below** Robert Redford in the film of *The Great Gatsby* (1974)
**Opposite** F. Scott Fitzgerald at his writing desk (c.1920s)

| **1896** Born Francis Scott Key Fitzgerald on 24 SEPTEMBER in St Paul, Minnesota, USA, and later educated at Newman School, New Jersey, and Princeton | **1920** Publication of his first novel, *This Side of Paradise* | **1925** Publication of his most famous novel, *The Great Gatsby* | **1937** Moves to Hollywood intending to remake his fortune as a scriptwriter | **1940** Dies, aged 44, on 21 DECEMBER, before completing his last novel, *The Last Tycoon* (pub. 1941) |

■ TIMELINE: F. SCOTT FITZGERALD

**DID YOU KNOW?**

● In his short story *The Rich Boy*, Fitzgerald wrote: 'Let me tell you about the very rich. They are different from you and me.' In one of his notebooks he recorded Ernest Hemingway's rejoinder to that comment: 'Yes, they have more money'

After his death, the undeniably great style and observation of his prose restored his literary reputation, but the changes in his last will and testament tell the sad story of his last years. In 1937 Fitzgerald moved to Hollywood as a scriptwriter, and in an optimistic moment he wrote a will including a request regarding his send-off: that it should be 'a funeral and burial in keeping with my station in life'. That ambiguous request could have been taken to imply a funeral in keeping with either fortune or destitution, but a later amendment makes it clear which Fitzgerald had originally intended. In 1940, the year of his death, he amended his will to request 'the cheapest funeral ... without undue ostentation or unnecessary expense'. The funeral of the spokesman of the Jazz Age cost just $613.25.

**The Last Bequest of**

Nobel prizewinning dramatist George Bernard Shaw is famous for the social observation and political insight shown in his writing, but he was also a great lover of language itself. When he died in 1950, he left money in his will to fund the development of a phonetic alphabet.

# GEORGE BERNARD SHAW

Playwright, critic, social commentator and wit, George Bernard Shaw (Ireland) was passionate about the English language and it is he who is attributed with the famous quotation: 'England and America are two countries divided by a common language.' To illustrate the shortcomings of written English, Shaw pointed out that it is perfectly feasible for a word spelt *ghoti* to be pronounced 'fish': *gh* as in 'tough', *o* as in 'women' and *ti* as in 'station'. To avoid such absurdities, he proposed that instead of 26 letters, English spelling should be reformed and that the language should adopt a more efficient phonetic alphabet of at least 42 letters so that each sound in the spoken language would be represented by a separate symbol.

Shaw died in 1950, bequeathing part of his fortune for the development of the 'Shavian Alphabet', which, although it has not been adopted as standard English, was developed into a 48-letter alphabet that was used for a 1962 edition of his 'religious pantomime' *Androcles and the Lion*. In the year 2000 a Revised Shaw Alphabet was published with 72 characters, a symbol to be used instead of a capital letter to indicate a name, and a stop sign to replace the comma and full stop.

Shaw also bequeathed a third of his royalties each to the Royal Academy of Dramatic Art (Britain), where he had served on the managing council, the National Gallery of Ireland and the British Museum. He died on 2 November 1950, when his last words, spoken to his nurse, were: 'Sister, you are trying to keep me alive as an old curiosity. But I'm done, I'm finished. I'm going to die.'

**Left** The slave Androcles removes a thorn from the lion's paw in a production of Shaw's play *Androcles and the Lion*, based on a Roman legend (1 September 1913)

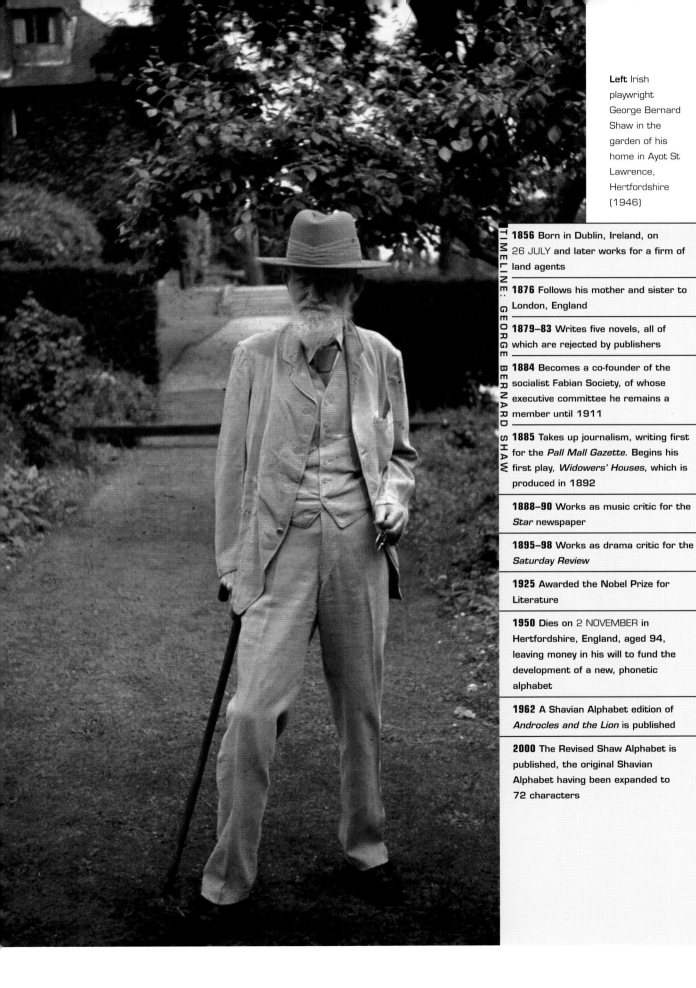

**Left** Irish playwright George Bernard Shaw in the garden of his home in Ayot St Lawrence, Hertfordshire (1946)

**TIMELINE: GEORGE BERNARD SHAW**

**1856** Born in Dublin, Ireland, on 26 JULY and later works for a firm of land agents

**1876** Follows his mother and sister to London, England

**1879–83** Writes five novels, all of which are rejected by publishers

**1884** Becomes a co-founder of the socialist Fabian Society, of whose executive committee he remains a member until 1911

**1885** Takes up journalism, writing first for the *Pall Mall Gazette*. Begins his first play, *Widowers' Houses*, which is produced in 1892

**1888–90** Works as music critic for the *Star* newspaper

**1895–98** Works as drama critic for the *Saturday Review*

**1925** Awarded the Nobel Prize for Literature

**1950** Dies on 2 NOVEMBER in Hertfordshire, England, aged 94, leaving money in his will to fund the development of a new, phonetic alphabet

**1962** A Shavian Alphabet edition of *Androcles and the Lion* is published

**2000** The Revised Shaw Alphabet is published, the original Shavian Alphabet having been expanded to 72 characters

Albert C. Barnes was a doctor, inventor, businessman and art collector whose revolutionary ideas about art and education infuriated the more conservative of his fellow Philadelphians. The conditions attached to his last bequest made him as controversial in death as he was in life.

# ALBERT C. BARNES

During his lifetime, Albert Coombs Barnes (USA) amassed one of the world's great art collections, establishing The Barnes Foundation in 1922 to house and administer his treasures and to 'promote the advancement of education and the appreciation of fine arts and horticulture'. He also alienated many individuals and institutions within the established Philadelphia art community through the unusual organization and content of his eclectic collection.

Before his death in 1951, Barnes specified various conditions governing the way in which his last bequest, The Barnes Foundation, should be run: the Foundation should continue to operate as an educational institution and not as a museum; works must be displayed exactly as he left them; works must not be sent on tour (this stipulation was broken in the 1990s to raise money); individual works must not be sold and, the subject of recent controversy, the collection must not be relocated.

Unfortunately, by the turn of the millennium the Foundation found itself in dire need of income and a rescue package was put together: three philanthropic institutions would help to raise $150 million for The Barnes Foundation if the collection was moved to the Benjamin Franklin Parkway, Philadelphia, close to a number of other cultural institutions including the Philadelphia Museum of Art. And so, more than 50 years after his death, the future of Barnes' last bequest is being contested in court, one party arguing that the collection should be relocated in the public interest of accessibility, the other that it should not be moved out of the setting its benefactor chose for it, against his express wishes, to become part of the art community that once disapproved of his revolutionary approach. The case was still ongoing at the time of going to press.

**Left** *Dr Albert C. Barnes*, by Italian artist Giorgio de Chirico in 1926
**Opposite** Inside The Barnes Foundation (1999)

| **1872** Born Albert Coombs Barnes in Philadelphia, Pennsylvania, the son of a butcher | **1892** Graduates as a doctor from the University of Pennsylvania Medical School, and later makes his fortune by developing an antiseptic treatment for eye infection, which is routinely used to prevent ophthalmic gonorrhoea in newborn babies | **1922** Establishes The Barnes Foundation in the town of Lower Merion, Pennsylvania | **1929** Sells his business, A.C. Barnes Company, shortly before the Wall Street Crash, realizing his fortune just in time | **1951** Dies after being hit by a truck | **2003** A court case begins in December to decide whether the terms of Barnes' Indenture may be overturned and the Foundation moved from its traditional home |

■TIMELINE: ALBERT C. BARNES

**Albert C. Barnes**

189

**The Last Bequest of**

# CALOUSTE GULBENKIAN

Calouste Gulbenkian was an oil baron, financier, industrialist, diplomat and art collector whose last bequest was to leave most of his fortune to establish the Gulbenkian Foundation in Portugal, which endows charitable, educational, artistic and scientific projects around the world.

**Below** The Portuguese Gulbenkian Ballet perfoming at the International Festival of Dance in Real Alcazar, Spain (17 July 2003)
**Opposite** Sculpture and statue of Gulbenkian outside the Gulbenkian Museum in Lisbon, Portugal

Calouste Gulbenkian (Armenia–Britain, b. Turkey) was born into an illustrious Armenian family and soon made his own fortune as a pioneer of Middle East oilfield development. He was a man who knew what he wanted and made sure he got it, even adopting the motto: *Only the best is good enough for me*. But as well as getting what he wanted, Gulbenkian also thought of others and died leaving a huge bequest for the education and enlightenment of thousands of people worldwide.

In 1942 Gulbenkian decided to make Lisbon, Portugal, his home for the twilight of his life and it was in Portugal that he made his last will and testament because, he wrote, he knew 'the extent to which a founder's wishes, in similar cases, are respected in Portugal'. Signed on 18 June 1953, the will bequeathed Gulbenkian's fortune, art collection and oil interests to the creation of a perpetual foundation in his name, which would become one of the world's twelve greatest such Foundations.

The Gulbenkian Foundation was established by decree in 1956 after its benefactor's death on 20 July 1955. Since then the Foundation has financed, among other things: the restoration of the Etchmiadzine Cathedral, Armenia; the construction of two Armenian cities, Nubarachene and Nor Guessaria ('New Caesarea') to house refugees; the Calouste Gulbenkian Museum in Lisbon, Portugal; Portuguese-based international orchestra, choir and ballet companies; the Centre Culturel Calouste Gulbenkian in Paris, France; and the Museum of Ancient Art in Baghdad, Iraq. The Foundation also provides educational and study grants as well as funding hospitals, libraries, arts centres and scientific institutions across Europe, the Middle East and Portuguese-speaking countries in Africa.

| **1869** Born Calouste Sarkis Gulbenkian on 23 MARCH in Scutari, Turkey, into a noble Armenian family whose ancestors include the Princes of Rechduni | **1887** Graduates with a first class degree from King's College, London, England | **1897–1920** Lives in London, England | **1898** Appointed Economic Adviser to the Ottoman embassies in London and Paris | **1902** Naturalized a British subject. Instrumental in the merger of Royal Dutch and Shell oil companies | **1916** Instrumental in arranging for France to enter the Turkish Petroleum Company in place of Germany, with whom the world is now at war. This leads to the founding of the Compagnie Française des Pétroles in 1924 |

**TIMELINE: CALOUSTE GULBENKIAN**

| **1920–42** Lives in Paris, France | **1921–28** Instrumental in arranging for the USA to enter the Turkish Petroleum Company | **1942–55** Lives in Lisbon, Portugal | **1953** Signs his last will and testament on 18 JUNE | **1955** Dies, aged 86, on 20 JULY in Lisbon, leaving a vast fortune to establish the Gulbenkian Foundation | **1956** The Gulbenkian Foundation is established by decree on 18 JULY | **1969** The Calouste Gulbenkian Museum opens on 2 OCTOBER in Lisbon, Portugal, bringing together most of Gulbenkian's vast art collection under one roof, as he had wished |

## The Last Bequest of BOB FOSSE

Bob Fosse's reputation as a choreographer and director of films and Broadway musicals came full circle in January 1999 with the opening of *Fosse*, a Broadway musical about his life and work. Fosse had died in 1987, leaving a characteristic last bequest – dinner for 66 of his friends.

For Bob Fosse (USA) there was no distinction between show business and 'real life'. Stage and screen musicals were his life, as performer, writer, director and choreographer – and in 1979 his life became a musical with the opening of the autobiographical *All That Jazz*. Four years earlier Fosse had suffered a heart attack during rehearsals for *Chicago*, and turned the experience into a musical about heart-attack suffering writer-director-choreographer Joe Gideon, although he denied that Gideon was based on himself, saying: 'On the surface, he looks like me, but he's not.'

Fosse's last day was 23 September 1987, when he died of another heart attack, having stated in his will that $25,000 was to be divided equally between 66 of his friends, who each duly received $378.79 with instructions to 'go out and have dinner on me'. The friends who had shared his love of life and now continued the party after his death included: Liza Minnelli, who had starred in Fosse's Oscar-winning film *Cabaret*; Roy Scheider, who had starred as Joe Gideon/Bob Fosse in *All That Jazz*; Janet Leigh, Elia Kazan, Dustin Hoffman, Melanie Griffith, Neil Simon and Jessica Lange (all USA).

Instead of all going out for 66 separate, quiet dinners, Bob's beneficiaries pooled their inheritance and threw a grand farewell party at The Tavern on the Green in Central Park, described in the Cadogan city guide to New York as: 'One of the tackiest smart restaurants in Manhattan, full of chandeliers, fairy lights and customers stooping under vast shoulder pads' – the perfect venue for the occasion, where a guest remembered: '[We] danced into the small hours, as Fosse wanted us to do.'

**Opposite** Bob Fosse behind the camera on the set of his film *Star 80* (1983)

**Below** The Tavern on the Green restaurant in Central Park, New York

TIMELINE: BOB FOSSE

**1927** Born Robert Louis Fosse on 23 JUNE in Chicago, USA, the son of a vaudeville entertainer

**1940** Begins performing on stage at the age of 13, touring with his own dance act, *The Riff Brothers*

**1940s** Serves in the US Navy and then attends acting school

**1950** Makes his Broadway debut in *Dance Me a Song*

**1954** Gets his big break as choreographer of *The Pajama Game* and becomes the talk of the town with his staging of the song 'Steam Heat'

**1972** Directs and choreographs the film *Cabaret*, for which he wins an Oscar for Best Director. He also wins a Tony for the stage musical *Pippin* and an Emmy for the TV special *Liza with a 'Z'*, starring Liza Minnelli

**1975** Hospitalized following a heart attack during rehearsals for *Chicago*, an experience that inspires him to write *All That Jazz*

**1977–79** Writes, directs and choreographs *All That Jazz*, but denies that the central character is based on himself

**1987** Dies on 23 SEPTEMBER, aged 60, leaving $378.79 to each of 66 friends with instructions to 'go out and have dinner on me'

**1999** The musical *Fosse* opens on Broadway, New York, USA

## DID YOU KNOW?

● Fosse's *Cabaret* won eight Oscars in 1972: Best Direction (Bob Fosse), Best Actress (Liza Minnelli as Sally Bowles), Best Supporting Actor (Joel Gray as the nightclub MC), Best Cinematography (Geoffrey Unsworth), Best Art Direction (Rolf Zehetbauer & Jurgen Kiebach), Best Editing (David Bretherton), Best Sound (Robert Knudson & David Hildyard) and Best Scoring (Ralph Burns), as well as a nomination for Best Set Direction (Herbert Strabl)

# JOAN KROC

Although she is invariably described as 'the widow of Ray Kroc, founder of the McDonald's fast food chain', Joan Kroc made her own decisions and was the driving force behind the couple's philanthropy. Her last bequest, the 'Kroc of Gold', broke several records for charitable donations.

**TIMELINE: JOAN AND RAY KROC**

**1902** Ray is born on 5 OCTOBER in Chicago, Illinois, USA

**1928** Joan is born Joan Beverly Mansfield in St Paul, Minnesota, the daughter of a railway worker

**1954** Ray Kroc (USA) makes his first visit to the McDonald brothers' Self-Service Restaurant, San Bernadino

**1957** Joan meets Ray when he eats in the restaurant where she is playing piano

**1969** Ray marries Joan, who is 25 years his junior

**1984** Ray dies, aged 82, on 14 JANUARY in San Diego, USA

**2003** Joan dies of brain cancer on 12 OCTOBER in San Diego

**2004** JANUARY: Joan's record-breaking last bequests are announced. These include: $1.5 billion to the Salvation Army, the largest donation it has ever received; $200 million to National Public Radio; $60 million to Ronald McDonald House Charities; and $50 million each to the universities of San Diego and Notre Dame, the largest donations ever received by either university

**Opposite top** Exhibit at the McDonald's museum in Des Plaines, Illinois, USA, where Ray Kroc opened the first McDonald's franchise (14 July 2000)

**Opposite bottom** During the celebrations for Ray's forthcoming 80th birthday, Ray and Joan Kroc are greeted by the mascot of the San Diego Padres, the baseball team owned by Ray (2 October 1982)

Joan Mansfield (USA) was the daughter of a railway worker who, though often out of work during the Depression, was determined that his daughter should be able to take piano lessons. The piano was to be Joan's pathway to another strata of society – in 1957, when she was 29, Joan was playing piano in a restaurant in her home town of St Paul, Minnesota, when one of the businessmen eating there caught her eye. He was Ray Kroc (USA), who had recently signed a deal with Richard and Maurice McDonald (both USA) to franchise McDonald's restaurants nationwide.

Ray and Joan married in 1969 and remained happily married until Ray, 25 years her senior, died in 1984. Over the next two decades Joan gave millions of dollars to charity and, after her death, the *Washington Post* newspaper (USA) reported: 'Though Ray Kroc had been committed to philanthropy, opening the Kroc Foundation in Chicago to support medical research, his wife took giving even more seriously.'

Joan's last bequests took many people by surprise, including the recipients, and broke a number of records. Very few people have donated a billion dollars to charity, but $1.5 billion, fully three-quarters of her $2 billion fortune, went to the Salvation Army with the stipulation that half the money be used to build from 30 to 50 recreational and educational facilities across America and the other half be invested in an endowment to subsidize the operating costs of the new facilities. She also gave a further $390 million to at least six other charities, the biggest single bequest among these being $200 million to National Public Radio. This gift, which amounted to almost twice NPR's annual operating budget, was described in an NPR press release as 'the largest monetary gift ever received by an American cultural institution'.

**DID YOU KNOW?**

● Ray Kroc was a milk-shake mixer salesman when he first met the McDonald brothers. Kroc was selling a unit capable of mixing five shakes at a time, and he could not understand why the McDonald brothers needed eight of them. In his autobiography he wrote of his feelings when he visited their restaurant and saw their so-called Speedee Service System, which was the beginning of the fast food phenomenon: 'I felt like some latter-day Newton who'd just had an Idaho potato caromed off his skull' – Kroc may not have defined the laws of gravity, but at that moment he had a vision of what McDonald's could and did become

# LAST BUT NOT LEAST...

## Lauren Bacall's Last Gift to Humphrey Bogart

The last film of Humphrey Bogart (USA) was *The Harder They Fall*, released in March 1956, less than a year before he died of throat cancer on 14 January 1957. At his funeral, his fourth and last wife, Lauren Bacall (USA, b. Betty Perske), placed in his coffin her last gift to him – a small gold whistle, inscribed: 'If you want anything, just whistle'. The significance of the whistle was not lost on film fans who remembered her line to Bogart in the film *To Have and Have Not*, in which they starred together in 1944, the year before they married.

**Right** Lauren Bacall and Humphrey Bogart in 1955

## James W. Rodgers' Last Request

Before facing the firing squad in 1960, convicted criminal James W. Rodgers (USA) was asked if he had a last request. His reply: 'Why yes – a bulletproof vest.'

## Henry Lucas' Last Bequest

Henry Lucas (England) was a 17th-century mathematician and MP for Cambridge University. When he died in December 1663 his last will and testament included the bequest of land to the university, intended to generate an income of £100 a year to endow a 'Professorship of Mathematick' that became known as the Lucasian Professorship, a post ratified by King Charles II in 1664. Since then, Lucasian professors have included Sir Isaac Newton (England), who established the nature of light and described the laws of gravity; Charles Babbage (England), the 'grandfather of the computer'; and Stephen Hawking (England), probably the world's most famous theoretical physicist.

## Georges Clemenceau's Last Request

Georges Clemenceau (France) was twice elected prime minister of France, and it was he who led France to its part in the Allied victory in the First World War. He was president of the Paris Peace Conference, and his fear that the terms of the Treaty of Versailles were not strong enough to prevent another German attack on France, which proved true in 1939, was reflected in his last request: 'I wish to be buried standing facing Germany.'

**Right** Georges Clemenceau in 1924

## Agatha Christie's Last Bequest

Dame Agatha Christie (England) died on 12 January 1976, three years after writing her last novel, *Postern of Fate*, and shortly after the release of her last novel to be published in her lifetime, the appropriately named *Curtain*. Christie had written *Curtain* c.1943 and stored the manuscript in a bank vault intending to have it published posthumously, it being the last case to be tackled by her creation, Belgian detective Hercule Poirot. (When *Curtain* was published in the USA, the

*New York Times* published Poirot's obituary on its front page.) But Christie still had one posthumous surprise for her readers. At about the same time as she wrote *Curtain*, during the Second World War, she had written and deposited for safekeeping the last case of another of her detectives, Miss Marple. *Sleeping Murder* (as in 'let sleeping murder lie'), the last of her novels to be published, was released after her death as her last bequest to her millions of faithful fans.

## John Nicholson's Last Bequest

Stationer John Nicholson (England) was extremely proud of his family name and left most of his estate for the benefit of various poor people named Nicholson. Part of his last bequest was £100 a year to be divided between poor boys or girls who wanted to learn a trade – if they were named Nicholson. Another £100 a year was to fund the weddings of impoverished couples who could not afford to marry – but only if both their names were Nicholson. Nicholson appointed five executors of his will. Their names: Nicholson, Nicholson, Nicholson, Nicholson and Nicholson.

## Vivien Leigh's Last Bequest and Request

Actress Vivien Leigh (Britain, b. India) died on 7 July 1967 at the age of 53. Her last will and testament was long, detailed and well organized, with bequests of money, paintings and possessions for her family, friends and servants, something that one family friend said 'demonstrated both her love for people and her awareness of their personal interests and needs'. She also bequeathed her eyes to be used for corneal grafting, but this bequest could not be accepted because of her medical history. Her last request was that she be cremated rather than buried, which was a huge blow to her mother, Gertrude, as it signalled Vivien's final rejection of Gertrude's Roman Catholic faith.

# Chapter Six

# Last Past
# the Post

There is a great deal of uncertainty as to the identity of Aesop and the authorship of the fables that are attributed to him. But regardless of who wrote them, Aesop's Fables are known throughout the world and one of the most popular is *The Hare and the Tortoise*.

**Last Past the Post**

# AESOP'S HARE

**6th century BC** According to tradition, Aesop (Greece, sometimes Esop) lives as a slave in Samos, Greece. Various fables are attributed to him, although their exact source is uncertain

**1st century AD** Aesop's Fables are translated, adapted and popularized by the Roman poet Phaedrus (b. Macedonia), who also writes many fables of his own

**2nd century** Babrius (Greece, b. Italy) collects a number of Aesop's Fables in a verse edition used in European medieval schools

**14th century** A Byzantine monk named Maximus Planudes writes a life of Aesop, which, though written nearly 2,000 years after Aesop's death, appears to be the source of a story, often related as fact, that Aesop was 'ugly and misshapen'

**1513** Desiderus Erasmus (Netherlands) publishes a Latin edition of Aesop's Fables

**1668–93** Aesop's Fables serve as the model for verse fables written by Jean de la Fontaine (France)

**1824–29** and **1853** Walter Savage Landor (England) writes *Imaginary Conversations* and *Imaginary Conversations of the Greeks and Romans*, which include two imaginary conversations between Aesop and his fellow slave Rhodope

Nothing is known for certain about the semi-legendary writer Aesop (Greece), but the historian Herodotus (Greece), writing some 100 years later, states that Aesop lived in the mid-6th century BC. Herodotus suggests that Aesop was probably the slave of a man named Iadmon who lived on the island of Samos, Greece, and that he was probably killed by the people of Delphi. Whoever Aesop was, his name became so closely connected with fables as a form of storytelling that any new fables, even those written long after his death, were attributed to him, and consequently many of the stories now known as Aesop's Fables were not, in fact, composed by him.

Fable literally means 'story' (from the Latin *fabula*), but since the time of Aesop the word has been used to refer to a particular type of story, usually involving animals that act and speak with human motives and emotions. All fables have a lesson or moral, either implicit in the narrative or, in later times, appended to the main story.

One of the most popular fables is that of the tortoise and the hare, in which the hare brags about how fast he is and how easily he could win a race against the ponderous tortoise. The tortoise accepts the challenge and begins plodding towards the finish line, but the hare is so confident of his speed that he lies down for a rest. The tortoise slowly passes the sleeping hare and wins the race. And the moral of the story is that dedication and perseverance are even more important than natural ability alone.

**Left** *Aesop* painted by Velazquez between 1639 and 1640
**Opposite** *The Hare and the Tortoise*, illustration by Charles H. Bennett for an 1857 edition of *Aesop's Fables*

**DID YOU KNOW?**

● About 13 years before publishing a Latin edition of Aesop's Fables, the humanist and scholar Desiderus Erasmus coined a memorable phrase that is still in use five centuries later: *in regione caecorum rex est luscus* – 'in the land of the blind the one-eyed man is king'

**Last Past the Post**

There are more ways of coming last than being last past the post – another is to finish first, but then be disqualified. Three memorable Olympic disqualifications were those of Fred Lorz at St Louis in 1904, Dorando Pietri at the London Games in 1908 and Ben Johnson at Seoul in 1988.

# MANY THAT ARE FIRST SHALL BE LAST

**Below** Dorando Pietri is helped across the finishing line of the Marathon at the 1908 London Olympics. He is later disqualified for receiving 'external support'

**Opposite** Competitors line up for the start of the Marathon at the 1904 St Louis Olympics, with eventual gold medallist Thomas Hicks on the left wearing 20, and first-placed Fred Lorz, who was disqualified, next to Hicks wearing 31

## Dorando Pietri

Often misquoted, the Gospel of St Matthew, chapter 19 verse 30, says: 'But many that are first shall be last; and the last shall be first.' At the London Olympics in 1908 the first half of this warning proved true for marathon runner Dorando Pietri (Italy), who staggered across the finish line in first place only to be disqualified on a technicality. However, the manner in which he lost brought him at least as much acclaim as if he had won.

Arriving at the stadium way ahead of the other competitors, Pietri had only to complete one lap of the track to win, but he was so exhausted that, according to *The New York Times*: '[He] staggered along the cinder path like a man in a dream, his gait being neither a walk nor a run but simply a flounder.' Some 300 yards from the finish his legs buckled and he fell to the track. *The*

**DID YOU KNOW?**

● Thomas Hicks, who was awarded the gold medal for the 1904 Olympic marathon after the disqualification of Fred Lorz, won the race fuelled by a mixture of brandy and strychnine that his trainers had been feeding him as a stimulant. At the time, the use of stimulants was common practice and perfectly acceptable according to the rules

● The marathon course for the 1908 Olympics was to have been exactly 26 miles, from Windsor Castle to the royal box at the new White City stadium. However, at the request of Princess Mary, the course was extended by 385 yards so that the race would begin under the nursery window at the Castle. Those extra 385 yards made a huge difference to the outcome, because Dorando Pietri fell within 300 yards of the finish. In 1924 this strange distance was officially accepted as the standard length for marathon races

*Times* reported: 'It seemed inhuman to leave Dorando to struggle on unaided and inhuman to urge him to continue.' Pietri struggled to his feet, but fell several more times before finally stumbling across the line, held upright by a race official and still almost a minute ahead of second-placed Johnny Hayes (USA).

Pietri's determination won the hearts of the world – except for the American team, which contested the result. Pietri was disqualified for using 'external support' and the gold medal went to Hayes, but public support for Pietri was such that the following afternoon, in recognition of his heroic effort, Britain's Queen Alexandra presented him with a special gold cup that she had donated at her own expense.

## Fred Lorz

One of the reasons that the American team was so quick to protest against Pietri's gold medal may have been that at the previous Olympics, in St Louis, USA, the American 'winner', Fred Lorz, had been disqualified. However, in the case of Lorz the situation was more clear cut. He had been leading the field in the marathon when the runners left the stadium, and he was also the first man back, looking very fresh despite the 90 degree heat. The energy he displayed in his victory celebration raised suspicions and it was soon

**TIMELINE: OLYMPIC DISQUALIFICATIONS**

**1904** St Louis, USA. Fred Lorz (USA) crosses the line first in the marathon, but is disqualified for hitching a lift

**1908** London, England. Dorando Pietri (Italy) crosses the line first in the marathon, but is disqualified for using 'external support'

**1912** Stockholm, Sweden. Native American Jim Thorpe wins the pentathlon and decathlon and comes fourth in the high jump and seventh in the long jump. When presenting Thorpe with his medals, King Gustav V (Sweden) calls him 'the greatest athlete in the world', but six months later an American journalist reveals that Thorpe once played minor league baseball for money, which technically makes him a professional. Thorpe is controversially disqualified and stripped of his medals and titles, which many suspect is more for racial reasons

*continued...*

...continued

discovered that he had collapsed with cramp during the race and then taken a lift by car back to the stadium. Lorz was disqualified and banned for life (although the ban was lifted after only a year), and the gold medal went to second-placed Thomas Hicks (England–USA).

# Ben Johnson

Numerous records were broken during the 1988 Olympics in Seoul, Korea, including one that most Olympians would rather forget – a record 10 athletes were disqualified for drug offences. The highest profile of these was Ben

than sporting ones. In OCTOBER 1982 Thorpe is posthumously pardoned by the International Olympic Committee, his titles restored and his medals presented to his family

**1968** Grenoble, France (Winter Games). Skier Karl Schranz (Austria) is allowed a second run at the slalom after stopping during his first run, claiming that he was impeded in the fog by a man dressed in black. He wins the gold medal with his second run, but is disqualified when judges notice that he had missed two gates during the first run before the alleged incident; the judges rule that the missed gates, rather than a mystery figure, were the reason for his pulling up

**1988** Seoul, Korea. Ben Johnson (Jamaica–Canada) crosses the line first in the 100 metres, but is disqualified for using a banned substance

**1992** Barcelona, Spain. Khalid Skah (Morocco) crosses the line first in the 10,000 metres, but is disqualified because a fellow Moroccan, who had been lapped, interfered with race leader Richard Chelimo (Kenya), allowing Skah to pass Chelimo. Skah's victory is later reinstated when the committee decides that Skah had not colluded with his countryman in blocking Chelimo

**1996** Atlanta, USA. Reigning Olympic champion Linford Christie (Britain) is unable to defend his title when he is disqualified from the 100 metres final for causing two false starts. He says: 'I lost my Olympic title, but I can't say I was beaten because I wasn't even in the race. The crowd knew they'd been robbed of a race that would have been much better if I'd been in it'

Johnson (Jamaica–Canada), who appeared to have won the blue riband event of athletics, the 100 metres, in an unbelievable 9.79 seconds. Sadly, 'unbelievable' was indeed the case, literally as well as metaphorically – Johnson tested positive for the banned steroid Stanazolol and the gold medal was awarded instead to Carl Lewis (USA).

Johnson, who denied any wrongdoing, said: 'They can take away my medal, but they can't take away my speed.' However, his protestations of innocence rang hollow five years later when he was banned for life after failing another drugs test.

**Opposite** Jim Thorpe (centre), a double gold medallist at the 1912 Stockholm Olympics who was disqualified for 'professionalism', but posthumously pardoned 70 years later (*see: Timeline 1912.* Photo: 8 June 1932)
**Below** Ben Johnson leads the field in the 100 metres at the 1988 Seoul Olympics. He was later disqualified for using a banned substance (24 September 1988)

Often, the real heroes of the marathon are not those who cross the line first, but those who battle it out to cross the line at all. In 2002 Lloyd Scott came last in the London Marathon in the slowest time to that date, and the following year Michael Watson recorded an even slower time.

**Last Past the Post**

# MARATHON MEN

| 1961 Born in Stepney, London, England | 1978 Signs as an apprentice professional footballer with Leyton Orient Football Club, London | 1980 Named Leyton Orient's Young Player of the Year | 1985 Joins the London Fire Brigade | 1987 Receives a commendation for rescuing two boys from a fire. Diagnosed with chronic myeloid leukaemia | 1989 Undergoes a life-saving bone marrow transplant | 2000 Undergoes surgery to replace his right hip | 2002 Completes the London Marathon in a 59kg diving suit, finishing last in the slowest time recorded to that date |

▌TIMELINE: LLOYD SCOTT

## Lloyd Scott

When former footballer and fireman Lloyd Scott (England) was diagnosed with chronic myeloid leukaemia in 1987 while undergoing routine tests for smoke inhalation after rescuing two young boys from a house fire, he was given just a 10% chance of survival. Two years later, just three weeks before the bone marrow transplant that would save his life, he ran the London Marathon. The following year he ran it again, both to raise money for charity and to give hope and inspiration to other cancer and leukaemia sufferers.

Then in 2002, two years after undergoing a hip replacement, he achieved something that eclipsed even his earlier marathon triumphs – raising £100,000 for charity by 'running' the London marathon in a deep-sea diving suit, which, at 59kg, was so heavy that he had to stop every 400 metres to regain his breath. Not surprisingly, he finished in last place in the slowest time recorded to that date: 5 days, 8 hours, 29 minutes and 46 seconds. As he crossed the line he was presented with his medal by Paula Radcliffe (England), who had won the women's marathon five days earlier. Never has last place been such a triumph, and as if that wasn't enough, just six months later he repeated his feat on the other side of the Atlantic in the New York Marathon.

## Michael Watson

A year after Lloyd Scott's celebrated effort, ex-boxer Michael Watson (England) recorded another heroic London Marathon-last in an even slower time: 6 days, 2 hours, 26 minutes and 18 seconds. Watson is still partially paralysed from injuries sustained in 1991 during a boxing match against Chris Eubank (England), after which he was told he would never walk again. It was a battle for him to complete 2.5 miles each morning and afternoon of his six-day effort, and he said afterwards: 'In participating in the marathon – a gruelling physical challenge for even the most able-bodied – I completed my greatest ever sporting feat.'

**Opposite** Lloyd Scott rests on the 59th Street Bridge during the New York City Marathon (6 November 2002)
**Right** Michael Watson (left) and Chris Eubank after Watson's feat of completing the London Marathon (19 April 2003)

**DID YOU KNOW?**

● As well as completing the London and New York marathons in his diving suit, since being diagnosed with chronic myeloid leukaemia Lloyd Scott has also completed the Snowdonia Marathon, the Everest Marathon, the Marathon des Sables (a 145-mile stage race through the Sahara Desert) and an underwater marathon in Loch Ness, as well as making expeditions to the North and South Poles. In December 2004 he completed a 50-day cycle ride from Perth to Sydney on a Penny Farthing bicycle, dressed in a Sherlock Holmes costume. So far he has raised more than £3 million for the charity CLIC – Cancer & Leukaemia in Childhood

● In completing the London Marathon, Michael Watson raised some £250,000 for the Brain and Spine Foundation, a charity founded by Peter Hamlyn, the neurosurgeon whose operations saved Watson's life

---

**TIMELINE: MICHAEL WATSON**

**1965** Born on 15 MARCH in London, England

**1991** Collapses at the end of a fight against Chris Eubank (England) on 21 SEPTEMBER for the vacant super-middleweight title. Undergoes six brain operations and remains in a coma for 40 days

**2003** Still partially paralysed, Watson walks the London Marathon, coming last in the slowest time to date. For the last mile, Chris Eubank walks alongside him. Eubank describes Watson's effort as: 'A miraculous feat of human endeavour'

**2004** Awarded the MBE in the New Year's Honours list in recognition of his achievement in completing the marathon

Jamaica's bobsleigh team burst onto the scene at the 1988 Winter Olympics with a spectacular last place that caught the imagination of the world. The nation's bobsleighers have since proved a force to be reckoned with, but Jamaica is still fondly remembered for that famous last place.

# JAMAICAN BOBSLEIGH TEAM

As a nation that has never experienced snow or ice, people on the Caribbean island of Jamaica did not have a longstanding tradition of winter sports when the country entered a bobsleigh team for the 1988 Winter Olympics in Calgary, Canada. At the opening ceremony the Mayor of Calgary, Ralph Klein (Canada), announced: 'The Olympics should be the best big party any of us has ever been to. If not, we may have missed the point.' Many people thought that the Jamaicans had only turned up for Klein's party, but in fact they took their sport very seriously and had trained hard for the event.

Lack of a winter sports tradition did not necessarily rule out the Jamaicans. The island does have a proud sprint tradition, and powerful sprinting is vital for the all-important push start – a fraction of a second saved during the 50-metre sprint and the leap onto the sleigh can result in a saving of three times that amount by the bottom of the run. In the end it was inexperience, rather than lack of athleticism or commitment, that defeated the Jamaican team as they spectacularly crashed their bobsleigh to record a memorable last place.

Had the Jamaicans finished second from last it would probably have passed without notice, but last place highlighted the unlikely scenario and caught the imagination of the world – including inspiring the Disney Corporation (USA) to make the comedy feature film, *Cool Runnings* (1993), which was loosely based on the team's story. But novelty value and last place was not enough for the Jamaicans, who now had a taste for the bobsleigh run, and in the 1994 Winter Olympics, in Lillehammer, Norway, they managed a creditable 14th place, ahead of such well-respected bobsleighing nations as France, Russia, Italy and the USA.

TIMELINE: JAMAICAN BOBSLEIGH TEAM

**1988** Calgary, Canada. Jamaica's first ever bobsleigh team crashes into last place in the four-man event

**1992** Albertville, France. Jamaica finishes in 34th place in the four-man event

**1994** Lillehammer, Norway. Jamaica finishes in 14th place in the four-man event

**1998** Nagano, Japan. Jamaica finishes 21st out of 32 in the four-man event and 29th out of 36 in the two-man event

**2002** Salt Lake City, USA. Jamaica finishes 28th out of 38 in the two-man event and does not compete in the four-man event

**Below** The Jamaican bobsleigh team at the opening ceremony of the 1994 Winter Olympics in Lillehammer, Norway (11 February 1994)

**Above right** A still from the 1993 film *Cool Runnings*, loosely based on the Jamaican bobsleigh team's debut at the 1988 Winter Olympics in Calgary, Canada

### DID YOU KNOW?

● Another unlikely entry at the Calgary Games of 1988 was a two-man bobsleigh team from Monaco, comprising His Serene Highness Prince Albert of Monaco and a croupier from one of the principality's famous casinos

● William 'Billy' Fiske, the American pilot who joined Britain's Royal Air Force during the Second World War and whose story was controversially fictionalized in 2004 for the film *The Few* (in which Fiske is played by Tom Cruise), was a member of the 1932 American four-man bobsleigh team

Had Derek Redmond won the semi-final of the 400 metres at the Barcelona Olympics he could hardly have been more famous than he was for finishing last – or, in fact, for finishing at all. After the Olympics he received more than 3,000 letters praising his courage and determination.

# DEREK REDMOND

**Above** Derek Redmond sits on the track in agony after injuring his hamstring in the semi-final of the 400 metres at the 1992 Barcelona Olympics
**Opposite** Jim Redmond helps his son Derek to complete his last competitive race (1992)

At the Barcelona Olympics in 1992 Derek Redmond (England) had something to prove – four years earlier he had been forced to withdraw from his 400-metre event at the Seoul Olympics because of problems with his Achilles tendon, and now, in Spain, he had the chance to show off his true talent. He had made it through to the semi-final and his fans were confident that he would take his place in the final.

Sadly, it was not to be. Almost a decade later, Redmond recalled what happened in what proved to be his last competitive race: 'I came out nice and low, like a plane taking off, and by the time I was upright I'd run 70 metres and I thought, "Blimey, I've only just got upright and I'm already here"… And all of a sudden I heard a clap in the crowd. Then, about three strides later, someone shot me in the back of the leg, or so I thought, and it turned out that clap was my hamstring popping … I remember thinking: "I ain't going out on a stretcher, not out of this stadium." I wasn't daft, I knew the race was over, but I said: "I've got to finish this race. I have to do this."'

Redmond could hardly walk, let alone run, but he was determined to complete the race. Officials tried to usher him from the track, but he pushed them away. His father, Jim, jumped over a barrier and ran to help him, half-carrying Derek for the last 100 metres and over the line in a human drama that far outweighed the result of the event. The official records say that Redmond abandoned the race, but he knows that while he may have been last he did achieve the goal he had set himself: 'I've got to finish this race. I have to do this.'

## DID YOU KNOW?

● Redmond's father later said of helping Derek across the line: 'For once you didn't have two people competing. You had two people joining together. And at that particular moment the world was seeing what the Olympics was all about'

**TIMELINE: 400 METRES' LASTS**

**1906** Athens, Greece. In the first and last of the so-called Interim or Intercalated Games, which are intended to be held in Greece in the interim between the official Olympiads, Paul Pilgrim (USA) is the last athlete to win the men's 400 metres in a time of more than 50 seconds

**1908** London, England. Wyndham Halswelle (Britain) wins the men's 400 metres in a rerun of the final, which is the first walkover in Olympic history and the last to date. Halswelle and three Americans ran in the first final, but the Americans were accused of impeding Halswelle and a rerun was ordered. The Americans refused to compete in the rerun and Halswelle crossed the line unopposed to win gold in a time of 50.0 seconds

**1972** Munich, Germany. Monika Zehrt (Germany) is the last athlete to win the women's 400 metres in a time of more than 50 seconds

**1980** Moscow, USSR. For the last time, Olympic athletic events are also the official world championships. In 1983 the International Amateur Athletics Federation inaugurates the first IAAF World Championships and from then on the two events are entirely separate. The last athletes to hold the joint title for the 400 metres are Viktor Markin (USSR, now Russian Federation) in the men's and Marita Koch (East Germany, now Germany) in the women's

**1992** Barcelona, Spain. Derek Redmond runs his last competitive race, the semi-final of the men's 400 metres

At the 1988 Winter Olympics in Calgary, Canada, Eddie Edwards, better known as Eddie the Eagle, made an art form out of coming last. Scorned by some for devaluing the Games, praised by others for having the courage to enter, he was given a paparazzi welcome when he returned home.

# EDDIE THE EAGLE

**TIMELINE: SKI-JUMPING**

**1866** Ski-jumping originates in Norway after Sondre Norheim (Norway) invents a heel-binding that makes jumping possible. The 'telemark position' used in ski jumping and the 'telemark turn' in skiing are both named after the home county of their originator, Norheim

**1924** The Winter Olympic Games are inaugurated, at Chamonix, France, with a 70-metre ski jump as one of the events

**1964** A second ski-jumping event, the 90-metre 'large hill', is introduced to the Winter Olympics

**1988** At the Calgary Winter Olympics in Canada Jan Boklev (Sweden) introduces the now-standard 'V' style for greater lift; previously the skis have been held parallel. Boklev's innovation is at first frowned upon, and is penalized by the judges. Eddie the Eagle comes last in both ski-jumping events

**1992** The height of the 'normal hill' is increased from 70 metres to 90 metres and the height of the 'large hill' from 90 metres to 120 metres

**DID YOU KNOW?**

● The Olympic flame at the Calgary Games of 1988 was the highest in Olympic history, burning throughout the Games at the top of the 191-metre tall Calgary Tower

To anyone who has ever watched ski-jumping it is obvious that it is not a sport for the faint-hearted. However, contrary to popular belief, neither is it simply a question of having the courage to stand at the top of a steep hill and let the skis do the rest. Jumpers must have at least a basic understanding of aerodynamics in order literally to fly through the air at up to 60mph, using their bodies and skis to create lift. They must also have the strength to adopt and hold the correct positions: ski tips rising on takeoff; body leaning forward and arms back during flight; adopting the 'telemark position' to absorb the shock on landing; and, of course, stopping successfully.

Taking all this into account, Michael 'Eddie' Edwards (England) was clearly not the idiot that many people made him out to be, although he did reinforce that image by playing the clown for the media. Edwards made his way into the Olympic record books for ski-jumping the shortest distances ever recorded in either of the two events he entered. He was placed 58th out of 58 in the 70-metre jump and 55th out of 55 in the 90-metre jump, although, since he was the first ever British competitor in the event, his distance of 71 metres (more than 20 metres shorter than everyone else in the competition) automatically became the British record.

By coming last in such spectacular fashion, Edwards became a cult hero, even recording a single after his return home, but many people were annoyed that he had stolen the limelight from the more accomplished competitors.

Edwards' answer to them: 'I know I'm just Eddie Edwards the plasterer, and sport is so professional now. But haven't I brought something back to Olympic sport? Like, what did they used to call it? Ah, yes. Taking part.'

**Left** Eddie 'the Eagle' Edwards gives a thumbs-up for the camera at the 1988 Winter Olympics in Calgary, Canada
**Opposite** Soaring like an eagle – Eddie Edwards in action in the 70-metre ski-jump

Like Eddie the Eagle before him, Eric the Eel achieved world fame in an event to which he was totally unsuited. In the process, he earned a place in *Guinness World Records*, won the hearts of sports fans around the globe and inspired the newspaper headline: 'Hail the conquering loser.'

**Last Past the Post** ERIC THE EEL

'Eric the Eel Makes a Big Splash. Many have been faster, higher and stronger but few will leave their mark on this or any other Olympics like the Central African thrashing solo in the Sydney water.' With these words *The Australian* newspaper summed up the heroic efforts of Eric Moussambani (Equatorial Guinea) in the heats of the men's 100-metres freestyle, which truly embodied the Olympic creed: 'The most important thing in the Olympic Games is not to win but to take part, just as the most important thing in life is not the triumph but the struggle. The essential thing is not to have conquered but to have fought well.'

Moussambani certainly fought well, although rather than fighting for a result he did seem to be fighting against the water itself. He had learned to swim just nine months earlier, in January 2000, and had never even seen an Olympic-size swimming pool before going to the Sydney Games in September that year. After his historic heat he told journalists: 'I didn't want to swim 100 metres, but my coach told me I should. I thought it was too much.'

Despite his pessimism, Eric even managed to 'win' his heat – because the

**1896** Athens, Greece. Swimming is one of the inaugural sports at the first modern Olympic Games. The swimming events are held in the sea in the Bay of Zea near Piraeus

**1900** Paris, France. The 200-metres obstacle race, won by Frederick Lane (Australia), and Underwater Swimming, won by Charles de Vendeville (France), are contested at the Olympics for the first and last time

**1904** St Louis, USA. Emil Rausch (Germany) is the last swimmer to win an Olympic freestyle swimming event using sidestroke, in the 1,500 metres, which he wins by more than one minute

**1908** London, England. The first Olympic swimming competition to be held in a pool takes place in a tank built alongside the running track at White City Stadium, London

only two other competitors were both disqualified for false starts. He had the pool to himself and completed his 100 metres in 1 minute 52.72 seconds: the slowest time ever recorded for the Olympic 100-metres freestyle and more than seven seconds slower than the winning time for the *200* metres. Eric was placed last in the event and did not progress to the finals because his time was outside the qualifying time for the competition, but he was delighted with the attention, saying: 'Before nobody knew me and now everyone does, so this is good for me and my people.'

**Opposite** Eric 'the Eel' Moussambani in action (19 September 2000)

**Below** Eric the Eel gets the full attention of the TV camera as he completes his heat of the men's 100 metres freestyle at the Sydney 2000 Olympics in first and last place, with the slowest time ever recorded (19 September 2000)

**1912** Stockholm, Sweden. Women's swimming is introduced to the Olympics

**1924** Paris, France. The first Olympic swimming competition to be held in a (now standard) 50-metre pool

**1948** London, England. The first Olympic swimming competition to be held in an indoor pool

**1980** Moscow, USSR. Jörg Woithe (Germany) is the last swimmer to win the men's 100-metres freestyle in a time of more than 50 seconds

**2000** Sydney, Australia. Eric Moussambani comes first and last in his heat for the 100-metres freestyle, in the slowest time ever recorded for the event

# LAST BUT NOT LEAST...

**Left** The Roman emperor Nero, by Antonius (1596)

## Nero's Olympic Chariot Race

Not satisfied with occupying the most powerful political position in the world, Roman emperor Nero also sought to distinguish himself as a poet, philosopher, actor, musician and charioteer. There is evidence that he had some talent as a poet, and he regularly staged musical and theatrical contests in which he himself competed. He also took part in the ancient Olympics in 67AD as a charioteer, although 'competed' is hardly an apt term for his participation. Not surprisingly, noone dared to race against the violent, tyrannical emperor and so he was the only entrant. He was drunk when he arrived for the 'race' and was crowned Olympic champion charioteer despite not managing to pass the post in first, last or any other position – he crashed his chariot and failed to finish. *See also: The Olympics, page 15*

## Dastardly and Muttley

Dick Dastardly and his sniggering hound Muttley were two of the most popular characters in the 1960s Hanna-Barbera cartoon *The Wacky Races*. The 'way out wacky racers', including such memorable characters as Peter Perfect, Penelope Pitstop and the Gruesome Twosome in their *Creepy Coupé*, battled it out over all sorts of unlikely terrain to win each race, most of them employing wacky gadgets and gizmos or equally wacky driving skills. But not Dastardly and Muttley, who resorted to scheming and cheating in their effort to win. However, not only did they never win, but they were always last past the post in the rocket-powered *Mean Machine*, usually after falling victim to their own dirty deeds. Dastardly's reaction to finishing last was always the same: 'Drat and double drat!'

## Mary Decker Slaney

In 1972 Mary Decker Slaney (USA) became America's youngest international runner at the age of just 14. By 1983 she was at her peak and at the 1984 Olympic Games in Los Angeles, USA, she was America's 'golden girl' and favourite for the 3,000 metres. With three laps to go, Decker was lying second behind controversial entrant Zola Budd (South Africa–Britain), who had provoked outrage before the Games when her application for British citizenship appeared to be fast-tracked to enable her to compete for Britain in the days when South Africa was banned from the Games due to its apartheid regime.

Decker made her move to pass Budd, but caught Budd's heel and fell at the side of the track, her dream of Olympic gold at an end, while Budd managed to keep her balance and finish the race. Decker claimed that Budd had deliberately tripped her (a difficult thing to do when the person you are allegedly tripping is behind you), but the endless television replays showed no evidence that this was the case. It was almost certainly an unfortunate accident, as a result of which both women lost their chances of a medal, Budd finishing a disappointing seventh and Decker being placed last, having failed to complete the race.

## The Eurovision Song Contest

Eurovision was launched on 6 June 1954 when television stations in Belgium, Britain, Denmark, France, Germany, Italy, the Netherlands and Switzerland were linked for a simultaneous broadcast of the Festival of Flowers from Montreux, Switzerland. The first Eurovision Song Contest took place two years later in Lugano, Switzerland, and the winner was – Switzerland. As in any competition, someone has to come last, but no country has come last in this contest more memorably than Norway in 1978 when the judges famously announced: 'Norway – nul points.'

From 1962 to 1970 no less than 20 songs had scored nul points, but the voting system was changed in 1975 with judges from all countries voting for all songs, making it much harder to score 'nul'. Despite the extra difficulty, Jahn Teigen (Norway) managed it three years later with the song *Mil Etter Mil* ('Mile After Mile'), not only singing a bad song badly, but adding to the embarrassment by twanging his braces throughout his performance. The last nation to date to score nul is Britain in 2003, with *Cry Baby* by Jemini.

**Above** Nul points – British pop duo Jemini performing 'Cry Baby' in the dress rehearsal for the Eurovision Song Contest in Latvia (23 May 2003)

# Chapter Seven

# Last Journeys

Ferdinand Magellan is famous for leading the first expedition to prove that Earth is spherical by sailing right around it, but he did not survive the journey, which thus proved to be his last. Juan Sebastian del Cano completed the epic voyage in Magellan's ship *Vittoria*.

## The Last Voyage of FERDINAND MAGELLAN

**TIMELINE: FERDINAND MAGELLAN**

**c.1480** Born near Villa de Sabrosa, Tras os Montes, Portugal, and later serves as a page in the court of John II (Portugal)

**1505** Enlists for a Portuguese voyage to India

**1509** Enlists for a Portuguese voyage to the Spice Islands (now known as the Maluku, or Moluccas)

**1512** Raised to the nobility with the rank of *fidalgo escudeiro*

**1513** Made lame in an attack on Azamur, Morocco, but accused of trading with the enemy

**1517** After four years of disfavour following the 1513 accusations, Magellan renounces his Portuguese nationality and approaches King Charles I of Spain with a scheme to find a westward passage to the Spice Islands

**1519** Departs Seville, Spain, on 20 SEPTEMBER

**1520** Discovers and names the Strait of Magellan. Names the Pacific Ocean

**1521** Reaches the Philippines where he is killed in a battle between rival Filipino groups on 27 APRIL

**1522** Juan Sebastian del Cano (Spain) arrives back in Seville on 6 SEPTEMBER, becoming the first captain to circumnavigate the globe

Royal courtier Ferdinand Magellan (Portugal) enlisted for his first major sea voyage, to India, at the age of 25. He quickly made a name for himself, rising through both the social and the maritime ranks, but fell out of favour with the Portuguese court in 1513 after being accused of trading with the enemy. Four years later he renounced his Portuguese nationality and approached King Charles I of Spain with a scheme to find a westward passage to the Spice Islands (now known as the Moluccas).

Magellan sailed in September 1519 with five ships, crossing the Atlantic and then heading south into the uncharted territory of South America. Just over a year later, on 21 October 1520, he discovered the tortuous passage now known as the Strait of Magellan. His fleet sailed for 38 days between reefs and snow-capped mountains, eventually reaching an ocean whose calm weather inspired him to name it the Pacific. He had discovered a westward passage, but it was to be another 98 days before the ships reached the Philippine island of Cebu, demonstrating that Earth was far bigger than anyone had thought possible.

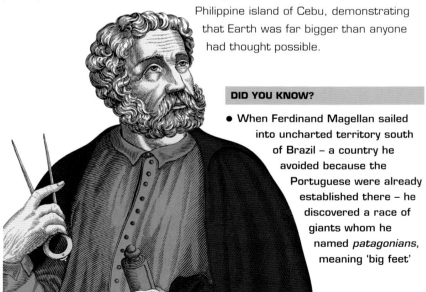

**DID YOU KNOW?**

● When Ferdinand Magellan sailed into uncharted territory south of Brazil – a country he avoided because the Portuguese were already established there – he discovered a race of giants whom he named *patagonians*, meaning 'big feet'

**Left** Undated engraving of Ferdinand Magellan

Magellan made an ill-judged alliance with the ruler of Cebu, who appeared to convert to Catholicism as proof of the strength of the alliance, but then persuaded Magellan to attack his rival on the island of Mactan under the guise of converting Mactan to Catholicism. Magellan was killed during the attack, after which his 'ally' killed several of the remaining expedition leaders. Two ships escaped, but only one made it back to Spain – not wanting to navigate the dangerous Strait of Magellan a second time, Juan Sebastian del Cano (Spain) continued the journey westwards, returning to Seville in September 1522 as the first captain to circumnavigate the globe.

**Below** A replica of Magellan's galleon *Vittoria*, built for the 1992 Seville Expo, leaves Seville for Japan, to be exhibited at the 2005 World Expo (12 October 2004)

# HORATIO NELSON

Admiral Lord Horatio Nelson had his finest and final hour against the French and Spanish fleets at the Battle of Trafalgar in 1805. The extremes of his last journey, from Trafalgar to his final resting place in St Paul's Cathedral, London, were a fitting tribute to the maverick naval hero.

**Below** *The Funeral of Lord Nelson, 1806*, by Daniel Turner
**Opposite top** HMS *Victory* during the Battle of Trafalgar, with Nelson lying on the deck, mortally wounded

'Sir, we have gained a great victory, but we have lost Lord Nelson' was how the news of Britain's triumph at the Battle of Trafalgar was delivered to the First Secretary of the British Admiralty. On 21 October 1805 Nelson (England) defeated the combined French and Spanish fleets off Cape Trafalgar, Spain, ensuring that Napoleon Bonaparte (France) would be unable to invade Britain. But during the battle, at approximately 13.15, Nelson was mortally wounded by a marksman from the French ship *Redoubtable*; he survived until 16.30 and died only after victory had been confirmed.

Debate has raged ever since about whether Nelson's last words, spoken to Admiral Hardy, were: 'Kiss me, Hardy', or 'Kismet, Hardy' (kismet meaning fate or destiny). In fact his last recorded words, on hearing news of the victory, were: 'Thank God I have done my duty.'

Nelson's final journey was as colourful as his often-controversial career had been. First he was pickled in a barrel of brandy to preserve his body on the voyage back to England. Then he was laid in state for three days in the famous Painted Hall of the Royal

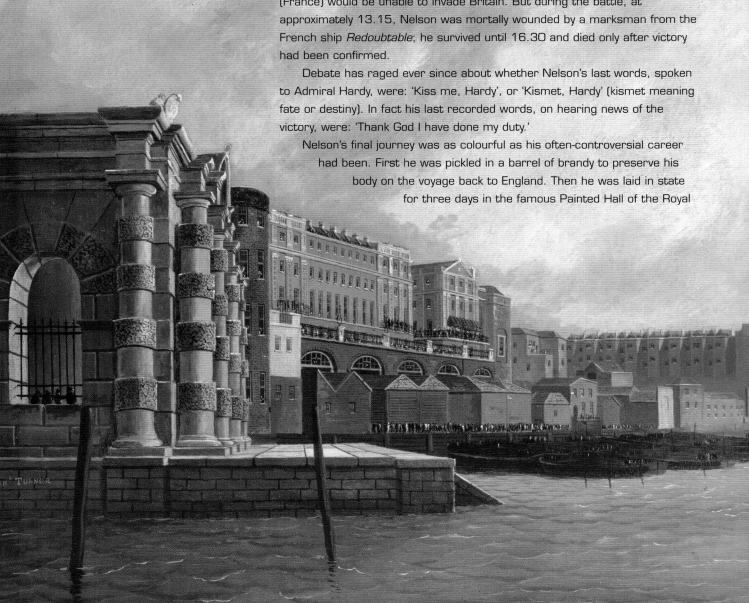

**1758** Born in Burnham Thorpe, Norfolk, England, on 29 SEPTEMBER, the third son of a rector

**1778** Given his first command, HMS *Badger*, during the American War of Independence

**1793** Takes command of HMS *Agamemnon* at the start of the Napoleonic Wars

**1794** Loses his right eye assisting the army ashore at the siege of Calvi, Corsica

**1797** Plays a distinguished part in the Battle of Cape St Vincent on 14 FEBRUARY, for which he is knighted. JULY, Loses his right arm attempting to seize a Spanish prize at Santa Cruz, Tenerife

**1798** Annihilates the French at the Battle of the Nile, on 1 AUGUST. As a result he is made Baron Nelson of the Nile, and the King of Naples makes him Duke of Bronte, Sicily

**1801** Famously disregards Admiral Parker's orders to win the Battle of Copenhagen on 2 APRIL

**1805** Leads Britain to victory against France and Spain at the Battle of Trafalgar on 21 OCTOBER, during which he is killed, at the age of 47

**1806** Laid to rest in St Paul's Cathedral, London, England

Naval Hospital in Greenwich (later the Royal Naval College), where each night his body was put on ice to prevent decomposition. Finally, he was rowed up the River Thames in the royal barge as part of a state funeral procession and laid to rest in the crypt of St Paul's Cathedral – appropriately, his coffin, which lies inside a black marble casket, was made from the mainmast of the French flagship *L'Orient*.

During the 1830s a newly created square near Charing Cross, London, was named Trafalgar Square in honour of the victory, and in 1843 a 5-metre statue of Nelson was raised to the top of the 50-metre column that now bears his name.

### DID YOU KNOW?

● Nelson's last piece of writing was Nelson's Prayer, composed on board the *Victory* less than an hour before the Battle of Trafalgar: 'May the Great God, whom I worship, grant to my Country, and for the benefit of Europe in general, a great and glorious Victory; and may no misconduct in anyone tarnish it; and may humanity after Victory be the predominant feature in the British Fleet. For myself, individually, I commit my life to Him who made me, and may His blessing light upon my endeavours for serving my Country faithfully. To Him I resign myself and the just cause which is entrusted to me to defend. Amen. Amen. Amen'

David Livingstone arrived in Africa as a naïve missionary and left as a celebrated explorer, having covered some 30,000 miles of the 'Dark Continent' in three major expeditions. Most famously, he was discovered by journalist Henry Stanley with the words: 'Dr Livingstone, I presume?'

**The Last Expedition of** DR LIVINGSTONE

David Livingstone (Scotland) worked in a cotton mill from the age of 10 until he was 24, after which, inspired by the writings of missionary Karl Gutzläff (Germany), he studied medicine and was ordained a missionary. He first visited Africa in 1841 where, by all accounts, he was a mediocre missionary, but in two great expeditions – 1852–56 and 1858–63 – he proved himself a great explorer. He returned to Africa for the third and last time in 1866 to collect data on Africa's river systems on behalf of the Royal Geographic Society (Britain).

This last expedition was dogged by bad weather, ill health and navigational problems until eventually Livingstone's deteriorating health forced him to recuperate at Ujiji (in what is now Tanzania). Meanwhile, outside Africa, no news had been heard of the expedition. The search for Livingstone became a cause célèbre, and the flamboyant editor of the *New York Herald*, Gordon Bennett (USA), told explorer and journalist Henry Morton Stanley (Wales–USA): 'Find Livingstone.' Stanley succeeded where three other expeditions had failed and found Livingstone at Ujiji on 10 November 1871 – his subsequent book *How I Found Livingstone* (1872) brought lasting fame to both men.

After Stanley's departure, Livingstone returned to his task of collecting data on the river systems, but ill-health returned, claiming his life on 1 May 1873. His last expedition was at an end, but there was still one last journey to make. His faithful African followers buried his heart close to where he had died and then embalmed his body and carried it 1,500 miles to the coast. Livingstone's body was then taken by ship to England, where it was buried with great ceremony in Westminster Abbey.

## DID YOU KNOW?

● Gordon Bennett Jr, who sent Stanley to find Livingstone, was a renowned journalist as well as the sponsor of sporting events such as balloon racing and the precursor of Formula One motor racing. He was said to be eccentric and boorish, characteristics often cited as the origin of the phrase 'Gordon Bennett!' as an expression of amazement

● Henry Stanley was born John Rowlands in a workhouse in Denbigh, Wales, and travelled as a cabin boy to New Orleans, where he was adopted by a man named Stanley. He served in the Confederate army and the US navy before becoming a journalist and explorer. From 1879 to 1887 he helped found the Congo Free State (later Zaire, now Democratic Republic of Congo) on behalf of King Leopold II of Belgium. He was naturalized a British subject in 1892 and later sat as Unionist MP for Lambeth, London. His last day was 10 May 1904

**Opposite** 'Dr Livingstone, I presume?' – Henry Stanley greets Dr Livingstone after tracking him down in Ujiji, Tanzania in November 1871

**Below** Inscription on a tree at Chitambo (in what is now Zambia), marking the site where Livingstone's heart was buried. The part of the tree carrying the inscription is now kept at the Royal Geographical Society in London, England (photograph c.1900)

TIMELINE: DAVID LIVINGSTONE

**1813** Born in Blantyre, Scotland, on 19 MARCH

**1823–37** Works in a cotton factory in Blantyre

**1837–40** Studies medicine in Glasgow, Scotland

**1840** Ordained a missionary by the London Missionary Society, England

**1841** First visits Africa, where he works as a missionary in Bechuanaland (now Botswana)

**1852–56** Travels widely in Africa, detailing flora, fauna and the native population. Discovers Lake Ngami and the Victoria Falls before returning to Britain

**1857** Publishes *Missionary Travels*

**1858–63** Serves as leader of a government expedition to explore the Zambezi, Shiré and Rovuma rivers. Discovers Lakes Shirwa and Nyasa

**1864** Returns to Britain

**1865** Publishes *The Zambezi and its Tributaries*

**1866** Returns to Africa to lead a Royal Geographic Society expedition to investigate the watershed of Africa and the sources of the Nile

**1867–68** Discovers Lakes Mweru and Bangweulu

**1871** Found by Henry Morton Stanley (Wales–USA) at Ujiji, near Lake Tanganyika

**1873** Still trying to determine the source of the Nile, dies on 1 MAY, aged 60, in Old Chitambo, in what is now Zambia. His heart is buried in Africa and his body in England

## The Last Expedition of CAPTAIN SCOTT

Captain Robert Falcon Scott's journey to the South Pole was intended to be a first, but proved instead to be a last. Hoping to be the first humans to reach the pole, Scott's team was beaten to that goal by Roald Amundsen and, crushed by disappointment, perished on the return journey.

**Below** Members of Roald Amundsen's team use a sextant and artificial horizon to confirm that they have definitely reached the South Pole

**Opposite** Captain Scott in his hut at base camp in Antarctica (1911)

When Captain Robert Falcon Scott (England) and his fellow explorers arrived at 'the bottom of the world' they did not need to check the location of the South Pole – it was well marked by a Norwegian flag left by their rivals, led by Roald Amundsen (Norway), who had arrived a month earlier. Scott and his team began what would be their last journey, the 800-mile trek back to One Ton Depot, the first food station, totally depressed, Scott writing prophetically in his diary: 'I wonder if we can make it.'

Bad weather and a shortage of rations sapped their energy. The largest member of the team, Petty Officer Edgar Evans, was the first to suffer frostbite and malnutrition, and died on 17 February. A few days later Captain Lawrence Oates made his legendary self-sacrifice. Knowing that his frostbitten feet were hindering the progress of the entire team, he left the tent during a blizzard with the famous last words: 'I am just going outside. I may be some time.' Scott wrote in his diary: 'We knew it was the act of a brave man and an English gentleman. We all hope to meet the end with a similar spirit, and assuredly the end is not far.' They were just 29 miles from One Ton Depot.

**TIMELINE: SCOTT & AMUNDSEN**

| 1868 Robert Falcon Scott is born near Devonport, England | 1872 Amundsen is born Roald Engelbreth Gravning Amundsen in Borge, Norway, and later abandons his medical studies for a life at sea | 1881 Scott joins the Royal Navy at the age of 13 | 1897 Amundsen serves with the Belgian Antarctic Expedition as first mate of the *Belgica* | 1901–04 Scott serves with the National Antarctic Expedition in *Discovery* | 1905 Amundsen locates the magnetic North Pole |

The last three members of the team battled on for 18 more miles, finally dying in their tent just 11 miles from safety. The last entry in Scott's diary read: 'We shall stick it out to the end, but we are getting weaker of course and the end cannot be far. It seems a pity, but I do not think I can write more.' And then, beneath his signature: 'For God's sake look after our people.' His last message for the public was more stoical: 'Had we lived, I should have had a tale to tell of the hardihood, endurance and courage of my companions that would have stirred the heart of every Englishman. These rough notes and our bodies must tell the tale.'

**1910** Scott embarks on a second Antarctic expedition, leaving London on 15 JUNE in *Terra Nova*. Amundsen organizes an expedition to reach the North Pole in *Fram*, but hearing that Robert Peary and Matthew Henson (both USA) have allegedly beaten him to it, he resolves instead to be the first to reach the South Pole and heads south, also in JUNE

**1911** Scott sets out towards the pole overland with Edward Wilson, Lawrence Oates, H.R. Bowers and Edgar Evans (all Britain) on 1 NOVEMBER. Amundsen and his team are the first humans to reach the South Pole, on 14 DECEMBER

**1912** Scott and his team reach the pole on 17 JANUARY. The last of Scott's team dies in MARCH, only 11 miles from One Ton Depot

**1928** Amundsen's last journey is on 20 JUNE, when his aeroplane disappears while he is searching for fellow explorer Umberto Nobile (Italy), whose airship *Italia* has gone missing while flying over the North Pole, but who is later found alive

George Mallory was the mountaineer who coined the legendary answer to the question why he wanted to climb Everest: 'Because it's there.' It is fitting, then, that his last journey, with fellow climber Andrew Irvine, was an attempt to be first to conquer the world's highest peak.

# MALLORY & IRVINE

Edmund Hillary (New Zealand) and Tenzing Norgay (Nepal) are world famous for being the first to climb Mount Everest, in 1953. But they may not have been the first. In 1924 George Mallory and Andrew 'Sandy' Irvine (both England) were lost in an attempt on the summit and noone knows whether or not they died on the way up or on the way back down. Mallory had made two attempts on the mountain, in 1921 and again in 1922 when strong winds and freezing temperatures forced him to turn back within 975 metres of the summit. In 1924 he returned for a third attempt and it may have been the memory of his disappointment two years earlier that drove him to press on upwards as the weather worsened, turning this third ascent into his last journey.

Mallory and Irvine were chosen by expedition leader Brigadier General C.G. Bruce (England) to make the final assault on the summit, and left the support team behind as they set out for the last leg of the climb. Less than 300 metres from the top, bad weather closed in. The last person to see Mallory and Irvine (until Mallory's body was discovered in 1999) was expedition photographer Noel Odell (Britain), who watched through his telephoto lens as the climbers disappeared into a swirling snowstorm on 8 June, still 'going strong for the top'.

Nobody knows what happened next, but it is a fact that more mountaineering accidents happen during the descent than the ascent. Mallory and Irvine may have perished soon after the snow closed in, but they may equally well have climbed through the snowstorm and stood on top of Everest before perishing on their way down, making their final journey a first as well as a last.

## DID YOU KNOW?

● In his book *The Fight for Everest 1924*, expedition photographer Noel Odell concluded: 'The question remains, "Has Mount Everest been climbed?" It must be left unanswered, for there is no direct evidence. But bearing in mind all the circumstances I have set out ... considering their position when last seen, I think myself there is a strong probability that Mallory and Irvine succeeded'

● Mallory borrowed a camera, which still lies somewhere on the slopes of Everest. If it is found, it may contain photographs that will prove whether or not Mallory and Irvine were indeed the first to conquer Everest

**Above** George Mallory (second from the left in the back row) and Andrew Irvine (far left in the back row) pose in front of a tent with other mountaineers during the 1924 British Expedition to Everest

**Left** Members of the 2nd Mallory and Irvine Research Expedition discover Mallory's body on Everest (1999)

There are so many versions of the *Titanic* story, from the conflicting newspaper reports of 1912 to the historically casual film of 1998, that it is difficult to separate the facts from the embellishments. But what is known for certain is that *Titanic's* maiden voyage was also its last.

230

**The Last Voyage of** *TITANIC*

**TIMELINE: TITANIC**

**1909** The White Star Line orders three *Titanic*-class liners from Harland & Wolff (Ireland, now Northern Ireland)

**1912:**

**2 April** *Titanic* leaves the Belfast shipyard

**10 April** *Titanic* departs Southampton, England, on its maiden voyage to New York, USA

**14 April** Nearing the Grand Banks, southeast of Newfoundland, Canada, *Titanic* receives four ice warnings; the fourth and last one does not reach the captain. At 23:40 the crow's nest reports an iceberg ahead and the First Officer orders a turn to port (left), but it is too late and *Titanic* strikes the iceberg with the starboard (right-hand) side

**15 April** *Titanic* sinks at 02:20. *Carpathia*, the first ship to arrive on the scene, arrives at 04:00

**1985** An expedition led by Robert Ballard (USA) and Jean-Louis Michel (France) discovers the wreck of the *Titanic* on 1 SEPTEMBER

**1998** The feature film *Titanic* is released to box office acclaim and accusations of distorting the truth

On 10 April 1912 the world's largest and most luxurious ocean liner, RMS *Titanic*, left Southampton, England, on its maiden voyage, bound for New York, USA. The pride of White Star Line's fleet, *Titanic* was said to be unsinkable because the hull was divided into 16 separate watertight compartments, but nature was to prove otherwise. Four days into the voyage, at 23:40 on 14 April, *Titanic* struck an iceberg on a calm, clear night while steaming at 22 knots and sank less than 2½ hours later, at 02:20 on 15 April.

Apart from these undisputed facts, all else is open to question. According to the British Board of Trade inquiry, 1,503 passengers and crew were killed and only 703 survived, but other tallies differ. Accepted thinking is that the iceberg ripped a hole through six of the watertight compartments, but according

**Below** Sketch of the sinking of the *Titanic*, by marine artist Willy Stoewer (undated)
**Opposite** The wreck of the *Titanic*, lying 4,000 metres below the surface (1985)

to Dr Robert Ballard (USA), co-discoverer of the wreck in 1985, it was a split seam, not a hole, that caused *Titanic* to sink – Ballard suggests that the hull buckled rather than ripping on impact, and that the rivets popped 'quietly but lethally' out of place. *Titanic* is often said to have been racing for a transatlantic record, but some maritime historians claim that there was not enough coal on board to do so. Some survivors remembered the band playing 'Nearer My God To Thee' as the ship went down, but others remember different tunes or that the band stopped before the ship sank: A.H. Barkworth (England) said: 'When I first came on deck the band was playing a waltz. The next time I passed … the members of the band had thrown down their instruments and were not to be seen.'

Whatever the truth of the details, and whether or not it was the result of culpable negligence or a genuine accident, the fact remains that this was one of the worst peacetime disasters of the 20th century, summed up in the last radio transmission from the stricken ship: 'Have struck iceberg. Badly damaged. Rush aid.'

**DID YOU KNOW?**

● In 1898, 14 years before the sinking of the *Titanic*, Morgan Robertson (England) wrote a story entitled *Futility*. Publishers repeatedly rejected it on the grounds that it was simply not credible – it involved the sinking of a supposedly unsinkable passenger liner named *Titan*, the biggest ship of its time. Like *Titanic* just over a decade later, *Titan* was carrying about 2,000 passengers across the Atlantic on its maiden voyage and sank after hitting an iceberg on the starboard (right-hand) side. Like the *Titanic*, Robertson's fictional ship was not carrying enough lifeboats and approximately two-thirds of the passengers perished

**The Last Voyage of** # *LUSITANIA*

The last voyage of RMS *Lusitania*, which ended when a German U-boat sank the luxury liner, was almost as great a disaster as the loss of the *Titanic*. The death toll was 1,198, including more than 100 US citizens, an outrage that helped bring the USA into the First World War.

## DID YOU KNOW?

● *Lusitania's* **full title was RMS *Lusitania*, RMS being a coveted prefix meaning Royal Mail Ship. Until the 19th century mail was carried in packet boats owned by the General Post Office (Britain), but with the advent of steam propulsion the GPO granted licenses to commercial operators because it proved too expensive for the GPO to build its own steamships. Licenses were granted to the fastest ships, which were usually passenger liners such as *Titanic* and *Lusitania***

Unlike the sinking of the *Titanic*, there was no doubt about where the blame lay for the loss of the *Lusitania*, which was cold-bloodedly sunk on 7 May 1915 by German submarine U-20 in direct contravention of the Hague Convention (*see: Timeline 1907*). President Woodrow Wilson (USA) described it as 'piracy on a vaster scale than the worst pirates of history', and successfully demanded an end to unrestricted German submarine warfare. However, the Germans reneged on this agreement on 1 February 1917, bringing the USA into the First World War on 6 April that year.

*Lusitania's* last voyage began on 1 May 1915, when it steamed out of New York harbour bound for Liverpool, England, with 1,978 passengers and crew. The previous Saturday, Count von Bernstorff, the German ambassador to the USA, had taken out a newspaper advertisement warning Americans not to sail on the *Lusitania*, but his warning was not taken seriously, partly because it was assumed that *Lusitania's* speed made the ship immune to torpedo attack and partly because the Hague Convention supposedly protected merchant vessels.

Six days later, as *Lusitania* approached the Old Head of Kinsale, Ireland, von Bernstorff's warning proved well founded. *Lusitania* had ignored instructions to sail a zigzag course and was steaming straight ahead when two torpedoes from U-20 hit the starboard (right-hand) side. Survivor Ernest Cowper (Canada) said that he had been chatting to a friend shortly after 14:00 when he noticed the conning tower of a submarine and then saw the track of the first torpedo approaching the ship. The two explosions were so severe that *Lusitania* sank within 20 minutes, at such a steep angle that many of the lifeboats could not be launched. Germany claimed that *Lusitania* was an armed troop carrier, and minted a special medal to commemorate the sinking.

**233**

**Below** The *Lusitania* leaving New York on what, six days later, proves to be the liner's last voyage (1 May 1915)
**Above right** Extras at the railings of a huge set built for the silent film *The Sinking of the Lusitania* (*see: Timeline 1918*).

**TIMELINE: THE SINKING OF THE LUSITANIA**

**1906** *Lusitania* is launched

**1907** *Lusitania* wins the Blue Riband for the fastest transatlantic crossing. The Hague Convention, signed in The Hague, Netherlands, outlaws the sinking of merchant vessels without first establishing whether or not they are carrying contraband and making provision for the safety of passengers and crew

**1915** *Lusitania* leaves New York, USA, on 1 MAY bound for Liverpool, England. *Lusitania* is torpedoed and sunk on 7 MAY by German submarine U-20. King George V (Britain) strips his cousin Kaiser Wilhelm (Germany) of the Order of the Garter on 13 MAY

**1916** In a diplomatic victory for President Woodrow Wilson (USA), Germany agrees on 4 MAY to restrict its submarine warfare

**1917** Germany resumes unrestricted submarine warfare on 1 FEBRUARY. The USA severs diplomatic relations with Germany on 3 FEBRUARY. Wilson asks Congress for a declaration of war 'to make the world safe for democracy'. The Senate approves the declaration 82–6 on 4 APRIL and the House 373–50 on 6 APRIL, bringing the USA into the First World War

**1918** The silent film *The Sinking of the Lusitania* is released

Crossing the Atlantic Ocean by airship was once considered the height of luxury, but the era of the 'flying hotel' never recovered from the loss of the world's largest airship, the *Hindenburg*, which exploded on landing at New Jersey on 6 May 1937 at the end of its last flight.

## The Last Flights of AIRSHIPS

**1913** The last flight of German Navy airship L1 is on 9 SEPTEMBER, when it crashes off Heligoland, Germany, killing 20 and leaving 6 survivors. The last flight of the German airship LZ18 is on 17 OCTOBER when it crashes after engine failure during a test flight near Berlin, Germany, killing 28 people

**1921** The last flight of British-built airship R38, which has been sold to the US Navy and renamed USN ZR-2, is on 24 AUGUST when it breaks in half near Hull, England, killing 44 of the 49 people on board

**1922** The last flight of the Italian-built airship *Roma*, which has been sold to the US Army, is on 21 February, when it crashes near Hampton Roads, Virginia, USA, killing 34 and leaving 11 survivors

**1923** The last flight of the French airship *Dixmude* ends on 21 DECEMBER when it disappears over the Mediterranean, presumed to have been struck by lightning, with the loss of 53 lives. Wreckage is found off Sicily a decade later

TIMELINE: AIRSHIPS' LAST FLIGHTS

# Last flights of the *Hindenburg* and *Graf Zeppelin*

For a brief period at the beginning of the 20th century it seemed that the future of commercial passenger air travel lay in hydrogen-filled dirigibles, or rigid airships, but the *Hindenburg* disaster of 1937 put an end to the era of the airship. The world's first airline, established in Germany by Count Ferdinand von Zeppelin (Germany), whose name became synonymous with airships, was regularly carrying passengers across the Atlantic to North and South America, and on 3 May 1937 two Zeppelin airships embarked on what turned out to be their last commercial flights.

*Hindenburg* left Frankfurt, Germany, on that day and arrived at Lakehurst, New Jersey, USA, three days later, on 6 May, having been delayed by headwinds over Newfoundland. *Hindenburg* circled Lakehurst airfield in a thunderstorm, waiting for a lull that would allow the crew to moor the airship to the mooring mast. As the mooring lines were dropped, witnesses on the ground saw a flash near the rear gondola; the hydrogen exploded and within minutes the airship had been destroyed. Amazingly, 61 of the 97 people on board managed to escape. The cause of the fire has never been established, but it is thought that static electricity may have built up during the thunderstorm and been discharged through the mooring lines, creating a spark.

Meanwhile, another airship, *Graf Zeppelin*, had also taken off on 3 May and was returning from Brazil to Friedrichshafen, Germany, carrying what proved to be the last scheduled commercial airship passengers. *Graf Zeppelin* landed safely, but as a result of the *Hindenburg* disaster, on 11 May Adolf Hitler (Germany) banned all further airship flights. The memory of the disaster, combined with the rapid development of the rival aeroplane, meant that the age of airship travel was at an end.

**Opposite** The *Hindenburg* flies over lower Manhattan on her maiden transatlantic flight
**Below left** The record sleeve of the eponymous debut album by rock group Led Zeppelin
**Below right** The wreckage of the US airship *Shenandoah* (see: Timeline 1925)

**1925** The last flight of *Shenandoah*, the first US-built airship, and the first to use helium instead of the more flammable hydrogen, ends on 3 SEPTEMBER when it breaks up during a storm, killing 14

**1930** The last flight of British airship R101 ends on 5 OCTOBER when it crashes into a hillside near Beauvais, France, en route to India

**1933** The world's worst airship disaster is the last flight of the US Navy airship *Akron*, which crashes into the sea off New Jersey on 4 APRIL during a storm, killing 73 and leaving only 3 survivors

**1937** The last use of airships as a commercial means of passenger transport comes with the last flights of the *Hindenburg*, which explodes on 6 MAY killing 36 people, and the *Graf Zeppelin*, which lands safely

Sadly, car crashes are now so common that they are rarely reported in the media unless there is a huge death toll or a celebrity is involved. Flowers are often left by the side of the road, whether for the anonymous thousands or for celebrities such as James Dean and Grace Kelly.

## Last **CAR JOURNEYS**

TIMELINE: LAST CAR JOURNEYS

**1927** The last journey of dancer and choreographer Isadora Duncan (USA, b. Angela Duncan) is on 14 SEPTEMBER when she goes for a drive in a red Bugatti in Nice, France. As the car pulls away she waves and calls: 'Adieu, my friends. I am going to glory!', but her shawl is caught in the spokes of the rear wheel and her neck is broken as soon as the wheels turn. She is either 49 or 50 (her d.o.b. is disputed)

**1955** The last journey of James Dean (USA) is on 30 SEPTEMBER when his Porsche Spyder crashes head-on with another vehicle near Cholame, California, USA. He is 21

**1956** The last journey of artist Jackson Pollock (USA), famous for his 'drip paintings', is on 11 AUGUST, when he is killed in a car crash in East Hampton, NY, USA. He is 44

**1960** The last journey of philosopher Albert Camus (France, b. Algeria) is on 4 JANUARY, when the car in which he is a passenger hits a tree. He is 46. His last, unfinished novel, *The First Man*, is found in his briefcase; it is later edited by his daughter Cathèrine and published in 1995. The last journey of rock'n'roll star Eddie Cochran (USA) is on 17 APRIL when he dies in a car crash in London, England, on his way to the airport; he is 21. Fellow rock'n'roller Gene Vincent (USA) injures his leg in the same accident

**1967** The last journey of actress Jayne Mansfield (USA) is on 29 JUNE, when she is killed in a car crash in Louisiana, USA. She is 34

*continued...*

### James Dean's last journey

Any sudden, unnatural death is a sad loss, but the word most often used when reporting car crash deaths is 'waste' – a feeling that such deaths ought somehow to be avoided. And road death statistics are no respecters of celebrity status, as film star James Dean (USA) discovered on 30 September 1955. That afternoon, Dean was travelling with his mechanic Rolf Wütherich from Los Angeles to Salinas Airport, California, where he was due to compete in a race. He had intended to tow his new Porsche 550 Spyder on a trailer behind his Ford, but at the last minute he decided to drive it to the race: his friends Sanford Roth and Bill Hickman followed in the Ford, all four men leaving Los Angeles in convoy at about 13.30.

Just outside Los Angeles both cars were stopped by the California Highway Patrol and Dean and Roth were ticketed for speeding. With hindsight it could be seen as a warning, but if so Dean did not heed it. As he approached the 'Y' intersection where State Highway 41 splits from Highway 466 (now 46), near a hamlet named Cholame, he was travelling at an estimated 85mph. Coming the other way was a Ford Tudor driven by student Donald Turnupseed (USA) who, not seeing the speeding silver Porsche in the twilight, crossed the centreline to take the fork onto Highway 41. The two vehicles collided head-on.

Turnupseed escaped with minor facial injuries, but the Porsche was thrown into a ditch where Roth, arriving minutes later, described it as looking 'like a crumpled pack of cigarettes'. Wütherich had been thrown from the car

**DID YOU KNOW?**

● James Dean once said of mortality: 'Death is the only thing left to respect. Everything else can be questioned. But death is truth. In it lies the only nobility for man and beyond it the only hope'

● At the time of his death, James Dean had been scheduled to play boxer Rocky Graziano in the film *Somebody Up There Likes Me*, but the role went instead to Paul Newman (USA)

**Opposite top** James Dean gives the thumbs-up from the driving seat of his Porsche Spyder, parked on Hollywood's Vine Street (September 1955)

**Opposite bottom** The wrecked Porsche in a garage in Paso Robles, California, USA (1 October 1955)

**1977** The last journey of Marc Bolan (England, b. Mark Feld), singer of glam rock band T. Rex, is on 17 SEPTEMBER when the Mini in which he is a passenger crashes into a tree near Barnes Common, London, England. He is 29

**1981** The last journey of 9-times world motorcycle champion and 14-times Isle of Man TT champion Mike Hailwood (England), a.k.a. 'Mike the Bike', and his nine-year-old daughter is on 23 MARCH, when his car collides with a lorry two miles from his home in Warwickshire, England. He is 40

**1982** The last journey of Grace Kelly (USA–Monaco) is on 13 SEPTEMBER when the car she is driving plunges off a mountain road into a ravine; she dies the following evening of her injuries. She is 52

**1984** The last journey of Nicholas Dingley (b. England), a.k.a. Razzle, drummer of Finnish glam rock band Hanoi Rocks, is in America on 8 DECEMBER when he is a passenger in a car crashed by drink-driver Vince Neil (USA), singer of US heavy metal band Motley Crue. Dingley is 24. Neil is convicted of manslaughter in 1985, but is allowed to finish a concert tour before serving time

**1997** The last living journey of Diana, Princess of Wales (England), is on 31 AUGUST when the car in which she is a passenger crashes in Paris, France. She is 36. *See also: Diana, Princess of Wales, page 240*

**1998** The last journey of Cozy Powell (Britain), drummer with rock outfits Jeff Beck, Rainbow, Whitesnake et al, is on 5 APRIL, when he is killed in a car crash. He is 50

**2004** The last journey of glamour and fashion photographer Helmut Newton (Germany–Australia) is on 24 JANUARY when he loses control of his Cadillac while leaving the Château Marmont Hotel in Hollywood, California, and crashes it into a wall. He is 83

and survived with several broken bones, but James Dean was pronounced dead on arrival at Paso Robles War Memorial Hospital. He was 24.

## Grace Kelly's last journey

In 1956, two years after winning her second Oscar for her role in *The Country Girl*, Grace Kelly (USA) retired from the screen to embark on a fairytale marriage to Prince Rainier III (Monaco), leaving Hollywood for a new life as Princess Grace of Monaco. Having visited Monaco in 1954 to film Alfred Hitchcock's *To Catch A Thief*, Kelly met her handsome prince the following year while promoting the film at the Cannes Film Festival. They immediately fell in love and married on 19 April 1956 in the second most widely televised royal wedding of the decade.

A quarter of a century later, on the night of 13 September 1982, Princess Grace was driving along the steep, winding corniche with her younger daughter, Stephanie, when, according to a witness who was driving behind the princesses, her car began to zigzag erratically. It then veered off

239

the road and plunged into a ravine, turning over several times. Reports at the time blamed brake failure for the accident, stating that Princess Stephanie had suffered only slight bruising and that Princess Grace was in a stable condition after suffering broken ribs, leg and collarbone. Sadly, it transpired that the situation was far worse. Princess Grace was not stable, and died of her injuries the following afternoon, while Princess Stephanie had, in fact, suffered severe fractures that left her too ill to attend the funeral. It was subsequently determined that Princess Grace had probably lost control of the car after suffering a stroke rather than because of any mechanical failure.

Conspiracy theorists and the superstitious noted that not only had the accident occurred on the 13th of the month but that it had also happened on the same stretch of road where, 17 years earlier, Grace had filmed a car chase and a picnic scene for her last Hitchcock movie, *To Catch a Thief*.

### DID YOU KNOW?

● **Eddie Cochran, who died in a car crash in 1960, was born Eddie Cochrane, but dropped the final 'e' from his surname when he appeared as one half of 'The Cochran Brothers' with Hank Cochran, who was no relation. In the 1979 feature film** *Radio On*, **Sting (England, b. Gordon Sumner) played the part of a petrol pump attendant with an Eddie Cochran fixation**

**The Last Journey of**

# DIANA, PRINCESS OF WALES

Diana, Princess of Wales, made two last car journeys. The one that killed her has become the world's most-discussed car crash, displacing even that of James Dean. The other was the motorcade that conveyed her body from her funeral to its last resting place at her family home, Althorp.

**Above** The underpass in which Diana's fatal car crash occurred

**Opposite** Diana's funeral cortège nearing the family home of Althorp (6 September 1997)

The funeral of Diana, Princess of Wales (England), took place at Westminster Abbey, London, on 6 September 1997. Afterwards, the funeral cortège made its way slowly northwards, a journey watched more closely by more people than any other in history. As well as the millions watching worldwide on television, thousands more lined the streets of London and the hard shoulder and bridges of the M1 motorway, which was closed in both directions.

As the motorcade drove slowly through London, the flowers thrown from the crowd piled up on the roof of the hearse or gathered on the windscreen and were intermittently swept aside by the wipers to clear the driver's view. When it reached the motorway, the cortège made an unscheduled stop to clear the windscreen, a pallbearer gently laying the pile of flowers at the roadside. And then the Daimler and its police outriders continued in splendid isolation at a steady 45mph along the middle lane of the motorway, usually busy but now empty.

When the motorcade arrived at Diana's ancestral seat of Althorp, Northamptonshire, the public part of this last journey was over. The flower-covered gates of the estate were closed to the world and, in sharp contrast to the funeral, the burial took place in private, in the familiar surroundings of Diana's childhood home. The final part of the journey was on foot, as members of the Princess of Wales' Royal Regiment bore her flag-draped coffin over a simple wooden bridge to an island set in an ornamental lake in the grounds of Althorp Park, where she was laid to rest in the peace and seclusion she had been unable to find in life.

| **1961** Born Lady Diana Frances Spencer on 1 JULY in Sandringham, England, and later educated in Switzerland | **1981** Marries Charles, Prince of Wales | **1982** Gives birth to William Arthur Philip Louis | **1984** Gives birth to Henry Charles Albert David | **1992** She and Charles separate | **1996** She and Charles divorce | **1997** Her last living journey is on 31 AUGUST when the car in which she is a passenger crashes in Paris, France. She is 36. Her very last journey is on 6 SEPTEMBER, when her body is taken from Westminster Abbey to her last resting place at the family home of Althorp, Northamptonshire |

TIMELINE: DIANA, PRINCESS OF WALES

Whereas car crashes are sadly so common as to be under-reported, media coverage makes plane crashes seem more common than they actually are for what is a remarkably safe form of travel. However, accidents still happen and, as with the car, celebrity is no passport to safety.

**Last** # PLANE JOURNEYS

TIMELINE: LAST PLANE JOURNEYS

**1908** The last journey of Lt Thomas Etholen Selfridge (USA) of the US Army Signal Corps is on 17 SEPTEMBER, when he becomes the first person ever to die in a powered aeroplane crash, at Fort Myer, Virginia, USA; the pilot, Orville Wright (USA), survives

**1910** The last journey of aviation and motoring pioneer Charles Stewart Rolls (England) of Rolls-Royce fame is on 12 JULY, when he becomes the first Briton to die in a powered aeroplane crash, during a flying competition near Bournemouth, England. He is 32

**1919** The last journey of Sir John Alcock (England), knighted for making the first non-stop transatlantic flight in June with Arthur Whitten Brown (Britain, b. Scotland of US parents), is on 18 DECEMBER, when he is killed in a plane crash near Rouen, France, en route to the Paris Air Show. He is 27

**1937** The last journey of Amelia Earhart (USA), famous as the first woman to fly the Atlantic solo (1932), is in JULY, when her aircraft disappears over the Pacific during an attempted round-the-world flight. She is 39

**1941** The last journey of Amy Johnson (England), famous as the first woman to fly solo from England to Australia (1930), is on 5 JANUARY, when the plane she is delivering from the factory to an RAF base ditches into the Thames Estuary, England. She is 37

**1944** The last journey of band leader Glenn Miller (USA) is on 15 DECEMBER, when the light plane in which he and

continued...

## Amelia Earhart's last journey

Amelia Earhart (USA) was an army nurse and a social worker before she took up flying. In 1928, as a passenger, she became the first woman to cross the Atlantic by air and four years later, on 21 May 1932, she landed her own plane in Londonderry, Ireland, having become the second pilot and the first woman to make a solo transatlantic flight. This and further pioneering flights made her a worldwide celebrity and a powerful spokeswoman for both aviation and feminism.

In 1937 Earhart embarked on her most ambitious project yet: a round-the-world flight. After an abortive westward attempt in March, she set off again on 21 May on what would prove to be

her last journey. With navigator Fred Noonan, she flew eastwards from Oakland, California, to Miami, Florida, and then south to Brazil for the shortest Atlantic crossing to Senegal, West Africa. They continued eastwards across the Sahara and the Arabian Peninsula to India, and then southeast to Darwin, Australia. From there they flew to Lae, New Guinea, to begin the longest over-water leg of the journey: 2,200 miles to the US-owned atoll of Howland Island, which would leave them with just two legs to complete the journey: Howland Island to Hawaii, and Hawaii back to Oakland.

However, they never made it to Howland Island. On 2 July Earhart radioed US Coast Guard ship USS *Itasca*, stationed off Howland Island to await their arrival: 'KHAQQ calling *Itasca*. We must be on you, but cannot see you … gas is running low…' An hour later she made her last radio communication before her plane disappeared without trace, never to be recovered: 'We are in a line position of 157'—337. Will report on 6210 kilocycles. Wait, listen on 6210 kilocycles. We are running North and South.'

**DID YOU KNOW?**

● In her last letter to her husband, Amelia Earhart wrote of her attempted round-the-world journey: 'Please know that I am quite aware of the hazards. I want to do it because I want to do it. Women must try things as men have tried. When they fail, their failure must be a challenge to others'

**Left** Fred Noonan and Amelia Earhart board their plane in San Juan, Puerto Rico, in readiness for the next leg of their round-the-world flight (1937)

*...continued*

two others are travelling to France to entertain Second World War troops disappears without trace over the English Channel. He is 40

**1958** The last journey of seven members of Matt Busby's Manchester United soccer squad, three members of the club's staff and eight journalists is on 6 FEBRUARY, when the plane carrying them on the last leg of their journey home from the European Cup semi-finals in Belgrade, Yugoslavia, crashes in an abortive takeoff from Munich Airport, Germany. England international Duncan Edwards dies two weeks later of his injuries

**1959** The last journey of rock musicians Buddy Holly, the Big Bopper and Ritchie Valens is on 3 FEBRUARY, when their charter plane crashes en route to a concert in Fargo, North Dakota, killing all three musicians and the pilot, Roger Peterson. Holly is 22, Big Bopper is 28 and Valens is 17

**1961** The last journey of UN secretary-general Dag Hammarskjöld (Sweden) is on 18 SEPTEMBER, when he dies in a plane crash in Northern Rhodesia (now Zimbabwe) during a peace mission to Africa. He is 56. He is posthumously awarded the Nobel Prize for Peace for 1961

**1967** The last journey of soul man Otis Redding (USA) and four members of his backing band, the Bar-Kays, is on 10 DECEMBER, when their plane crashes into an icy lake near Madison, Wisconsin, en route to a concert. Redding is 26

**1968** The last journey of Yuri Gagarin (USSR), the first man to orbit the earth, is on 27 MARCH, when he is killed in a plane crash while training near Moscow, Russia. He is 34

**1969** The last journey of undefeated world champion boxer Rocky Marciano, his friend Frank Farrell and pilot Glenn Belz (all USA) is on 31 AUGUST, when they are killed in a plane crash en route from Chicago to Des Moines. Marciano is 45

**1972** The last journey of Prince William of Gloucester, ninth in line to the

*continued...*

## Amy Johnson's last journey

Pioneer aviatrix Amy Johnson (England) wrote of her first flying lesson: 'I was scared stiff of my instructor, who never seemed to lose his first idea that I was a born idiot.' History proved him wrong, of course – Johnson was granted her pilot's licence on 6 July 1929 and less than a year later, on 24 May 1930, she landed in Darwin as the first woman to fly solo from Britain to Australia. She followed this with a number of record-breaking long-distance flights, but temporarily gave up flying when she heard about the fate of Amelia Earhart, writing to her mother: 'No more flights so no need to worry! Poor Amelia.'

But shortly after the outbreak of the Second World War Johnson, ineligible to fly in combat, enlisted as a pilot in the Air Transport Auxiliary, delivering aircraft from factories to RAF bases. Her last journey was on 5 January 1941, when she took off from Blackpool Aerodrome, England, in fog, heading for Kidlington RAF base in Oxfordshire, which should have been a 90-minute flight. She was next seen four hours later baling out of her twin-engined plane into the Thames Estuary, more than 70 miles off course.

How she drifted so far off course is a mystery, as is what happened next. HMS *Haslemere* was nearby and steamed to her rescue, but she could not grab the ropes they threw her. Lieutenant-Commander Walter Fletcher dived into the water, but could not reach her; he died of exposure after being plucked from the water and Johnson disappeared without trace, possibly having been dragged under the ship in the swell.

Johnson once told a friend: 'I know where I shall finish up – in the drink. A few headlines in the newspapers and then they forget you.' The first part of her gloomy prediction may have proved true, but the second part certainly has not.

## Buddy Holly's last journey

If 'waste' is the word most often associated with car crashes, then 'fate' is the one attached to air crashes. And fate (a.k.a. luck, or chance) had its part to play in the plane crash that killed rock musicians Buddy Holly, Ritchie Valens and the Big Bopper (all USA) on 3 February 1959. Holly's bassist Waylon Jennings (USA) had been due to fly, but at the last minute gave up his seat on the plane to the Big Bopper and travelled by bus instead,

and Holly's guitarist Tommy Allsup tossed a coin with Ritchie Valens for the third seat. Given his enormous and lasting influence on rock and pop music, it is amazing that Buddy Holly had been recording for only three years before embarking on this last journey. Having split from his band, the Crickets, Holly was touring heavily and, exhausted by the schedule, he chartered a plane from Dwyer Flying Service to take him from Clear Lake, Iowa, to Fargo, North Dakota, for his next concert; going by road was not only exhausting but the heating on the tour bus had broken. Flying with him were two of the acts with whom he was sharing the bill on 'The Winter Dance Party Tour' – Ritchie Valens, the Chicano rock legend also known by the name of his hit *La Bamba*, and Jiles P. Richardson, whose biggest hit, as the Big Bopper, was *Chantilly Lace*.

**DID YOU KNOW?**

● Years after the plane crash that killed Buddy Holly, his backing guitarist Tommy Allsup opened a club called The Heads-Up Saloon, in memory of the toss of the coin that saved his life

● Previous names of the band Lynyrd Skynyrd (*see: Timeline 1977*) included the Noble Five, the Wild Things and 1%. They eventually settled on the name of a teacher who had suspended them from school for having long hair – Leonard Skinner. The band's first album was entitled *Pronounced Leh-nerd Skin-nerd*

**Opposite top** A signed portrait of pioneer aviatrix Amy Johnson, by Ruth Hollick
**Left** Buddy Holly photographed c.1955
**Above** The wreckage of the plane crash that killed Buddy Holly, Ritchie Valens and the Big Bopper (3 February 1959)

...continued

British throne, is on 28 AUGUST, when he dies in an air crash in Staffordshire. He is 30. The last journey of racing driver Graham Hill (England), twice winner of the Grand Prix world championship, is on 29 NOVEMBER, when his plane crashes near London, England. He is 46

**1977** The last journey of blues/boogie singer Ronnie Van Zant (USA), two members of his band Lynyrd Skynyrd, and their road manager, is on 20 OCTOBER, when their charter plane crashes into a swamp near McCombe, Mississippi, en route to a concert. Van Zant is 28. The rest of the band survive

**1985** The last journey of pop/country singer Rick Nelson (USA, b. Eric Hilliard Nelson) and six others is on 31 DECEMBER, when his private jet crashes near De Kalb, Texas, en route to a concert in Dallas. He is 45

**1990** The last journey of blues guitarist Stevie Ray Vaughan (USA) is on 27 AUGUST, when he is killed in a helicopter crash. He is 35

**1997** The last journey of country singer-songwriter John Denver (USA, b. Henry John Deutschendorf) is on 12 OCTOBER when, having already survived two car crashes in his Porsche, he crashes his light aircraft into Monterey Bay. He is 53

**1999** The last journey of John F. Kennedy Jr, his wife and her sister is on 16 JULY, when the plane he is piloting crashes off Martha's Vineyard, USA. He is 38. On 25 OCTOBER twice-US Open golf champion Payne Stewart (USA) takes his last journey when the plane in which he is travelling crashes in South Dakota, killing all on board. He is 42

Sadly, the three stars never arrived in Fargo. After taking off in snow at about 01:00, the plane crashed soon afterwards near Mason City, Iowa, depriving the music world of three of its fastest rising stars. That February day became known as 'the day the music died', as commemorated in one-time paper-boy Don Maclean's song 'American Pie':

> But February made me shiver,
> With every paper I'd deliver,
> Bad news on the doorstep...
> I couldn't take one more step.
> I can't remember if I cried
> When I read about his widowed bride
> But something touched me deep inside,
> The day the music died.

---

**DID YOU KNOW?**

● There is some good news among the bad – plane crashes are survivable. Celebrities who have survived plane crashes include: Palestinian politician Yasser Arafat; soccer players and managers Sir Matt Busby (Scotland) and Sir Bobby Charlton (England), who both survived the Munich air disaster (*see: Timeline 1958*); racing driver David Coulthard (Scotland); jockeys Frankie Dettori (Italy) and Ray Cochrane (Northern Ireland); actor and director Clint Eastwood (USA); businessman, film producer, aviator and recluse Howard Hughes (USA); opera singer Luciano Pavarotti (Italy); film star Elizabeth Taylor (USA, b. England); rock star Sting (England, b. Gordon Sumner); actor Patrick Swayze (USA); and aviation pioneers the Wright brothers (USA), who survived a number of crashes

**Below** A crane lifts the wreckage of Otis Redding's Beechcraft H18 light aircraft out of Lake Monona, Wisconsin (10 December 1967, *see: Timeline 1967*)

**Opposite** Muscovites queueing to pay their last respects to former cosmonauts Yuri Gagarin and Vladimir Seryogin (29 March 1968, *see: Timeline 1968*)

Concorde was a triumph of international cooperation, a technological milestone and one of the world's best-loved aircraft. Hundreds of people made their way to Heathrow Airport on 24 October 2003 to watch the last commercial flight of the world's first supersonic passenger airliner.

## The Last Flight of CONCORDE

It began with an argument over whether to use the French or English spelling of the word concord (meaning 'agreement, peace or harmony') and it ended with a year-long goodbye that lasted from the retirement of the Air France fleet of Concordes in May 2003 to the last journey of the last British Airways (BA) Concorde in April 2004.

On 22 October 2003 more than 1,000 people gathered to watch Concorde's last commercial takeoff from Heathrow Airport, London, at 19:20 BST, bound for JFK Airport, New York. Two days later the return flight from New York was the last of a trio of Concordes to land at Heathrow, marking the end of an era. The first of the trio to land was a special flight from Edinburgh, Scotland, carrying competition winners and BA staff. The second was another special, a supersonic round trip that had left Heathrow $1^3/_4$ hours earlier. And the last was Flight BA002 from New York, the last commercial flight of Concorde.

The farewells continued as BA's Concordes made their last flights from Heathrow to their new homes. On 31 October G-BOAC flew to Manchester en route to Manchester Aviation Viewing Park; on 3 November G-BOAG flew to JFK and then on 5 November from JFK to Boeing Field, Seattle, en route to Seattle's Museum of Flight; on 10 November G-BOAD flew to JFK en route to the Intrepid Museum, New York; on 17 November G-BOAE flew to Barbados Airport; and on 26 November G-BOAF flew to Filton Airfield, Bristol, from where the first British-built Concorde had made its first test flight 27 years earlier.

G-BOAB was to remain at Heathrow, which left just one last journey to be completed. In April 2004 G-BOAA left Heathrow by lorry, was transferred to a barge for the journey down the River Thames and round the coast to Scotland and then went by a purpose-built road to the Museum of Flight at East Fortune.

### DID YOU KNOW?

● **The last flight of the USSR's second preproduction Tupolev Tu-144 supersonic transport plane, known as 'Concordski', was on 3 June 1973, when it exploded in the air at the Paris Air Show, France, killing all six crew and nine spectators**

**Opposite top** Concorde makes its last commercial takeoff from Charles de Gaulle Airport in Paris, France, bound for New York's JFK Airport. The last ever commercial flight of an Air France Concorde is the return flight from JFK the following day (30 May 2003)

**Opposite bottom** The last BA Concorde nears the end of its last journey as it travels to the Museum of Flight at East Fortune, near Edinburgh, on a road specially built by the British Army (19 April 2004)

The first space shuttle, *Columbia*, successfully took to the skies on 12 April 1981 and NASA's shuttle programme maintained an unblemished safety record until 28 January 1986, when compromised safety procedures resulted in the explosion of *Challenger* just over a minute after liftoff.

## The Last Flight of CHALLENGER

**Below** The five astronauts and two payload specialists who made up the crew of *Challenger* for the fatal mission STS 51-L: (left to right front row) astronauts Michael J. Smith (pilot), Francis R. (Dick) Scobee (mission commander) and Ronald E. McNair; (left to right back row) astronaut Ellison S. Onizuka, payload specialists Christa McAuliffe and Gregory Jarvis, and astronaut Judith A. Resnik (November 1985)

By 1986, five years into NASA's space shuttle programme, shuttle flights were fairly routine, and NASA had even launched a Space Flight Participation programme to enable ordinary citizens to fly in the shuttle. US President Ronald Reagan announced that the first space flight participant should be a schoolteacher, and Christa McAuliffe (USA), a 37-year-old teacher from Concord High School, New Hampshire, was chosen from among 11,000 teachers who had applied for a place on the shuttle. Her husband and two children could only watch in horror and disbelief with the families of the other astronauts as *Challenger* exploded 73 seconds into the flight.

*Challenger* took off as normal at 11:38 EST, quickly accelerating to about twice the speed of sound and climbing to a height of some 10 miles before suddenly exploding in a massive ball of flame and smoke. The crew reported nothing unusual prior to the explosion, but photographs taken from tracker planes showed that a small flame had appeared on one of the booster rockets immediately after liftoff, spreading to become a circle of fire around the base of the booster and finally igniting the booster's thousands of tons of liquid oxygen and hydrogen fuel – NASA later revealed that the rockets had no sensors to warn of trouble.

The space shuttle programme was suspended for more than two years after the *Challenger* disaster, and the ensuing investigations pinpointed the cause of the disaster as an insufficiently robust rubber 'O-ring seal' on the booster rocket. The report said that NASA should have changed the design of the seal after previous warnings that it might be faulty, and accused NASA of compromising safety procedures in order to retain public funding. As a result, NASA reviewed its procedures and relaunched its manned space flight programme under the slogan: 'Nice And Safe Attitude'.

**TIMELINE: COUNTDOWN TO DISASTER**

**T=0.0** Ignition

**T+0.7 seconds** Photographic evidence shows abnormal black smoke near the O-ring joint in the right-hand solid rocket booster

**T+59 seconds** Film from tracker planes shows a 'well-defined intense plume' of exhaust on the right-hand booster. Investigators later cite this as clear evidence of O-ring joint failure. Flames appear on the right-hand booster

**T+60 seconds** Pressure in right-hand booster begins to drop due to the fast expanding hole in the failed O-ring joint

**T+1 minute 4 seconds** The flame on the booster changes shape suddenly, indicating that the liquid hydrogen tank has been breached and begun to leak

**T+1 minute 12 seconds** The right-hand booster breaks away from one of the struts connecting it to the external fuel tank. Tracking cameras show a large ball of orange flame

**T+1 minute 13 seconds** The last recorded voice communication is from pilot Michael J. Smith: 'Uh oh...' It is thought he may be responding to indications of falling pressure in the external fuel tank. Tracking cameras show a sudden flash between the shuttle and the external fuel tank, followed by a yellow and red fireball. A ball of white flame appears from beneath the nose of the shuttle

**T+1 minute 14 seconds** The nose of the shuttle and crew compartment are engulfed in flame. *Challenger* explodes

**T+3 minutes 25 seconds** The first pieces of debris fall into the Atlantic

**T+3 minutes 58 seconds** The crew cabin hits the sea at about 200mph, disintegrates and sinks

**Left** A trail of smoke leading upwards from Cape Canaveral to the point where *Challenger* exploded (28 January 1986)

# TIMOTHY LEARY & GENE RODDENBERRY

Sadly, many attempts at pioneering firsts turn out to be the last living journeys of the pioneers. But not for Timothy Leary and Gene Roddenberry – they died before their shared last journey, having signed up to be among the first group of people to have their ashes blasted into orbit.

On 21 April 1997 the 'cremains' (cremated remains) of counter-culture guru Timothy Leary and *Star Trek*-creator Gene Roddenberry (both USA) were among those of 24 deceased people whose cremains boldly went where no cremains have gone before. Their collective last journey, a trip to outdo any of those that Leary famously took in the Sixties, was also a world first, being the first ever space 'burial'.

At 13:00 local time, a Lockheed L-1011 TriStar named *Stargazer* took off from Spain's Gando Air Force Base on the Canary Islands with an air-launched Pegasus XL space-rocket strapped beneath it. At 38,000 feet the rocket was released from the plane and ignited, carrying into orbit a Spanish research satellite and a canister owned by pioneering space 'burial' company Celestis Inc. (USA) containing 24 capsules of human ashes. These 24 people, or their families, had paid c.$5,000 each to have 7 grams of ashes taken into space in an engraved capsule for what, on re-entry to the earth's atmosphere, would become a second cremation.

Leary is said to have learned about Celestis just two days before he died in 1996 and to have immediately embraced the idea, saying: 'I'll be a space pioneer. I will be the light.' Appropriately for the man who coined the Sixties mantra: 'Turn on, tune in, drop out', the inscription engraved on his capsule was: 'Peace Love Light YouMeOne' [sic]. Roddenberry's read simply: 'With love from Majel and Rob.' Together they orbited the earth more than 25,000 times, once every 96 minutes, before re-entry to the atmosphere to the northeast of Australia on 20 May 2002. Appropriately for Roddenberry, it had been almost exactly a five-year mission.

**1997** Celestis Inc. (USA) launches *Earthview 01*, 'The Founders' Flight', on 21 APRIL

**1998** Celestis launches *Lunar 01* on 6 JANUARY, delivering the ashes of astronomer Dr Eugene Shoemaker (USA) to the moon, and *Earthview 02*, 'The Ad Astra Flight', on 10 FEBRUARY

**1999** Celestis launches *Earthview 03*, 'The Millennial Flight', on 20 DECEMBER

**2001** Celestis launches *Earthview 04*, 'The Odyssey Flight', on 21 SEPTEMBER

**2004** Celestis launches *Earthview 05*, 'The Pioneers' Flight', in JANUARY 2005

## DID YOU KNOW?

● Legend has it that before his death, Timothy Leary programmed his computer to send a posthumous e-mail to his friend, philosopher Robert Anton Wilson (USA), which arrived a month after Leary's death saying: 'Robert, how is everything? Greetings from the other side... It's not what I expected. Nice but crowded... Hope you're well. Love, Timothy'

● As well as sending ashes into orbit, Celestis also enabled Dr Eugene Shoemaker to posthumously fulfil his dream of visiting the moon. Shoemaker, a pioneer in the exploration of the solar system, is most famous as the co-discoverer of Comet Shoemaker-Levy 9, which hit Jupiter in 1994. NASA's 1998 *Lunar Prospector* mission carried a Celestis capsule containing part of Shoemaker's ashes, which eventually hit the moon near its south pole, creating a permanent and personal monument to a scientist who, during his lifetime, had yearned to visit the moon and study its geology first-hand

**Opposite** Portrait of Timothy Leary by Douglas Kirkland (undated)
**Above** The Pegasus XL rocket on its journey into space, carrying a satellite and the ashes of 24 people
**Below** Portrait by Douglas Kirkland of Gene Roddenberry with a model of the starship *Enterprise* (January 1988)

Most people's very last journey on earth is in a coffin, either to a crematorium or to a grave. In death as in life many public figures are surrounded by other public figures, and many celebrities have a star-studded line-up of pallbearers to carry them on that last journey.

# PALLBEARERS

Audrey Hepburn and Hubert de Givenchy attend the 1985 Council of Fashion Designers of America Awards in New York (24 October 1985)

## Audrey Hepburn's funeral

In life she eclipsed many of her co-stars and in death she upstaged the president. Actress and children's aid worker Audrey Hepburn (Belgium, b. Edda Van Heemstra Hepburn-Ruston) died at home in Switzerland on 20 January 1993, the day that Bill Clinton was sworn in as president of the USA, and news of her death interrupted broadcasts of his inauguration ceremony. Her family received flowers from the Dutch royal family, condolences from four US presidents and eulogies from two James Bonds. Prince Sadruddin Aga Khan spoke at her funeral and Tiffany's, referring to her film *Breakfast at Tiffany's*, placed advertisements in the newspapers and in their storefronts around the world saying:

> AUDREY HEPBURN
> 1929–1993
> *Our huckleberry friend*
> TIFFANY & CO.

Her funeral was to be held in her home town, Tolochenaz-sur-Morges, Switzerland, on 24 January, where the service would be presided over by Pastor Maurice Eindiguer (Switzerland) who had performed the marriage ceremony for Audrey in 1954, baptized her son Sean in 1960 and had come out of retirement to give Audrey the last rites four days earlier. Hundreds lined the route from her house to the church and from the church to the cemetery.

At midday Audrey began her last journey, borne to the church in her coffin by her partner Robert Wolders (they had considered marriage, but she said: 'Robbie it's not necessary...you're closer than any husband'), her sons, Sean and Luca, her brother, Jan van Ufford, and her long-term friends, lawyer Georges Müller and fashion designer Hubert de Givenchy. Hepburn and

| **1827** Composer Franz Schubert (Austria) is a pallbearer at the funeral of fellow composer Ludwig van Beethoven (Germany) | **1898** The Prince of Wales, later King Edward VII (Britain), is a pallbearer at the funeral of former British prime minister William Gladstone (England) | **1928** Authors J.M. Barrie (Scotland) & George Bernard Shaw (Ireland) are pallbearers at the funeral of fellow author Thomas Hardy (England) | **1959** Phil Everly (USA), of pop/ country and western duo the Everly Brothers, is a pallbearer at the funeral of Buddy Holly (USA) | **1960** Film stars James Stewart and Spencer Tracy (both USA) are pallbearers at the funeral of fellow film star Clark Gable (USA) | **1981** Stage and screen stars Rock Hudson, Frank Sinatra, Gregory Peck & Fred Astaire (all USA), Laurence Olivier & David Niven (both England) & Elia Kazan (Turkey–USA) are pallbearers at the funeral of film star Natalie Wood (USA) |

■ TIMELINE: PALLBEARERS

## DID YOU KNOW?

● Formula One racing driver Ayrton Senna was a national hero in Brazil, and his funeral was a grander affair than many state funerals in other countries, with a team of elite Formula One pallbearers. Senna was killed in the San Marino Grand Prix on 1 May 1994 when his car hit a concrete barrier at 140mph. At his funeral some one million Brazilians lined the streets of São Paulo to watch the cortège pass, and when his body was laid to rest in the Morumbi Cemetery the Brazilian Air Force performed a fly-past in his honour, sky-writing an 'S' and a heart high above the cemetery (*see: Timeline 1994*)

**Below** Eight of the world's top motor racing drivers act as pallbearers at the funeral of Ayrton Senna (5 May 1994)

Givenchy had begun a legendary association in 1953, of which fashion designer Ralph Lauren (USA) said: 'I truly feel Audrey gave Givenchy a look. As time went on, they collaborated, but I think she picked what was Audrey out of Givenchy.' For her part, Audrey once said: 'I depend on Givenchy in the same way that American women depend on their psychiatrists.'

**1993** Fashion designer Hubert James Marcel Taffin de Givenchy (France) is a pallbearer at the funeral of film star Audrey Hepburn (Belgium, b. Edda Van Heemstra Hepburn-Ruston)

**1994** Racing drivers Emerson Fittipaldi & Rubens Barrichello (both Brazil), Damon Hill, Derek Warwick & Johnny Herbert (all England), Gerhard Berger (Austria), Alain Prost (France) & Jackie Stewart (Scotland) are pallbearers at the funeral of fellow racing driver Ayrton Senna (Brazil). Tennis player John McEnroe (USA) is a pallbearer at the funeral of fellow tennis player Vitas Gerulaitis (USA)

**2000** Former soccer players Sir Bobby Charlton, Sir Tom Finney & Nat Lofthouse (all England) are pallbearers at the funeral of fellow former soccer player Sir Stanley Matthews (England)

# LAST BUT NOT LEAST...

## Howard Hughes' Last Journey and the Last Flight of *Spruce Goose*

At the age of 18 Howard Hughes (USA) inherited millions of dollars and immediately began making them into millions more. He produced several Hollywood films and then turned his attention to aviation, breaking most of the world's air speed records as a pilot from 1935 to 1938 as well as designing and building a number of aircraft. One of his designs was the famous eight-engined all-wooden Hughes H-4 Hercules known as *Spruce Goose*, the largest seaplane ever built, which made its first and last flight on 2 November 1947 when it flew approximately one mile over Los Angeles harbour, USA.

After being badly injured in a plane crash in 1946, Hughes became, paradoxically, the world's most famous recluse. His last journey was on 5 April 1976 when he died of a stroke in his private jet en route from Mexico to Texas where he was due to see a medical specialist for an illness that was never disclosed. Hughes' last public statement was made four years earlier in a telephone interview refuting that a purported biography was his true story (the authors were later imprisoned for fraud): 'I'm not going to continue being quite as reclusive as I have been, because it has apparently attracted so much attention that I have just got to live a somewhat modified life in order not to be an oddity ... for one thing I would like to see an accurate story of my life printed.' What he would have thought of the 2004 film *The Aviator* is a matter of conjecture.

**Above** Howard Hughes in the cockpit of *Spruce Goose* (6 November 1947)

## Abraham Lincoln's Last Journey

Abraham Lincoln (USA) was the first US president to be assassinated, when he was shot by militiaman, spy and Shakespearean actor John Wilkes Booth (USA) as he watched a performance of *Our American Cousin* with his wife at the Ford's Theater in Washington, DC. His last words, in reply to his wife's question whether the audience would laugh at their holding hands in the box, were: 'They won't think anything about it.' The last journey of Lincoln's corpse, from Washington to his home town of Springfield, Illinois, was by rail, in the plush surroundings of a newly invented Pullman carriage. George Pullman (USA), who received a patent for his invention later the same year, was thereby given a huge publicity boost and soon afterwards his name became a byword around the world for luxury rail travel.

*See also: Lasts of the US Presidency, page 140*

## Laika's Last Journey

The last journey of Laika (USSR), the first dog in space, began on 3 November 1957 and ended in April 1958, although it is uncertain how much of the journey Laika survived. Rounded up as a stray to be trained as a cosmonaut, Laika was nicknamed 'Muttnik' by the American press after travelling to an altitude of nearly 2,000 miles in the Soviet satellite *Sputnik II*. *Sputnik*'s telemetry system began to fail five hours into the flight, so nobody can be certain exactly what happened, but there are various theories as to Laika's fate: she died when the oxygen ran out; she died of heat exhaustion when ground control failed to remedy rising humidity and temperature; or she died of food poisoning after being fed poisoned meat by the automatic feeder on board. What is certain, however, is that the Kremlin's story that Laika survived to see the 40th anniversary of the October Revolution is not true – the capsule burned up on re-entry to Earth's atmosphere in April 1958.

**Right** Russian postage stamp depicting Laika (1957)

## Walter Raleigh's Last Trip to the Tower of London

Having once been the court favourite of Queen Elizabeth I, Sir Walter Raleigh (England, also recorded as Ralegh) fell out of favour in 1587 and subsequently made three involuntary journeys to the Tower of London. The first was in 1592, for having a secret affair with one of the Queen's maids-of-honour, Bessy Throckmorton (England), whom he later married. The second was in July 1603, just four months after James I succeeded Elizabeth I. Raleigh was condemned to death, but as he stood on the scaffold awaiting execution the sentence was commuted to life imprisonment. In 1616 he was released from the Tower to make his last expedition, to South America, an expedition sometimes referred to as 'the last great Elizabethan adventure' despite the fact that it took place during the reign of James I.

However, Raleigh's men broke the terms of the expedition by clashing with Spanish forces, which gave King James the excuse he needed to reinvoke Raleigh's suspended death sentence. When Raleigh returned to England in June 1618 he was sent to the Tower for the third and last time, before being beheaded on 29 October 1618. Raleigh's last words are attributed in various orders and for various reasons. Feeling the edge of the axe, he said: 'It is a sharp remedy, but a sure one for all ills.' Either immediately before or immediately after this, and either because someone objected to the position of the block or because he was asked which way he preferred to lay his head, Raleigh said either: 'What matter how the head lie, so the heart be right?' or: 'So the heart be right, it is no matter which way the head lieth.'

# Chapter Eight

# Last Words

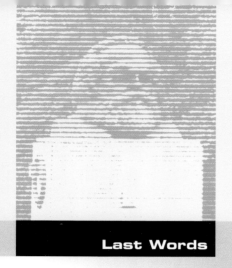

In death, as in life, the world takes more notice of some people than of others. Many celebrities rehearse their dying words in readiness, but others disapprove of the idea – including Karl Marx, whose last words are recorded as: 'Last words are for fools who haven't said enough.'

260 **Last Words**

# WITH THEIR LAST BREATH...

## King Albert I
(BELGIUM, d. 1934)

Albert I was an active king, commanding the Belgian Army in the field throughout the First World War and leading the Belgian and French Armies in the final offensive to retake the Belgian coast at the end of the war. He was killed in a climbing accident in the Ardennes. Before leaving his companions to take his own route he said:

> If I feel in good form I shall take the difficult way up. If I do not, I shall take the easy one. I shall join you in an hour.

## Meher Baba
(INDIA, d. 1925)

Guru Meher Baba's last words, which have since been turned into a pop song, were spoken 44 years before his death in 1969. Before executing his vow of silence, his last words were:

> Don't worry, be happy.

## Ambrose Bierce
(USA, d. 1913)

Short-story writer and journalist Ambrose Bierce is most famous for his *Cynic's Word Book*, since republished under the better-known title *The Devil's Dictionary*. In 1913 he went to Mexico, to report on the rise of Pancho Villa's revolutionary army, where he vanished without trace. In his last letter before his disappearance, he wrote prophetically:

> To be a gringo in Mexico. Ah, that is euthanasia.

**Below** 'Don't worry, be happy': the last words of Meher Baba
**Opposite** Rex Harrison, playing Julius Caesar, is stabbed to death in the Roman Senate, in the historical epic film *Cleopatra* (1963)

## Billy the Kid

(USA, d. 1881)

William H. Bonney, better known as Billy the Kid, was one of America's legendary outlaws. After Bonney escaped from prison in April 1881, former friend turned lawman Pat Garrett began a pursuit that is the subject of Sam Peckinpah's film *Pat Garrett & Billy the Kid*. At midnight on 14 July Garrett entered the bedroom of Pete Maxwell, a mutual acquaintance, to quiz him about Billy's whereabouts. Shortly afterwards Billy entered the room; Garrett recognized his voice in the dark and shot him dead. Billy's last words were a question to Maxwell about the figure in the darkness:

> *Who is it? Who is it?*

## Anne Boleyn

(ENGLAND, d. 1536)

The second of Henry VIII's six wives, Anne Boleyn, mother of Elizabeth I, was executed for adultery on 19 May 1536, when she said hopefully:

> *The executioner is, I believe, very expert; and my neck is very slender. Oh God, have pity on my soul.*

## John Wilkes Booth

(USA, d. 1865)

John Wilkes Booth is infamous as the assassin of US President Abraham Lincoln in April 1865. Booth escaped to Virginia, but was tracked down and, when he refused to surrender, was shot dead. His last words were his explanation and personal assessment of his crime:

> *Tell my mother that I died for my country. I thought I did it for the best. Useless! Useless!*

## Julius Caesar

(ITALY, d. 44BC)

In 45BC the Roman General Julius Caesar became all-powerful, being given the title 'Father of his Country', made consul for 10 years thereafter and dictator for life. However, 'for life' proved to be a short reign when, on the ides (15th) of March the following year, he was assassinated by a group of conspirators led by his former confidante Marcus Junius Brutus. Caesar's last words, as Brutus stabbed him, were:

> *Et tu, Brute?*

## Donald Campbell

(ENGLAND, d. 1967)

Sir Malcolm Campbell broke the land-speed record no less than eight times between 1924 and 1935 and the water-speed record four times between 1937 and 1939, but discouraged his son, Donald, from trying to emulate his feat, saying, prophetically, that

Donald was so accident-prone he would kill himself if he tried. Donald ignored his father's advice, breaking the water-speed record six times between 1955 and 1964 and in 1964 becoming the first person and the last to date to break both land- and water-speed records in the same year. Having broken the 200mph water-speed barrier in 1955, Campbell decided in 1967 to attempt the 300mph barrier in his turbojet hydroplane *Bluebird*, but sadly he died in the attempt. A recording of his last radio transmission was released in 1997:

> Roger, Paul. I am starting the return run now. Nose is up. Pitching a bit down here as I drive over my own wash... Tramping like mad, full power, tramping like hell here. I can't see much. The water's very dark... green... I can't see anything... Hello, the bow's up. I have gone...

## Miguel de Cervantes
(SPAIN, d. 1616)

Cervantes was perhaps Spain's greatest writer, author of the comic epic *Don Quixote*, which has been described as 'the greatest book of the 17th century', 'one of the best books in the world' and 'the most carelessly written of all great books'. It is also sometimes described as the first novel. Cervantes' last words were written to his patron:

> Already my foot is in the stirrup. Already, great Lord and master, the agonies are upon me as I send these lines. Yesterday they administered to me the last rites. Today I am writing this. Time is short. Agony grows. Hope lessens. Only the will to live keeps me alive. Would that life might last until I might kiss the feet of your excellency. Seeing your excellency back in Spain, hale and hearty, might restore me to life. But if it be decreed that I must die, heaven's will be done. May your excellency know at least what my wish was and know also that he had in me a servant so faithful as to have wished to have served your excellency even after death.

## Cherokee Bill
(USA, d. 1896)

Before he was hanged, outlaw Cherokee Bill's penultimate words were: 'The quicker this thing's over, the better.' Then, in reply to the question whether he had any last words, he said:

> No. I came here to die, not make a speech.

## Erskine Childers
(IRELAND–ENGLAND, d. 1922)

Erskine Childers is probably best remembered today for *The Riddle of the Sands*, his 1903 spy novel about a German invasion of Britain, which was made into a feature film starring Donald Sutherland. However, he was first and foremost not a novelist but an Irish nationalist and politician, working before the First World War for Irish Home Rule and afterwards becoming a Sinn Fein member of the Irish Parliament. He joined the IRA in opposition to the establishment of the Irish Free State and was executed in Dublin. His son, Erskine Hamilton Childers, later became the fourth president of Ireland. Childers' last words, as he faced the firing squad, were:

> Take a step forward, lads. It will be easier that way.

**Left** Portrait of Miguel de Cervantes by Juan de Jáuregui y Aguilar

**Opposite above** Noël Coward in the Nevada Desert during his debut season in Las Vegas (22 June 1955)

## Winston Churchill

(ENGLAND, d. 1965)

Sir Winston Churchill was not simply a great British prime minister and wartime leader, he was an international statesman and man of letters – the last serving MP to have sat during the reign of Queen Victoria and the last public link with the British Empire, and the last British prime minister to date to be awarded the Nobel Prize for Literature. Churchill's last day in the House of Commons was 27 July 1964. His last words are not recorded, but those spoken on his 75th birthday remained appropriate:

> I am ready to meet my Maker. Whether my Maker is prepared for the ordeal of meeting me is another matter.

*See also: The Last Post, page 276*

## Noël Coward

(ENGLAND, d. 1976)

Cheerful and optimistic to the end, actor, playwright, composer and wit Noël Coward uttered as his last words:

> Goodnight my darlings, I'll see you in the morning.

## Dr Henry Hawley Crippen

(USA, d. 1910)

Crippen is infamous as the US dentist who murdered his second wife, Cora Turner, because he had fallen in love with his secretary, Ethel le Neve. He and le Neve fled to Antwerp, Belgium, whence they sailed for Quebec, Canada, on board the transatlantic liner *Montrose* under the guise of Mister and Master Robinson. The captain was

suspicious of the couple and liaised by radio with police (the first time radio had been used to catch a criminal), who were waiting to arrest Crippen on his arrival in Canada. Before being hanged in 1910, Crippen wrote:

> In this last letter to the world, written as I face eternity, I say that Ethel le Neve loved me as few women love men and that her innocence of any crime, save that of yielding to the dictates of her heart, is absolute. My last prayer will be that God will protect her and keep her safe from harm and allow her to join me in eternity.

## James Croll

(SCOTLAND, d. 1890)

Physicist and geologist James Croll

was a lifelong teetotaller, but decided on his deathbed to sample a little of the water of life:

> I'll take a wee drop of that. I don't think there's much fear of me turning to drink now.

## Leon Czogolsz

(USA, d. 1901)

Like those of presidential assassin John Wilkes Booth, the last words of Leon Czogolsz, anarchist and assassin of US President William McKinley, were an explanation of his crime:

> I killed the President because he was the enemy of the good people, the good working people. I am not sorry for my crime.

## Sir William D'Avenant

(ENGLAND, d. 1668)

Poet and playwright William D'Avenant was born in Oxford, where his father ran a tavern at which William Shakespeare used to stay, provoking the rumour that D'Avenant was, in fact, Shakespeare's illegitimate son. D'Avenant was appointed Poet Laureate in 1638 after the death of Ben Jonson the previous year, knighted by Charles I in 1643 and imprisoned in the Tower of London for two years during the interregnum. His last words, as he stopped work on the poem he was composing, were:

> I shall have to ask leave to desist, when I am interrupted by so great an experiment as dying.

## Leonardo da Vinci

(ITALY, d. 1519)

Painter, sculptor, architect, anatomist, scientist and engineer Leonardo da Vinci was one of the most accomplished artists of all time. His last words reveal the perfectionism that drove him to create works such as the Mona Lisa and The Last Supper:

> I have offended God and mankind because my work did not reach the quality it should have.

## Georges Danton

(FRANCE, d. 1794)

Revolutionary leader Georges Danton became Minister of Justice in the First French Republic and was among those who voted to execute the king, but later lost power to Maximilien Robespierre. In 1794 he was arrested for conspiring to overthrow the government, and his last words before his execution were typically defiant:

> Be sure to show my head to the people. It is worth showing. (sometimes translated as: It will be a long time ere they see its like.)

## René Descartes

(FRANCE, d. 1650)

Philosopher and mathematician René Descartes, often referred to as 'the father of modern philosophy', died of pneumonia in Stockholm, Sweden. His last words are sometimes quoted as:

> So, my soul, a time for parting,

although they are also rendered more philosophically as:

> My soul, thou hast long been held captive. The hour has now come for thee to quit thy prison, to leave the trammels of this body. Then to this separation with joy and courage.

## Queen Elizabeth I

(ENGLAND, d. 1603)

The last words of Elizabeth I show that riches and power mean little in the overall scheme of things:

> All my possessions for one moment of time.

## Douglas Fairbanks Snr

(USA, d. 1939)

Film star and producer Douglas Fairbanks Snr was famous for his swashbuckling roles in films such as The Three Musketeers, Robin Hood and The Thief of Baghdad, and was a co-founder of United Pictures. Optimistic to the end, his last words were:

> I've never felt better.

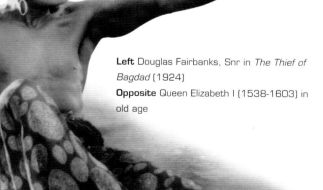

**Left** Douglas Fairbanks, Snr in *The Thief of Bagdad* (1924)
**Opposite** Queen Elizabeth I (1538-1603) in old age

## Bernard le Bovier de Fontenelle

(FRANCE, d. 1757)

Writer Bernard de Fontenelle, author of, among other things, *New Dialogues of the Dead*, lived for 100 years, a remarkable age in the 18th century. In the light of his longevity, his last words are perhaps not surprising:

*I feel nothing except a certain difficulty in continuing to exist.*

## Henry Fox, Lord Holland

(ENGLAND, d. 1774)

London's Holland House and Holland Park take their name from the title of Henry Fox, 1st Baron Holland, who was a Liberal politician, writer and translator of Spanish works. A competitive politician to the end, his last words were:

*If Mr Selwyn [a political rival] calls again, show him up. If I am alive I shall be delighted to see him, and if I am dead he would like to see me.*

## Benjamin Franklin

(USA, d. 1790)

US Founding Father, statesman, diplomat, printer, publisher, inventor and scientist Benjamin Franklin died at the age of 84. In 1731, at the age of 25 and with his greatest achievements yet to come, Franklin had amused himself by composing this epitaph:

*The body of Ben Franklin, Printer (like the cover of an old book, its contents torn out and stripped of its lettering and gilding) lies here, food for worms. But the work shall not be lost, for it will (as he believed) appear in a new and more elegant edition, revised and corrected by the author.*

## Clark Gable

(USA, d. 1960)

Clark Gable managed no less than 12 film appearances in his Hollywood debut year, 1931. He won an Oscar three years later and was voted 'King of Hollywood' three years after that, in 1937. Most famous for his Oscar-nominated role as Rhett Butler in *Gone With The Wind* (1939), he appeared with Marilyn Monroe in his last film, *The Misfits* (1961). His last words on screen are particularly apt:

Marilyn Monroe: *How do you find the way back in the dark?*
Clark Gable: *Just head for the big star straight on. The highways under it take us right home.*

## Paul Gauguin

(FRANCE, d. 1903)

During the 1870s Paul Gauguin was a successful Paris stockbroker, but during the following decade he abandoned this profession, his Danish wife and five children for art. He visited Martinique and then lived for a decade in Tahiti before moving in 1901 to the Marquesas Islands, where he died alone two years later. His last words were in the form of a note to a missionary:

*Would it be too much to ask you to come and see me? My eyesight seems to be going and I cannot walk. I am very ill.*

## King George V

(BRITAIN, d. 1936)

Among the various last words attributed to King George V are his two-word reply to suggestions that his health was improving and that he might soon be well enough to visit his favourite resort, Bognor Regis:

*Bugger Bognor.*

**Right** Detail of statue of Nathan Hale at Connecticut Hall, Yale University

## William Graham
(BRITAIN, d. 1856)

William Graham was a passenger on board the steamship *Pacific*, which sank in an icefield during a voyage from Liverpool, England, to New York, USA. His last written words were a message in a bottle, later washed ashore in the Hebrides:

*On board the* Pacific *from Liverpool to NY. Ship going down. Confusion on board. Icebergs around us on every side. I know I cannot escape. I write the cause of our loss that friends may not live in suspense. The finder will please get it published.*

## Pope Gregory VII
(ITALY, d. 1085)

The son of an Italian carpenter, Hildebrand was appointed Pope in 1073, taking the name Gregory VII. His reforms led to conflict with Holy Roman Emperor Henry IV, who excommunicated him in 1076. Gregory withdrew to Salerno, Italy, where he died after uttering the last words:

*I have loved justice and hated iniquity, therefore I die in exile.*

## Nathan Hale
(USA, d. 1776)

A statue of Nathan Hale, the unofficial patron saint of US intelligence agencies, stands outside the headquarters of the CIA in Langley, Virginia. Hale fought for the Continental Army in the American War of Independence and volunteered to spy for George Washington behind British lines on Long Island. After being captured, his last words before being hanged as a spy were:

*I regret that I have but one life to give for my country.*

## Henrik Ibsen
(NORWAY, d. 1906)

Henrik Ibsen was a brilliant poet, dramatist and social critic who revolutionized European drama, but his last words were neither poetic nor dramatic. When his nurse assured visitors to his sickbed that his health was improving, Ibsen's last words were:

*On the contrary.*

## Andrew Jackson
(USA, d. 1845)

In his last words, former US President Andrew Jackson remembered firstly the man who had stood against him in the presidential election of 1832 and secondly his own vice president, who had resigned after an argument over policy:

*I have only two regrets ... that I have not shot Henry Clay or hanged John C. Calhoun.*

## Thornton Jones
(WALES, d. 1924)

Jones was a solicitor who somehow – unless it was an elaborate way of committing suicide without seeming to do so – managed to cut his own

Left Ned Kelly in his home-made armour

throat in his sleep. After waking, he survived long enough to write:

*I dreamt that I had done it; I woke to find it true.*

## Ned Kelly
(AUSTRALIA, d. 1880)

Ned Kelly, the Australian son of a transported Irish convict, became an unlikely folk hero after shooting three policemen and pulling off two armed bank robberies. Kelly was captured, in his famous home-made suit of armour, while attempting to hold up a train in Glenrowan, Victoria. His last words before being hanged in November 1880 were:

*Ah, well. I suppose it had to come to this. Such is life.*

## Martin Luther King Jr
(USA, d. 1968)

On 28 August 1963 clergyman and civil rights leader Martin Luther King, who championed a Gandhi-like philosophy of non-violent, passive resistance to racial intolerance, delivered one of the greatest speeches of the 20th century. The following year he was awarded an honorary doctorate from Yale University, the Kennedy Peace Prize and the Nobel Peace Prize. He was assassinated on 4 April 1968 in Memphis, Tennessee. The last sentence of his 'I Have A Dream' speech was:

*When we let freedom ring, when we let it ring from every village and every hamlet, from every state and every city, we will be able to speed up that day when all of God's children, black men and white men, Jews and Gentiles, Protestants and Catholics, will be able to join hands and sing the words of the* old negro spiritual, *'Free at last! Free at last! Thank God Almighty, free at last'*.

King's own last words were spoken to his friend the Reverend Jesse Jackson:

*Be sure to sing* Precious Lord *tonight and sing it well.*

## King Louis XIV, the 'Sun King'
(FRANCE, d. 1715)

The reign of Louis XIV, who ascended the throne at the age of five, was the longest in European history to that date. Louis outlived his son and grandson, and was therefore succeeded by his five-year-old great-grandson, Louis XV. Louis'

**Below** Martin Luther King waves to the crowd during the March on Washington on the day that he delivered his famous 'I Have a Dream' speech (28 August 1963)

**Opposite** The grave of Karl Marx in Highgate Cemetery, London, England

last words were:

*Why weep you? Did you think I would live forever? I thought dying would have been harder.*

## King Louis XVI
(FRANCE, d. 1793)

Louis XVI was deposed by the French Revolution and executed for treason against the Republic, ending more than 1,000 years of French monarchy. His last words are variously recorded as, firstly:

*I shall drink the cup to the last dregs.*

implying a continuation of the self-indulgence that in part precipitated the Revolution, and, secondly, a protestation of his innocence of treason:

*Frenchmen, I die guiltless of the crimes imputed to me. Pray God my blood fall not on France.*

## Maccail
(SCOTLAND, d. 1668)

Scottish Covenanter Maccail was tortured to death for his religious beliefs. His last words were poetic, childlike and strangely haunting:

*Farewell moon and stars, farewell world and time, farewell weak and frail body. Welcome eternity, welcome angels and saints, welcome saviour of the world, welcome God, the judge of all.*

## Niccolò Machiavelli
(ITALY, d. 1527)

Statesman, writer and political philosopher Niccolò Machiavelli gave the world the adjective machiavellian, from the political theory, outlined in his book *The Prince*, that political ends justify any means necessary. His contempt for the existing order was revealed in his last words:

*I desire to go to hell and not to heaven. In the former place I shall enjoy the company of popes, kings and princes, while in the latter are only beggars, monks and apostles.*

## Marcus Aurelius

(ITALY, d. 80AD)

The last words of Roman emperor and philosopher Marcus Aurelius, whose most famous work was *Meditationes*, were suitably philosophical:

*Go to the rising sun, for I am setting. Think more of death than of me.*

## Karl Marx

(GERMANY, d. 1883)

Social, political and economic theorist Karl Marx, who wrote one of the most influential political works of the 19th century, *Das Kapital*, also spent 37 years as European correspondent for the *New York Daily Tribune*. His last words were spoken to his housekeeper, who asked if he had a last message to give to the world:

*Go on, get out! Last words are for fools who haven't said enough.*

## Somerset Maugham

(BRITAIN, b. FRANCE OF IRISH ORIGIN, d. 1965)

Somerset Maugham is known primarily as a playwright and author, but he was also a qualified surgeon who spent a year practising in the 19th-century London slums. He served as a spy in both world wars, and travelled to Russia hoping to prevent the outbreak of the revolution. Little wonder that he found the idea of death rather boring:

*Dying is a very dull, dreary affair.*

*And my advice to you is to have nothing whatever to do with it.*

## Wolfgang Amadeus Mozart

(AUSTRIA, d. 1791)

The two sets of last words attributed to Mozart both refer to his unfinished Requiem Mass:

*You spoke of a refreshment, Emile; take my last notes, and let me hear once more my solace and delight.*

This is sometimes rendered more prosaically as:

*Did I not tell you I was writing this for myself?*

*See also: Lasts of Classical Music, page 102*

## Emperor Nero

(ITALY, d. 68AD)

Power corrupted Nero, who began as an able emperor but soon descended into tyrany. While the story that he fiddled while Rome burned is probably untrue, his reign of debauchery and murder eventually became too much for the Praetorian Guard, which rose against him in 68AD. Nero had nurtured ambitions as a poet, philosopher, actor and musician and his last words before committing suicide to spare himself the ignominy of execution were:

*Qualis artifex pereo – 'how great an artist dies in me'*

## Sir Isaac Newton

(ENGLAND, d. 1727)

One of the world's greatest scientists, Sir Isaac Newton was knighted for the advances he made in mathematics, for establishing the nature of light and for describing the laws of gravity, yet for all his knowledge he remained humble to the last about the things he did not know:

*I don't know what I may seem to the world. But as to myself I seem to have been only like a boy playing on the seashore and diverting myself in now and then finding a smoother pebble or a prettier shell than the ordinary, whilst the great ocean of truth lay all undiscovered before me.*

## Eugene O'Neill

(USA, d. 1953)

In 1936 Eugene O'Neill became the first American playwright to be awarded the Nobel Prize for Literature. He then released nothing else for a decade while he worked on two of his most important plays, *The Iceman Cometh* (1946) and *A Moon for the Misbegotten* (1947). His masterpiece *Long Day's Journey Into Night* was first performed in 1956, three years after his death in a hotel room, where his last words were:

> I knew it. I knew it. Born in a hotel room and, God damn it, died in a hotel room.

## Lord Palmerston

(ENGLAND, d. 1865)

Henry John Temple, 3rd Viscount Palmerston, was junior Lord of the Admiralty and Secretary at War under five different prime ministers including Spencer Perceval, the last British prime minister to date to be assassinated. Palmerston was twice elected prime minister, on the second occasion remaining in office until his death, when he told his doctor:

> Die, my dear Doctor? That's the last thing I shall do.

## Carl Panzram

(USA, d. 1930)

Panzram was a self-confessed mass murderer who, while he was on death row awaiting execution, became the focus of a campaign by the Society for the Abolition of Capital Punishment to commute his sentence. However, Panzram wanted none of it, writing to the campaigners:

> I do not believe that being hanged by the neck until dead is a barbaric or inhuman punishment. I look forward to

that as a real pleasure and a big relief to me ... when my last hour comes I will dance out of my dungeon and onto the scaffold with a smile on my face and happiness in my heart ... the only thanks that you and your kind will ever get from me for your efforts is that I wish you all had one neck and I had my hands on it.

Panzram's actual last words, when asked on the gallows whether he had anything to say, were:

> Yes. Hurry it up, you Hoosier bastard. I could hang a dozen men while you're fooling around.

## Gram Parsons

(USA, d. 1972)

Singer, songwriter, bandleader, guitarist, keyboard player and all-round influential rock musician Gram Parsons died in a motel room in Joshua Tree, California, of heart failure brought on by 'burning the candle at both ends'. Earlier, when he had been told that continuing his drug habit would prove fatal, he said:

> Death is a warm cloak, an old friend. I regard death as something that comes up on a roulette wheel every once in a while.

## Anna Pavlova

(RUSSIA, d. 1931)

The last words of prima ballerina Anna Pavlova referred back to her most famous role, The Dying Swan, which she created in 1907:

> Get my Swan costume ready.

## Luigi Pirandello

(ITALY, d. 1936)

Among the many works of playwright, novelist, short-story writer and Nobel laureate Luigi

Pirandello was the play *Six Characters in Search of an Author*. On his deathbed, Pirandello named three further characters in search of that author:

> The hearse, the horse, the driver and – enough!

## Pope Pius X

(ITALY, d. 1914)

When he was elected Pope in 1903, Giuseppe Sarto took the name of Pius X. A committed pacifist, he died of a heart attack while berating Franz Joseph, Emperor of Austria and King of Hungary, whose actions following the assassination of his son Franz Ferdinand had precipitated the First World War earlier the same month:

> Get out of my sight! Get out of my sight! Away! Away! We grant blessing to noone who provokes the world to war.

## Plato

(GREECE, d. c.348BC)

Were it not for Athenian philosopher Socrates, the adjective 'platonic' might have referred to metre or rhyme rather than a philosophical ideal, for it was Socrates who persuaded Plato to abandon poetry for philosophy – a debt remembered in Plato's last words:

> I thank the guiding providence and fortune of my life, first, that I was born a man and a Greek, not a barbarian nor a brute; and next, that I happened to live in the age of Socrates.

## William Pope

(BRITAIN, d. 1797)

Ironically for a man of his surname, William Pope was a committed

**Opposite** Anna Pavlova in her most famous role as the dying swan (c.1910)

atheist who established a cult whose main purpose was the desecration of religious places and objects. To the last, he was committed to his cause:

*I cannot pray God will have nothing to do with me. I will not have salvation at his hands. I long to be in the bottomless pit, the lake which burneth with fire and brimstone. I tell you I am damned. I will not have salvation. Nothing for me but hell. Come eternal torments! Oh God do not hear my prayers for I will not be saved. I hate everything that God has made!*

## François Rabelais
(FRANCE, d. 1553)

The monk, physician and satirist Rabelais remained humorous to the end. The last line of his will read: 'I have nothing. I owe much. The rest I leave to the poor', while his last words were:

*I am going to seek the great perhaps...*

and then, echoing the last words of the Greek philosopher Demonax:

*Bring down the curtain, the farce is over.*

## King Richard I, 'the Lion-Heart'
(ENGLAND, d. 1199)

Richard the Lion-Heart spent less than a year of his 10-year reign in England, and there is some doubt that he spoke English, yet he is a popular national hero. He was killed while besieging the castle of Chalus, France, by an archer named Bertrand de Gourdon, who was subsequently captured. Richard's last words were to pardon his killer:

*Youth, I forgive thee. Take off his chains, give him 100 shillings, and let him go.*

## Ethel & Julius Rosenberg
(USA, d. 1953)

The Rosenberg espionage trial of 1951 sparked demonstrations across America both for and against the verdict, as well as appeals for leniency from several western European nations. Husband and wife Ethel and Julius Rosenberg, Ethel's brother David Greenglass, and their colleague Morton Sobell were accused of passing atomic secrets to the USSR. In return for leniency, Greenglass testified against the other three, whom Judge Irving Kaufmann sentenced to death for 'a diabolical conspiracy to destroy a God-fearing nation'. Sobell's sentence was commuted to 30 years' imprisonment, but the Rosenbergs, who had two young sons, were executed in the gas chamber on 19 June 1953. In a petition to President Eisenhower, Julius wrote:

*We are innocent. That is the whole truth. To forsake this truth is to pay too high a price even for the priceless gift of life. For life thus purchased we could not live in dignity.*

Ethel's last words were:

*We are the first victims of American fascism.*

## Siward
(DENMARK–ENGLAND, d. 1055)

Siward was a Danish adventurer who, after settling in England, was made Earl of Northumberland. There are two versions of his last words and both attest to his disappointment at a ruminant death:

*Lift me up that I may die standing, not lying down like a cow.*

This is sometimes rendered more poetically as:

*Shame on me that I did not die in one of the many battles that I have fought, but am reserved to die with the disgrace of the death of a sick cow. At least put on my armour of proof, gird the sword by my side, place the helmet on my head, let me have my shield in my left hand and my axe in my right, that the bravest of soldiers may die in a soldier's garb.*

## Socrates

(GREECE, d. 399BC)

The questions raised by the great philosopher Socrates eventually led to his trial, at the age of 70, for 'impiety'. He was sentenced to die by drinking hemlock and his last words displayed not philosophical wisdom but human good faith:

*Crito, I owe a cock to Asclepius. Will you remember the debt?*

## Mark Twain

(USA, d. 1910)

Samuel Langhorne Clemens, better known by his pseudonym Mark Twain, was one of America's best-loved and most influential writers and the author of *Tom Sawyer* and *Huckleberry Finn*. He left a written memo by his deathbed:

*Death, the only immortal, who treats us all alike, whose peace and refuge are for all. The soiled and the pure, the rich and the poor, the loved and the unloved.*

## Voltaire

(FRANCE, d. 1778)

Voltaire was the pseudonym of 18th-century French writer, satirist and historian François Marie Arouet, whose best-known work is *Candide*. In 1762 he published the first of a number of anti-religious writings, and this rejection of religion explains his last words, spoken to a priest who visited his deathbed hoping that he might repent:

*In God's name let me die in peace!*

Then, looking at the lamp burning at his bedside, he said:

*The flames already?*

**Opposite** Portrait of Oscar Wilde by N. Sarony (c.1882)

**Right** A scene from the 1936 film *The Great Ziegfeld*

## Oscar Wilde

(IRELAND, d. 1900)

Dramatist and wit Oscar Wilde died as he lived – with humour. At the time most people considered the year of his death, 1900, to be the last year of the 19th century rather than the first of the 20th, which explains the use of the conditional tense in his last words, spoken shortly before his death on 30 November 1900:

*It would really be more than the English could stand if another century began and I were still alive. I am dying as I have lived … beyond my means.*

## Virginia Woolf

(ENGLAND, d. 1941)

As a novelist Virginia Woolf was one of the great innovators of her day with works such as *Mrs Dalloway*, *To The Lighthouse* and *The Waves*. Her last novel, *Between The Acts*, was published posthumously in 1941, the same year that she succumbed to her long-term depression and drowned herself in the River Ouse, Sussex. Her suicide note took the form of three last letters, one of them to her husband:

*I have a feeling I shall go mad. I cannot go on any longer in these terrible times. I hear voices and I cannot concentrate on my work. I have fought against it but cannot fight any longer. I owe all my happiness to you, but cannot go on and spoil your life.*

## Florenz Ziegfeld

(USA, d. 1932)

Impresario and theatre manager Florenz Ziegfeld created a theatrical phenomenon new to the USA – the revue, which he based on the French *Folies Bergères*. Ziegfeld's Follies proved hugely popular and helped launch the career of W.C. Fields among others. Judging from Ziegfeld's last words, he was happily imagining himself back in the theatre as he died:

*Curtain! Fast music! Lights! Ready for the last finale! Great! The show looks good, the show looks good!*

The Last Post contains the lasts that did not have a home in earlier chapters, but without which no book of lasts would be complete. It is a collection of lasts that defy categorization, some of which are not lasts in the usual sense, but qualify as lasts by name rather than by definition.

**And Finally...**

# THE LAST POST

## Mariners' and Cobblers' lasts

For seafarers and shoemakers the word 'last' has another meaning apart from the final or most recent example of something. Mariners (and others, including farmers) use the word to denote an inexact unit of measurement for a load generally weighing about 1,800kg, deriving from the Old English word *hlæst*, meaning a load or burden.

A cobbler's last is a three-dimensional model of a foot made from wood or metal, which is used for making and repairing shoes. The tool itself dates back several thousand years, but the word is more recent, deriving from the Old English *læst*, meaning footprint. Interestingly, 'last' in the sense of 'continue' or 'endure' derives from another form of the same Old English word – *læstan*, meaning 'to follow a track (of footprints)'.

## The Last Rose of Summer

The original reference to 'the last rose of summer' comes in the poem '*Tis the Last Rose*, by Thomas Moore (Ireland):

> *'Tis the last rose of summer*
> *Left blooming alone;*
> *All her lovely companions*
> *Are faded and gone.*

## The Last Straw

The metaphor 'the last straw' derives from the proverb: 'It is the last straw that breaks the camel's back', meaning that the final difficulty that makes a situation completely unendurable could be something as insignificant as a single piece of straw. The first use of this phrase in print was in the 1848 novel *Dombey & Son* by Charles Dickens (England): 'As the last straw breaks the laden camel's back, this piece of underground information crushed the sinking spirits of Mr Dombey.' However, more than 50 years earlier, in 1793, a similar phrase appeared in *Publications of the Colonial Society of Massachusetts* (USA): 'It is certainly true that the last feather will sink the camel.' And more than a century before that, in 1655, J. Bramhall (Britain) wrote: 'It is the last feather may be said to break an Horses back.'

## Obituaries: the last word?

Obituaries are usually thought to be the last words on a person's life, but that is not always the case – several luminaries have had the disturbing experience of reading their own obituaries long before they died. Alfred Nobel (Sweden) read that he was 'a merchant of death' and was stung into establishing the Nobel Foundation that still funds the annual Nobel Prizes (*see also: Alfred Nobel, page 176*). Mark Twain (USA) was in the fortunate position of being able to describe reports that he had died as 'greatly exaggerated', and Ernest Hemingway (USA) read his obituary

**Left** Celebrated Italian shoemaker Salvatore Ferragamo (1898–1960) with some of the lasts used to make shoes for his distinguished clients, who include Sophia Loren, Ava Gardner and Greta Garbo (1956) **Opposite** Almost the last straw... an overloaded camel near Bagram, Afghanistan (25 May 2003)

on two separate occasions before obliging the obituarists by committing suicide in 1961 (*see also: Authors' Last Novels, page 110*). Others lived so long that their obituaries had been prepared for years and were regularly updated in readiness for their death; they included HRH Queen Elizabeth the Queen Mother (Britain), who died on 30 March 2002 at the age of 101, and Bob Hope (England–USA), who died on 27 July 2003, at the age of 100.

## Predicting his last day

On 24 January 1950, between terms as British prime minister, Winston Churchill (England) pointed out to his companions that this was the day his father, Lord Randolph Churchill, had died just over half a century earlier, in 1895 and he predicted that it would be the day

that he, too, would die. He fulfilled his prediction exactly 15 years later, on 24 January 1965. *See also: With Their Last Breath..., page 263*

## Famous last words

Although the phrase 'famous last words' can be applied to the dying words of famous people, such as those listed in chapter 8 of this book, it is more usually applied to a bold statement that has been, or is likely to be, proved incorrect by subsequent events. One case where both meanings apply is that of General John Sedgwick (USA), a Union commander in the American Civil War, who was killed at the Battle of Spotsylvania, USA, while looking over the parapet of the Court House and announcing his military assessment of the danger from the enemy: 'They couldn't hit an elephant at this dist...'

Famous last words that were not words of the dying include the following:

Film producer Irving Thalberg, head of production at MGM, advised Louis B. Mayer (both USA) not to bother bidding for the film rights to *Gone With the Wind*: 'Forget it, Louis. No Civil War picture ever made a nickel.'

Dick Rowe (Britain), A&R man at Decca, turned down the Beatles, saying: 'We don't like their sound. Groups with guitars are on their way out.' (Rowe did redeem himself the following year by signing The Rolling Stones.)

Film producer Darryl F. Zanuck (USA) refused to sign Cary Grant (England–USA) to Warner Brothers, saying: 'His ears are too big. He looks like an ape.'

Disc jockey Jono Coleman (Australia) was one of the first people to play *The Locomotion* by Kylie Minogue (Australia) on the radio, but then said: 'She's a great little actress, but I don't think she'll be giving up the day job any time soon' – *The Locomotion* spent seven weeks as Australian No.1 and Minogue went on to have 13 consecutive UK and Australian Top 10 hits.

British Prime Minister Neville Chamberlain signed the Munich Agreement on 29 September 1938 and returned to Britain saying: 'I believe it is peace for our time … peace with honour.' Less than a year later the Second World War began.

Professor Dionysius Lardner (Ireland) predicted in the early 19th century that: 'No steamship could be built large enough to carry sufficient coals for a voyage across the Atlantic.'

Charles H. Duell (USA), an official at the US Patent Office, is often quoted as saying in 1899 (although whether he said this is disputed): 'Everything that can be invented has been invented.'

Marshal Ferdinand Foch (France), Allied commander in chief at the end of the First World War, said: 'Aeroplanes are interesting toys, but have no military value.'

## The Last Post

The Last Post means one thing to postal workers and something entirely different to the armed forces. The military Last Post is the last of a number of bugle calls marking the phases of the day, and is the counterpart of the first bugle call of the day, the reveille (from the French *réveillez*, meaning 'wake up'). The Last Post is now a ritual in its own right, but is thought to have evolved as the final part of an

evening routine dating back to the 17th century, when the duty officer would do the rounds, sending off-duty soldiers to their billets and checking that the sentry posts were manned. The First Post was sounded on the bugle when the duty officer started his rounds, a drumbeat accompanied the rounds (from which the American military practice of 'taps' originated) and another bugle call, the Last Post, was sounded when the duty officer reached the last sentry post, completing his rounds. Later, the Last Post was incorporated in military funeral and memorial services as a final farewell, signifying that life, not just the day's duty, is over.

**Opposite** *The Death of General Sedgwick*, by Civil War veteran Julian Scott (see: *Famous Last Words*)
**Right** A bugler of the Indian army plays the Last Post (8 June 1946)

# SELECTED BIBLIOGRAPHY

**General lasts & lasts facts**

Cosmopulos, Stavros. *The Book of Lasts*. Penguin, 1995

Green, Jonathon. *Famous Last Words*. Kyle Cathie Ltd, 2002

Lenman, Bruce P. (consultant ed.). *Chambers Dictionary of World History*. Chambers, 2000

Parry, Melanie (ed.). *Chambers Biographical Dictionary*. Chambers, 1999

Reader's Digest Association. *Reader's Digest Book of Facts*. Reader's Digest Association Ltd, 1985

Slee, Christopher. *The Guinness Book of Lasts*. Guinness Publishing Ltd, 1994

Symons, Mitchell. *That Book*. Bantam Press, 2003

**Specific subjects.**

Barner, Klaus. 'Paul Wolfskehl and the Wolfskehl Prize'. Translation of article originally appearing in *Mathematische Schriften Kassel, Vordruckreihe des Fachbereichs 17*, Preprint Nr. 4/97, Mar-97

Calouste Gulbenkian Foundation. *Calouste Sarkis Gulbenkian The Man and His Achievements*. Calouste Gulbenkian Foundation, 1999

Chown, Marcus. 'Did falling comet cause rumble in the jungle?' Article in *New Scientist*, 11-Nov-95

Clarke, Donald (ed.). *The Penguin Encyclopedia of Popular Music*. Penguin, 1998

Fane-Saunders, Kilmeny (ed.). *Radio Times Guide to Films*. BBC

Worldwide, 2003

Gammond, Peter (ed.). *The A–Z of Classical Composers*. Bramley Books, 1997

Kemp, Peter (ed.). *The Oxford Companion to Ships & The Sea*. OUP, 1979

Little, Alan. *This is Wimbledon*. All England Lawn Tennis & Croquet Club, 2002

Mankowitz, Wolf. *Dickens of London*. Weidenfeld & Nicholson, 1976

Ross, David. *'The Willing Servant' A History of the Steam Locomotive*. Tempus Publishing Ltd, 2004

Sacks, David. *The Alphabet*. Hutchinson, 2003

Singh, Simon. *Fermat's Last Theorem*. Fourth Estate, 1997

# ACKNOWLEDGEMENTS

Dedicated to the memory of all those who have suffered as a result of the lasts described in this book.

With thanks to Barbara Dixon for (as always) expert advice that goes well beyond the call of editorial duty; to Thomas Keenes for designing with the maximum of impact and the minimum of cuts to the text; to project editors Anna Cheifetz and Victoria Alers-Hankey for such a seamless handover of power; and to Sue Bosanko and Vickie Walters for editorial help and picture research. Thanks also to the following people and organizations for their help in researching *The Book of Lasts*: Marjorie Caygill (British Museum); Andrew Colquhoun (Imperial War Museum); George Crosbie; Ben Grindley; Pat Hammond; John Handford; Phil Harrison; Mary Harrison; Louisa Hooper (Calouste Gulbenkian Foundation UK); Roddy Langley; Geraint Lewis; Sally Lewis; Richard Penfold; Katy Rawdon-Faucett (Barnes Foundation); Simon Rogers; David Shepherd; Andrew Stewart (Barnes Foundation); Tim Tanner. Lyrics for 'American Pie' (page 246) © Don Maclean.

## Picture credits

Every effort has been made to contact copyright holders, however please contact the publishers if any omissions have inadvertently been made.

**AKG, London 103**, **200** top left, **200** bottom centre; /Archiv K.Wagenbach **180** top, **180** bottom.
**The Barnes Foundation**/Dr. Albert C. Barnes, Giorgio de Chirico, BF#805 (c) reproduced with the Permission of The Barnes Foundation TM, All Rights Reserved. **188** top left, **188** bottom.
**Bridgeman Art Library, London (www.bridgeman.co.uk) 14** top left, **38** top left, **44** top left, **82** centre; /Jauregui y Aguilar/Private Collection **262**; /Bibliotheque Nationale, Paris **122** top left, **123** top right; /Central St. Martins College, London **108** bottom; /English School, Corsham Court, Wiltshire **265**; /Giraudon Private Collection **38**; /Guildhall Art Gallery, Corporation of London, UK **222-223**; /The Wellington Museum, London **122-123**; /Louvre, Paris **95** top centre; /Musee de la Revolution Francaise, Vizille, France **25**; /Musee Municipal Antoine Vivenel, Compiegne, France, Lauros/Giraudon **15** bottom right; /National Library of Australia, Canberra, Australia **39**; /Philip Mould, Historical Portraits Ltd, London,UK **148** bottom; /Private Collection **45**, **46**; /Rijksmuseum Vincent van Gogh, Amsterdam **94**, **94-95** bottom; /Santa Maria della Grazie, Milan **126** top left, **126-127**.
**Corbis UK Limited 10**, **10** top left, **18**, **20** top left, **22** top left, **24**, **24** top left, **30** top left, **34**, **36** top left, **40** top left, **48** top left, **50**, **110-111**, **120** centre left, **152** top left, **153** right, **166** centre, **176** top, **177**, **226**, **226** top left, **228** top, **235** bottom right, **267**, **268**, **272**; /(c) National Gallery Collection: by kind permission of the Trustees of the National Gallery, London **21** top, **170** top, **171**; /Academy of Natural Sciences of Philadelphia **129**; /Adam Woolfitt **152-153**; /Alinari Archives **16**; /Applewhite Denise **96** top left, **97**; /Archivo Iconografico, S.A. **41**, **42-43**, **56** left, **102** centre, **112** top left, **113**; /BBC **131**; /Bettmann **14-15**, **23**, **26-27** top, **30**, **40**, **55** top, **58-59** bottom, **60** centre left, **66** top left, **67** top, **68** top left, **69**, **72-73** bottom, **76** centre, **78** top left, **79** top, **82** top left, **83**, **93** top right, **96** bottom centre, **109**, **118** centre left, **142** top left, **143** top, **144** top left, **145**, **154**, **154** top left, **155**, **157** bottom, **172**, **173**, **182** bottom, **184**, **184-185**, **194** top left, **195** bottom, **202** top left, **204** top left, **204-205**, **225** bottom, **230** top left, **230** bottom, **231**, **232** top left, **232-233**, **234**, **236** top left, **237**, **237** top, **239** right, **242-243**, **246**, **247**, **250**, **261**, **271**; /S. Carmona **210** centre left; /Charles E. Rotkin **37** bottom; /Conde Nast Archive **158** bottom; /Gianni Dagli **56** top left, **57**; /Alexander Demianchuk **84**, **85**; /Aubert Dominique **67** bottom; /Julio Donoso **64** top left, **65**; /Douglas Kirkland **252**, **253** bottom; /Francis G. Meyer **11**; /Farrell Grehan **164** top, **165**; /Historical Picture Archive **51** bottom; /Angelo Hornak **98** bottom; /Hulton Collection **88**, **108** top left; /Image **144** bottom; /Image (c) Andy Warhol Foundation Artwork (c) The Andy Warhol Foundation for the Visual Arts **31**; /Robbie Jack **112** bottom; /Jerry Ohlinger/Sygma **238-239**; /Jose F. Poblete **48** bottom; /JP Laffont/Sygma **33** inset; /Bob Krist **189**; /Lee Snider/Photo Images **168-169** bottom; /Liba Taylor **181**; /Pawel Libera **166** top, **167**; /Stefan Lindblom **176** centre; /Macduff Everton **142-143** bottom; /Manchete **255**; /Mike Powel/Sygma **241**, **241** top left; /Francoise de Mulder **79** bottom; /NASA/CalTech **137**; /Pierre Vauthey/Sygma **254**; /Ralph White **230-231**; /Steve Raymer **102** top left, **104**; /Reuters **13** top, **27** bottom, **62** top left, **63**, **70** top left, **71** top right, **71** bottom, **81**, **86** top left, **87** top left, **206** bottom, **214** centre right, **249** top, **275**; /Zuckerman Robert **117**; /Anders Ryman **86-87**; /Shannon Stapleton/Reuters **28**; /Lee Snider/Photo Images **266**; /Stapleton Collection **216**, /The State Russian Museum **54** top left, **55** bottom; /Stefano Bianchetti **220** top left, **220** bottom /Sygma **240** centre; /Ted Spiegel **20-21** bottom; /Peter Tumley **62** bottom; /Underwood & Underwood **37** top, **273**; /Peter M. Wilson **190** top, **191**; /Jim Zuckerman **105**.
**Empics 148** top left, **150-151** bottom, **203**.
**Mary Evans Picture Library 135** bottom, **182** top, **183**.
**Getty Images 12** top left, **16** top left, **32** top left, **33**, **68** bottom, **72** top left, **73** top, **74** top left, **74** bottom, **75**, **80** top left, **80** bottom, **89**, **92**, **93**, **98** top left, **99**, **100**, **101** top, **101** bottom, **106** top left, **107** top, **107** bottom, **114** top left, **115**, **120** top left, **121**, **124** top left, **124** bottom, **125** top, **125** centre, **130**, **136** top left, **140** top left, **146-147** bottom, **151** left, **158** top left, **159**, **160**, **164** bottom, **170** centre, **173** top right, **186** top, **186** bottom, **187**, **195** top, **196**, **197**, **222** top left, **223** top, **224**, **224** top left, **225**, **228** top left, **228** bottom, **233**, **242** top left, **244** top, **244-245**, **249**, **256**, **257**; /AFP **12-13**, **136**, **161**, **190** centre; /Ralph Crane **168** top, **169** top right; /Steve Dunn/Allsport **208-209**; /Paul Gilham **206** top left, **207**; /Henry Groskinsky/Time Life Pictures **276**; /Sergei Guneyev **64** bottom; /Time Life Pictures **58** top left, **59** centre, **76** top left, **77**, **111** top right; /Warner Bros./Handout **192** bottom, **192** top; /Mark Harwood **178** top, **179**; /Terry Husebye **260** bottom; /IOC/Allsport **202** bottom /Keystone **274** top left; /Gray Mortimore/Allsport **210** top left, **211**, **212** top left, **212** bottom centre, **213**; /Merlyn Severn/Picture Post **274** top left, **277**; /Janek Skarzynski/AFP **217**; /Billy Stickland/Allsport **214** top left, **215** /Time Life Pictures **17**, **22**.
**Illustrated London News Picture Library 60** top left, **61**.
**Kobal Collection 28** top left, **114** centre left, **118** top left, **118-119**; /Lorimar **29**. **North Wind Picture Archives 146** top left, **147** top.
**Orbital Sciences Corporation 253** top.
**The Picture Desk Limited 46** top left; /Advertising Archives **51** top, **174** top, **174** bottom; /Art Archive **201**; /Bibliotheque Municipale Moulins/Dagli Orti **47**; /Cathedral of Santiago de Compostela/Dagli Orti **49**; /Eileen Tweedy **149**; /Kobal Collection **28** top left, **114** centre left, **118** top left, **118-119**; /Lorimar **29**; /Paramount **156** top left, **157** top, **184** bottom, **208** top left, **209** top right; /United Artists **264**.
**Rex Features 116**, **245** top; /Nigel R. Barklie **260** top left, **269**; /SIPA **140** top left, **141**.
**James Richardson 193**.
**Science Photo Library 138** top left; /NASA **138** top, **139** bottom.
**David Shepherd 34** top left, **35**.
**TopFoto 18** top left, **19**.
**Warner Bros** /Harvest **36** bottom. William K. Hartmann **134** top left, **135** top. **Winchester Mystery House** /San Jose, C.A. **175**, **178** centre.